Joint Ventures in Europe

Joint Ventures in Europe

A Collaborative Study of Law and Practice
prepared by the law firms

— ASHURST MORRIS CRISP

— BÄR & KARRER

— BRUCKHAUS WESTRICK STEGEMANN

— DECHERT PRICE & RHOADS

— ESTUDIO JURIDICO CASTELLANA

— GIDE LOYRETTE NOUEL

— NAUTA DUTILH

— STUDIO LEGALE BISCONTI

Butterworths
London, Dublin, Edinburgh
1991

United Kingdom	Butterworth & Co (Publishers) Ltd, 88 Kingsway, London WC2B 6AB and 4 Hill Street, Edinburgh EH2 3JZ
Australia	Butterworths Pty Ltd, Sydney, Melbourne, Brisbane, Adelaide, Perth, Canberra and Hobart
Canada	Butterworths Canada Ltd, Toronto and Vancouver
Ireland	Butterworth (Ireland) Ltd, Dublin
Malaysa	Malayan Law Journal Sdn Bhd, Kuala Lumpur
New Zealand	Butterworths of New Zealand Ltd, Wellington and Auckland
Puerto Rico	Equity de Puerto Rico, Inc, Hato Rey
Singapore	Malayan Law Journal Pte Ltd, Singapore
USA	Butterworth Legal Publishers, Austin, Texas; Boston, Massachusetts; Clearwater, Florida (D & S Publishers); Orford, New Hampshire (Equity Publishing); St Paul, Minnesota; and Seattle, Washington

A CIP Catalogue record for this book is available from the British Library.

ISBN 0 406 11612 1

Typeset by BP Integraphics Ltd, Bath, Avon
Printed by Bookcraft (Bath) Ltd, Midsomer Norton, Avon

Foreword

This book has been produced in recognition of the widespread use of joint ventures in the European Community. It seeks to offer a practical guide to the selection and use of differing joint venture structures in France, Germany, Italy, the Netherlands, Spain, Switzerland and the UK. To achieve this aim the book brings together a group of contributors who are leading practitioners in the field of joint ventures in their respective jurisdictions. In order to harmonise what would otherwise have been a very disparate work and to make possible comparisons between jurisdictions, each country chapter follows a standard format, addressing discrete issues such as the advantages or disadvantages of a given joint venture structure or specific intellectual, tax or national competition law issues. European competition law, since it has application in all the Member States, has been addressed in a separate chapter. The law is stated as at December 1990.

Edward Kling
Dechert Price & Rhoads
London

Julian Ellison
Ashurst Morris Crisp
Brussels

Contents

CHAPTER 1

European Community joint ventures

Competition lies at the heart of the common market. It is, in the words of the EC Commission ('the Commission'), 'essential in securing all of the benefits linked with the single market'.[1]

The removal of competitive distortions in the EC is a fundamental means by which the single market is to be achieved. Article 85(1) of the Treaty of Rome ('the Treaty') thus prohibits agreements between enterprises which have as their object or effect the prevention, restriction or distortion of competition; and Article 86 of the Treaty prohibits abuses of dominant positions by enterprises who enjoy that market status. These Treaty Articles, whose text is set out in full at the end of this chapter, form the basis of joint venture control at the EC level.

1. 'JOINT VENTURES' – DEFINITION

As its name suggests, 'joint venture' implies the carrying out of some commercial endeavour by two or more parties. In that sense, virtually any commercial agreement between two or more parties may constitute a 'joint venture'. For present purposes, the notion must be narrowed. Yet it is difficult to draw universally acceptable lines of division between joint ventures and other types of commercial cooperation.

In this chapter, the term 'joint venture' will be used to denote a form of cooperation between two or more parties whose primary effect is the creation of a means to facilitate an on-going pooling or exchange of resources.

Excluded from the definition are agreements which do not *per se* have as their primary effect an on-going pooling or exchange of resources – for example, agency, distribution, franchising, patent and know-how licensing agreements – although many of these agreements may themselves form ancillary features of broader 'joint ventures'.[2]

The definition, on the other hand, is wider than a number of others and includes not only forms of cooperation which do, but also forms of cooperation

---

[1] 19th Report on Competition Policy (1990), page 34.
[2] The Commission has promulgated a number of group exemptions covering agreements of this sort. *See*, e.g., Regulation 1983/83 (exclusive distribution agreements); Regulation 1984/83 (exclusive purchasing agreements); Regulation 2349/84 (patent licensing agreements); Regulation 4087/88 (franchise agreements); Regulation 556/89 (know-how licensing agreements).

which do not, involve the creation of business enterprises altogether separate from the parties who create them.

EC competition law is generally not concerned with the *form* the arrangements between the parties may take, but rather focuses on their *substantive economic effects.*[3] Accordingly, whether a joint venture is to be achieved by way of a new jointly-owned company, a partial merger or acquisition, a partnership or a contract is essentially irrelevant to the analysis.

2.   COMPETITION POLICY AND JOINT VENTURES

The Commission's attitude toward joint ventures is less easy to divine than its general policy of free competition between Member States. Whilst the latter is clearly documented in the opening provisions of the Treaty, joint ventures are not specifically the subject of any EC legislation. ('Legislation' in this context refers to Regulations implemented by the EC Council and the Commission.)

In its 15th Report on Competition Policy (1986), the Commission expressed favour for those joint ventures which contribute towards market integration, risk sharing, innovation, technology transfer, development of new markets, improvements in competitiveness, strengthening of small and medium-sized firms and the elimination of structural over-capacity within the EC.

However, the same Report also noted that there are dangers to the free movement of goods within the Community inherent in any joint venture. These dangers include market sharing, the raising of barriers to market entry and the intensification of market power.

It is necessary to engage in a balancing exercise in order to determine whether a particular joint venture will be considered advantageous or disadvantageous to the EC free market. The virtues of risk sharing, market integration, etc. must be weighed against the perils of anti-competitive harm.

Whilst joint ventures are not specifically the subject of legislation *per se*, references to them feature frequently in policy documents and rulings of the Commission and the European Court of Justice ('the ECJ'). They include (illustratively):

(a)   Specialisation Agreements (which are referred to more fully in 7.1 below).

(b)   Joint Research and Development Agreements (which are referred to more fully in 7.2 below).

(c)   Joint Purchasing Agreements, which provide for the purchasing of products through a pool to enhance participants' purchasing power.

(d)   Joint Sales Agreements, which involve pooling of sales efforts, often by granting exclusive selling rights and the power to fix prices to a jointly-owned body (such as a trade association or a joint subsidiary).

---

[3] *See, GEC-Weir Sodium Circulators*, OJ L327/20.12.77, p. 26.

The Commission generally regards such agreements with great suspicion.[4]

(e)   Joint Production Agreements.

(f)   Joint After-Sale Service Agreements, which as between non-competitors the Commission generally regards as unobjectionable.[5]

Joint ventures will be analysed on the basis of the principles noted in 3 below.

3.   EC COMPETITION LAW – BASICS

Article 85 calls for a two-tiered analysis of any agreement that may prevent, restrict or distort competition. Article 85(1) prohibits agreements that have this object or effect; and it will therefore be necessary first to determine whether the agreement in question is in this sense anti-competitive or not. Article 85(3) provides for an exemption from the prohibition when agreements, notwithstanding their anti-competitive effect, produce outweighing objective benefits in terms of increased or improved productivity, technology or economic progress, with a fair share of the resulting benefit going to consumers; and it will therefore be necessary to determine whether the agreement in question will nonetheless produce sufficient benefits to be permitted.

Article 86, which prohibits without exemption abuses of dominant market positions, may apply to joint ventures involving parties in dominant positions whose activity in relation to the venture would constitute an abuse.

These Treaty provisions are administered by the Commission,[6] in the first instance by its Directorate-General IV ('DG IV'), whose decisions are subject to the review of the ECJ.

By the EC Council's adoption of Regulation 17 in 1962, the Commission was empowered to operate a system whereby parties to agreements could 'notify' them to the Commission, and seek a formal or informal statement of the Commission's opinion that they did not infringe Articles 85(1) or 86 ('negative clearance') and/or that their proposed agreements should be granted 'exemption' under Article 85(3).

Notification has a number of advantages. It enables parties to questionable agreements to know at a relatively early stage whether their proposed arrangements will be regarded with hostility or not. Further, agreements notified to the Commission are automatically entitled to 'provisional validity' from the date of notification – that is, the parties to them will be immune from penalties during the period of the Commission's deliberation and until the Commission rules negatively on the parties' application. Perhaps most importantly, the Commission has the *exclusive* competence to grant exemptions under Article 85(3).

---

[4] *See Bayer Gist-Brocades*, OJ L23/5.2.76, p. 13.
[5] *See* Commission Notice on Cooperation between Enterprises (1968).
[6] Article 155, Treaty.

However, the Commission is powerless (save in a very narrow range of cases)[7] to grant an exemption under Article 85(3) with effect *prior to the date of notification*. Parties to anti-competitive or arguably anti-competitive arrangements, intending to justify the pursuit of them on the basis of the benefits they will produce, must therefore notify their agreements immediately: Otherwise, even if they subsequently notify their agreements (for example, *after* some problem arises), and even if they then succeed in showing an entitlement to an exemption, they will nonetheless be unable to escape the consequence of an illegal arrangement during the period from its inception to the subsequent notification date.

4.   COMMISSION NOTICES AND GROUP EXEMPTIONS

The notification system naturally imposes a great administrative burden on the Commission. To alleviate this burden and more generally to promote efficiency, the Commission has over the years published Notices and promulgated Regulations which enable parties to know the Commission's position in advance, and thereby either to determine that their proposed agreements will not need to be notified, or to formulate their agreements in such a way as to bring them within a group of agreements to which the Commission has granted an exemption *en masse*, thus making notification unnecessary. Examples of such arrangements are noted in 6 and 7 below.

5.   SUSPECT PROVISIONS IN JOINT VENTURE AGREEMENTS

The Commission generally regards as anti-competitive the following effects which may result from the creation of a joint venture:[8]

  (a)   limitations on the extent to which the joint venture parties may compete with one another or with the joint venture company itself; and
  (b)   adverse consequences for third party competitors.

The Commission is in general also likely to be concerned with the following ancillary provisions which commonly appear in joint venture agreements:

  (a)   overt non-competition provisions;
  (b)   provisions requiring the coordination of the venture's investment policy;
  (c)   post-termination provisions;
  (d)   provisions concerning the licensing and exchange of technical information;
  (e)   provisions concerning joint price fixing;
  (f)   provisions imposing purchase and supply obligations;

[7] *See* Article 6, Regulation 17.
[8] *See*, generally, Jones, Van Der Woude and Lewis, *EEC Competition Law Handbook*, Sweet & Maxwell (1990), Part X.

(g) provisions concerning the grant of exclusive distribution rights; and
(h) territorial restrictions.

6. JOINT VENTURES NOT WITHIN ARTICLE 85(1)

Agreements which automatically escape the prohibition in Article 85(1) include:

6.1 Domestic agreements

Agreements between parties situated in a single Member State, which do not involve imports or exports between Member States, have no effect on EC trade and therefore are regarded as not infringing Article 85(1).[9]

6.2 International agreements

Where the effects of an agreement lie only within the territory of one Member State and the territory or territories of non-Member States, there is not considered to be any effect on trade between Member States, and the agreement will not offend Article 85(1).[10]

6.3 Agreements of minor importance

Agreements which have such little economic significance that their effect on trade between Member States is 'negligible' or 'without an appreciable impact' will not offend Article 85(1). This is primarily determined by reference to market share and the turnover of the enterprises concerned. The Commission Notice on Agreements of Minor Importance[11] provides that agreements between enterprises engaged in the production of goods or the provision of services generally do not fall within Article 85(1) where 'the goods or services ... together with the participating undertakings' other goods or services which are considered by users to be equivalent in view of their characteristics, price and intended use, do not represent more than 5% of the total market for such products, and the aggregate annual turnover of the participating undertakings does not exceed 200 million ECU'.

7. GROUP EXEMPTIONS

The Commission has promulgated two group exemptions of direct relevance to specific types of joint ventures (as defined).

---

[9] Article 4 of Regulation 17/62, as amended by Regulation 2822/71.
[10] DG IV: Principles governing the assessment of joint ventures under the Competition laws, 1985, p. 3.
[11] 3 September 1986, OJ C231/2.

7.1   Specialisation agreements – Regulation 417/85

Under this Regulation, the Commission granted a group exemption to certain specialisation agreements which conform to its terms. A specialisation agreement is one which provides that each of the parties will not manufacture certain products specified, and will instead obtain them from the other. The Regulation does not cover agreements where only one party merely agrees not to manufacture.

Specialisation agreements have substantial potential benefits: They permit various economies of scale and the rationalisation of production. Accordingly, the Regulation's exemption will apply notwithstanding the appearance of the following otherwise potentially offensive provisions:[12]

(a)   an obligation not to enter into another specialisation agreement for an identical or equivalent product;

(b)   an obligation to obtain the product in question only from one of the parties or a joint venture entity;

(c)   an obligation to grant an exclusive distribution right to the other party (provided that intermediaries and users are not precluded from supply); and

(d)   an obligation to maintain minimum inventories and to provide customer services.

The Regulation will *not* apply when the combined market share of the products in question exceeds 20%, or when the aggregate turnover of the participants exceeds 500 million ECU.

7.2   Joint research and development – Regulation 418/85

R&D collaboration has been perceived by the Commission to have the potential for profound economic benefit.[13] The large expense and risk involved in R&D projects may be reduced significantly by several firms entering into agreements for the pursuit of R&D jointly. Furthermore, separate venturers who have already embarked upon specific R&D projects may share the results achieved to date. On a broader scale, R&D cooperation between firms of more than one Member State facilitates the Community goal of a greater opening-up of national markets; and cooperation with non-EC firms can lead to access within the EC to technology that might not otherwise have been available.

The manifest benefits of joint R&D ventures are contrasted by the Commission with potential anti-competitive burdens, such as where:

(a)   'powerful firms ... enter into R&D agreements with potentially very innovative rivals in order to be able to control technological progress

---

[12] Article 2.
[13] *See*, for example, the 13th and 15th Reports on Competitive Policy (1984 and 1986).

... (or where) R&D collaboration may raise entry barriers to non-participating competitors';[14]

(b) 'R&D collaboration ... facilitate(s) coordination of pricing and production and enable(s) abnormal profit to be made from innovations. ... In such cases, cross-frontier collaboration at the R&D stage may give way to geographical divisions of the market on national lines for the product resulting from the R&D';[15]

(c) joint participants enter into agreements to restrict their own independent R&D activities or the use of their results;

(d) R&D collaborators exclude the grant of licences to third parties.

Taking into account these advantages and disadvantages, the Commission promulgated Regulation 418/85, which grants joint R&D agreements that conform to its terms exemption from Article 85(1) infringement. The group exemption covers agreements which relate both to the conduct of the R&D and the exploitation of the results.[16]

In order to enjoy the benefit of the exemption:[17]

(a) the joint R&D must be carried out within a framework of a programme defining the objectives of the work and the field in which it is to be carried out;

(b) all parties to the work must have access to its results;

(c) each party must be free to exploit the results of the work (together with pre-existing technical knowledge) independently of the other;

(d) where there is joint exploitation of the R&D results, such results must be protectable by intellectual property rights or constitute know-how which substantially contributes to technical or economic progress *and* the results must be decisive for the manufacture or the application of the contract product or processes; and

(e) in cases where the parties manufacture by way of specialisation in production, they must fulfil orders for supplies from all parties concerned.

The block exemption is not available in cases involving joint selling or to agreements between competing manufacturers who at the time of entering into the agreement have a combined production exceeding 20% of the market for such products in the EC or a substantial part of it.[18] In cases of collaboration between non-competing manufacturers, the arrangement in relation to joint exploitation may continue until the later of five years from the date relevant products are put on to the market or the time when such products gain a 20% or greater market share.[19]

[14] 15th Report on Competition Policy (1986).
[15] *Ibid.*
[16] Article 1.
[17] Article 2.
[18] Article 3(2).
[19] Article 3(1) and (3).

The Regulation's exemption will apply notwithstanding the appearance in the agreement of the following otherwise potentially offensive provisions:[20]

(a) an obligation not to carry out independently R&D covered by the joint programme;
(b) an obligation not to enter into R&D agreements with third parties in the same field;
(c) an obligation to procure the contract products only from the venture parties, the venture itself or third parties jointly charged with their manufacture;
(d) an obligation not to manufacture contract products in territories reserved to other venture parties;
(e) an obligation to limit manufacture of contract products for specific applications;
(f) an obligation not actively to solicit sales for contract products in territories reserved to other venture parties; and
(g) an obligation to exchange information about experiences in dealings in contract products, and to grant non-exclusive licenses for further improvements.

Some restrictions in agreements are not permissible; and the benefit of the group exemption will not apply where any of the following so-called 'black clauses' appear.[1]

(a) an obligation not to carry out independently any R&D outside the field of collaboration;
(b) an obligation not to challenge the validity of the intellectual property rights in any of the R&D;
(c) an obligation limiting the amount of contract products that may be manufactured or sold;
(d) an obligation limiting the freedom to determine prices of contract products;
(e) an obligation restricting customers who may be served; and
(f) an obligation not to allow third parties to manufacture contract products.

Joint R&D agreements which fall outside the Regulation are to be analysed, notified or otherwise dealt with on a case-by-case basis in accordance with the principles noted above. Similarly, the Commission reserves the power to declare that conforming agreements in any particular instance are no longer covered by the Regulation, and as such susceptible of individual evaluation.[2]

[20] Article 4.
[1] Article 6.
[2] Article 7(6).

8.   JOINT ACQUISITIONS/PARTIAL MERGERS

The Commission has long held the view that where two or more actual or potential competitors form a joint venture, Article 85(1) will normally apply:

> ... (T)he creation of a joint venture generally has a notable effect on the conduct of the parent parties. ... Within the field of the joint venture and in related fields such parties are likely to coordinate their conduct and be influenced by what would otherwise have been their independent decisions.[3]

When two parties combine to take over an existing enterprise, the potential anti-competitive harm may be no different than had the two parties created the venture operation afresh. Joint acquisitions are therefore very much the subject of Commission review.

After substantial debate at both the EC and Member State levels, the EC Council recently promulgated the so-called 'merger regulation', Regulation 4064/89. Unilateral acquisitions by single enterprises of target enterprises, resulting in an ultimate 'concentration' of commercial interests, had been the subject of EC regulation, if at all, under Article 86. For various reasons, concern was widespread that the Commission's regulatory powers were inadequate. The Regulation is a response to that perceived deficiency.

The Regulation distinguishes between 'concentrations' where two or more previously independent enterprises merge, or one acquires sufficient control of the other to result in the loss of the other's independence, on the one hand; and operations between two or more independent enterprises involving the 'coordination' of their competitive behaviour whilst the independence of each subsists, on the other hand.[4]

The creation of a joint venture which performs on a lasting basis all of the functions of an autonomous economic entity, and which does *not* give rise to any coordination of competitive conduct either between the venturers or between any one of them and the venture itself, will be treated as a 'concentration' for purposes of the Regulation.[5]

'Concentrations' are subject to the Regulation; 'coordinations' are not (and will therefore continue to be regulated under the principles of Article 85 noted above).

The Regulation requires the notification to the Commission of all concentrations which have a 'Community dimension' not more than one week after the conclusion of the agreement or the announcement of a public bid.[6] A

---

[3] *GEC/Weir Sodium Circulators*, op. cit.
[4] Article 3(1) and (2).
[5] Article 3(2). See, also, Commission notice regarding concentrative and cooperative operations (OJ C203/10 14.8.90). This is in line with the Commission's earlier *Memorandum on Concentrations*, where 'partial concentrations' were said to avoid Article 85(1) if (a) the venturers have transferred to the venture a complete business, constituting the venture as an independently viable entity, (b) the venturers permanently withdraw from the business the venture will conduct, (c) the venture has its own management, free to determine the venture's business policies independently (the venturers' interest being as wholly passive investors) and (d) the arrangement will not lead to cooperation between the venturers in other fields.
[6] Article 4.

transaction has a 'Community dimension' when the aggregate worldwide turn-over of all enterprises involved exceeds 5 billion ECU *and* their aggregate EC turnover exceeds 250 million ECU *unless* each of the enterprises involved achieves more than two-thirds of its EC turnover in one and the same Member State.[7]

The Commission will then appraise the proposed concentration from a competition policy point of view. In short, a concentration which will not create or strengthen a dominant position as a result of which competition would significantly be impeded will be declared compatible with the common market, and *vice versa*.[8]

Concentrations which do not have a 'Community dimension' will continue to be scrutinised (if at all) under the normal rules of the Member States involved and the Commission under Article 86.

Similarly, 'coordinations', which fall outside the scope of the Regulation, will continue to be subject to review under Article 85 as noted above.

9.   EUROPEAN ECONOMIC INTEREST GROUPINGS

Although this chapter is principally concerned with the regulation of joint ventures at the EC level as a *substantive* matter of competition policy, the EC has recently introduced a new *form* of joint venture operation which should also be included. This is the European Economic Interest Grouping, or 'EEIG'.

9.1   Introduction

An EEIG is neither a partnership nor a company although it bears some of the hallmarks of each. The structure of EEIGs is derived from the French Groupement d'Intérêt Economique introduced in 1967 which has been used in large-scale international cooperative activities such as Ariane Espace and Airbus Industrie. Essentially, the EEIG is a hybrid type of undertaking perhaps aptly described as a form of partnership incorporated at Community level.

An EEIG is not made subject to the regulation of the individual national company laws of the Member States: its formation depends simply upon a contract drawn up by its participating members. There is no minimum capital requirement; there is no necessity of preparing or filing EEIG accounts; and the entity has tax transparency, i.e. its profits or losses are those of its individual members taxable upon their proportion according to the national law of each member. The legal liability of the members is unlimited, joint and several.

The intention behind EEIGs is that they should facilitate and develop the business activities of their members, while respecting their legal and economic independence. EEIGs were created by EC Council Regulation 2137/85 under the authority of Article 235 of the Treaty. One of its primary aims was to

[7] Article 1.
[8] Article 2.

facilitate further cross-frontier joint research and development, marketing and manufacture. Professional groups such as lawyers which are currently barred from cross-border mergers have begun to use the form as a vehicle for European-wide cooperation. The autonomy of the EEIG members ensures that there is no outside interference in the internal affairs of the members. Such independence should lessen potential conflict between disparate national rules applicable to members.

9.2   Membership

Two or more of any combination of a company, corporation or natural person in the EC may form an EEIG. Membership must be drawn from at least two Member States and such States may place an upper limit of twenty members in their territory. There is an upper limit of 500 employees. (Ironically, Airbus Industrie is not an EEIG.) Membership is not open to parties based in non-Member States, although this difficulty may be overcome by external companies setting up a subsidiary in a Member State which would become the EEIG member. Member States may, on grounds of public interest, limit the formation of EEIGs in certain sectors, e.g. insurance or banking.

Unlike companies and other business entities, an EEIG may not be established with the principal object of profit-making. It may, of course, make a profit; but this cannot be its stated primary purpose. It must carry on the economic activities of its members. It may not be used to create a new activity bearing no connection with the members' current activities: this would require the formation of a company. Furthermore, an EEIG must neither replace nor overtake the economic activities of the members. If the members of an EEIG become dependent on it, the grouping would behave more like a company under the guise of an EEIG, which would not be permissible under Regulation 2137/85.

9.3   Formation and internal organisation of an EEIG

An EEIG must be registered at an address within the Community and the registration must be published in the EC *Official Journal*. Furthermore, provision is made for an EEIG to transfer its address within a Member State and to change its registration from one Member State to another without dissolution.

The EEIG agreement must set out its objectives and the contractual relationship of members in respect of contributions to costs and apportionment of profits. The EEIG's purposes may be as broad or narrow as members decide, and may be ancillary either to the whole of their business or to only a part of it.

Internal arrangements between members within the EEIG are for their own choice, unlike many of the constricting requirements of company law at national level. Each member must have at least one vote but the contract may permit a member to have more than one provided no one member has a majority of votes. Patterns of voting power may be decided by the members reflecting the contributions of each to the cooperative endeavour. Altering the original contract will require a unanimous vote, as will matters such as changing the objects, the voting pattern, the life of the EEIG and the obligations of a member.

The management of an EEIG must be made up of persons not disqualified by national law from holding comparable office. The conditions for appointment and removal of the managers, and their powers, must be set out in the EEIG contract or in a subsequent unanimous decision of the members. Only the managers may represent the EEIG in dealings with third parties.

9.4   Liability

By way of balancing the absence of any capital requirement, the members have unlimited joint and several liability. Debts to third parties, however, must be those of the EEIG; and creditors may proceed against an individual member only after a request for payment by a fixed deadline from the EEIG has been unsuccessful. A member who withdraws from membership nevertheless retains liabilities for debts incurred during his period of membership for a period of five years thereafter. A new member may be excluded from liabilities arising prior to his membership, but such an exclusion must be registered to be effective against third parties.

An EEIG may borrow from a bank and issue medium-term notes. It is not permitted, however, to raise capital by the issuance of bonds or other securities for sale to the public. Where expenditure exceeds income, each member must contribute according to proportions laid down in the contract or if silent, then in equal shares. National law will govern matters relating to insolvency but the commencement of insolvency proceedings against an EEIG will not of itself entitle commencement of proceedings against the individual members.

9.5   EEIG and competition law

The form of cooperation between the members established within an EEIG may be caught by Article 85(1) of the Treaty. EEIGs do not *per se* enjoy the benefit of any group exemption. They may, however, sometimes benefit from an existing group exemption, e.g. for joint R&D agreements; or they may seek and obtain individual exemptions under Article 85(3). As EEIGs are not required by regulation to have pre-determined periods of life, members will need to take note of the time restrictions that some group exemptions impose on covered transactions as well as the expiry date of the exemptions themselves.

When the formalities of registration have taken place, the EEIG has the capacity to make contracts in its own name, to sue and be sued, and to operate as if it had corporate personality.

TREATY
establishing
THE EUROPEAN ECONOMIC COMMUNITY
(Rome, 25 March 1957)
ARTICLE 85

1. The following shall be prohibited as incompatible with the common market: all agreements between undertakings, decisions by associations of undertakings and concerted practices which may affect trade between Member States and which have as their object or effect the prevention, restriction or distortion of competition within the common market, and in particular those which:

(a) directly or indirectly fix purchase or selling prices or any other trading conditions;
(b) limit or control production, markets, technical development, or investment;
(c) share markets or sources of supply;
(d) apply dissimilar conditions to equivalent transactions with other trading parties, thereby placing them at a competitive disadvantage;
(e) make the conclusion of contracts subject to acceptance by the other parties of supplementary obligations which, by their nature or according to commercial usage, have no connection with the subject of such contracts.

2. Any agreements or decisions prohibited pursuant to this Article shall be automatically void.

3. The provisions of paragraph 1 may, however, be declared inapplicable in the case of:

- any agreement or category of agreements between undertakings;
- any decision or category of decisions by associations of undertakings;
- any concerted practice or category of concerted practices;

which contributes to improving the production or distribution of goods or to promoting technical or economic progress, while allowing consumers a fair share of the resulting benefit, and which does not:

(a) impose on the undertakings concerned restrictions which are not indispensable to the attainment of these objectives;
(b) afford such undertakings the possibility of eliminating competition in respect of a substantial part of the products in question.

ARTICLE 86

Any abuse by one or more undertakings of a dominant position within the common market or in a substantial part of it shall be prohibited as incompatible with the common market in so far as it may affect trade between Member States. Such abuse may, in particular, consist in:

(a) directly or indirectly imposing unfair purchase or selling prices or other unfair trading conditions;
(b) limiting production, markets or technical development to the prejudice of consumers;
(c) applying dissimilar conditions to equivalent transactions with other trading parties, thereby placing them at a competitive disadvantage;
(d) making the conclusion of contracts subject to acceptance by the other parties of supplementary obligations which, by their nature or according to commercial usage, have no connection with the subject of such contracts.

CHAPTER 2

French joint ventures

1. GENERAL INTRODUCTION

Although there is no legal definition in French law, a joint venture may be described as an agreement of cooperation between independent parties (generally of similar economic weight) who venture into a common objective and who negotiate as equals.

1.1 The three types of joint ventures

There are three types of joint ventures in France which can be organised in the following forms:

- – a simple contractual relationship,
- – a partnership agreement,
- – a joint corporation.

These three forms are all based on contractual documents, but generally, a distinction is made between a simple contractual joint venture which does not give rise to a common entity and a joint venture which does give rise to a common entity.

Joint ventures which result in a common entity are organised either in the form of a partnership (in French, 'société de personnes') or in the form of a corporation (in French, 'société de capitaux'). For the purposes of this study, these last two types of entities shall be hereinafter referred to as 'common entities'.

1.2 Contractual documents

A joint venture is set up by following several steps: negotiation – pooling of existing resources (information, know-how, employees, etc.) – cooperation in order to expand on a joint basis (obtaining contracts, developing new products, generating new clients, etc.) – and, finally, actual work in common in a particular business sector.

The agreements on which a joint venture is based are generally the following:

(i)   A letter of intent or a general agreement setting out the purpose of the joint venture and referring to a number of other documents.

(ii)   The actual contractual documents of cooperation namely:
- a contract in the case of a contractual joint venture,
- Articles of Incorporation and Shareholders Agreements for corporations and Articles of Association and Partnership Agreements for partnerships.

(iii) Miscellaneous collateral agreements, and more particularly in the case of a joint venture in the form of a common entity, agreements pertaining to the relations between each joint venturer and the common entity.

Collateral agreements consist generally of loan agreements, supply agreements (for raw materials, goods or services), data processing agreements, cash management agreements, agreements related to insurance, licences of industrial property rights, technical, commercial or administrative assistance agreements, secondment of employee agreements and leases of premises or equipment, to name a few. Generally, drafts of the collateral agreements appear as exhibits to the agreements mentioned in (ii) above.

1.3   Choice between the forms of joint ventures in France

1.3.1 Factors affecting choice

Among several factors, the following should be taken into consideration:

(i)   *Size and complexity of the proposed joint venture*: Is a common entity justified or is a simple contractual joint venture sufficient?

(ii)   *Anticipated length of the contemplated joint venture*: A contractual joint venture is often only a first step, which, if successful, will give rise to a common entity.

(iii) *Relationship between the joint venturers*: Anticipated problems of management/control, compatibility of the parties' interests, relative size and commercial weight of the parties.

In practice, the common entity will have greater independence and autonomy when in the form of a joint corporation (as opposed to a partnership). The extent to which the parties require such 'independence and autonomy' is in itself a factor affecting choice (*see further* 1.3.2(ii) below).

(iv)   *Use of tax benefits*: If an immediate deduction of start-up expenses for the joint venture is a significant factor, the form of a partnership is likely to be the most appropriate structure.

(v)   *Cash flow*: If income from the joint venture can be accumulated and distribution of profits deferred, a common entity in the form of a corporation would be preferable.

1.3.2 Differences between a contractual joint venture and a common entity

The main characteristic of a common entity is that in most cases, it is a *separate legal vehicle* which is independent from the joint venturers, operating in terms of its own interests.

(i)   This entails the following consequences:

- the common entity can trade in its own name with third parties (within the limits agreed upon by the joint venturers);
- in principle, the common entity is not dissolved if a joint venturer goes bankrupt or enters into liquidation;
- the common entity is an ideal vehicle for future expansion; it can, for instance, merge with other entities, be listed on the Stock Exchange, and have its own subsidiaries;
- the common entity can contract loans, in most cases with borrowings being guaranteed by a pledge of its assets (or of its business);[1]
- there is an argument that a common entity is better placed to establish market presence and reputation and to monitor and adapt to enduring market forces;
- it is easier for the joint venturers to transfer all or part of their interest in the common entity and by the same token to bring in new joint venturers or investors.

(ii)   The principle that a common entity must be independent from the interests of its members under French law was reaffirmed in the well-known Fruehauf case[2] where the court insisted that the shareholders are only one component of a company and that companies have their own specific identity, along with other components such as the State, the work force, suppliers and clients. In any case under French company law, the majority shareholders are not permitted to commit an 'abusive use of their majority position' (decision contrary to the interests of the common entity and taken in the sole interest of the majority shareholders), nor engage in 'abusive use of corporate assets' (use of the assets or credit of the common entity in a manner which is contrary to the interests of the entity, for personal ends and in bad faith). The abusive use of corporate assets is a criminal offence, while the abusive use of a majority position may only result in the nullity of the decision concerned and/or in the payment of damages, depending

---

[1] Pledge of a business (in French, 'nantissement de fonds de commerce') is specific to French law. This is a charge without transfer of title covering the goodwill, lease and trade name (and possibly other assets) of an undertaking made in favour of a creditor. Such charge, which must be registered with the Trade and Companies Register allows such secured creditor to have priority for payment of his claims from the proceeds of the sale of the business and also to request that the commercial court order the sale of the business by way of public auction.

[2] Decision of the Court of Appeal of Paris made on 22 May 1965 (Dalloz 1968 page 147): the Court held that the American parent company of Fruehauf France was guilty of abusive use of its majority position by forcing (under pressure from the US Government) Fruehauf France to terminate an agreement for delivery of trailers to the People's Republic of China.

on the case. It should be noted that the above rules apply to partnerships as well as companies.

Decisions of a common entity, taken in agreement between the joint venturers can thus be challenged by a liquidator, by the Public Prosecutor (in French, 'Procureur de la République') or by any third parties having an interest on the ground that those decisions are contrary to the interests of the entity: this is, however, in practice, exceptional.

1.3.3 Differences between a common entity in the form of a partnership and a common entity in the form of a corporation.

See 3.1 below.

1.4 General tax considerations

In addition to the specific rules described in the following sections for contractual joint ventures, and joint ventures in the form of a partnership or a corporation, it is necessary to clarify that French law has several specific sets of rules with respect to distribution of income from French sources to beneficiaries who are tax-wise not residents of France.

In particular, a withholding tax applies on income from securities and income from industrial property rights at rates which are in most cases reduced substantially where tax treaties apply.

2. CONTRACTUAL JOINT VENTURES[3]

2.1 Introduction – general characteristics

(i) A contractual joint venture is created by a direct contractual relationship between joint venturers through one or several contracts (hereafter the 'jv contracts') without formation of a joint venture entity such as a partnership or corporation. It is in fact a simple contract of cooperation between two or several partners pursuing the same objectives.

However, in addition to a statement on their objectives and the means to be taken to achieve them, the parties must define 'who does what' in a very precise manner as by definition there is no common entity through which the parties' joint endeavours will be channelled. This constitutes a fundamental difference with the other types of joint ventures which give rise to legal entities having an independent legal status.

In spite of the absence of a separate legal entity, the joint venturers have certain obligations, which, if not complied with pursuant to the jv contracts, will entail general penalties under the applicable contractual law and possibly

[3] In French, 'accords de coopération'.

specific penalties which may be stipulated in such contracts,[4] enforceable through court proceedings or, more often, arbitration proceedings.

Under French law, contractual joint ventures are known as *'undesignated' contracts*[5] as they are not specifically categorised in the French Civil Code.

(ii) Jv contracts generally include various provisions for the purpose of reaching sufficient financial and market strength through the pooling and supply of resources by the different parties.

However, although rights and obligations of the joint venturers may be defined in several contracts, the *unity of the jv contracts* is typically an essential aspect and it is only in the light of the totality of their mutual obligations that the parties can assess whether their contractual relationship will be equally balanced.

(iii) Common features of jv contracts. Contractual joint ventures are diverse and numerous. However, an analysis of jv contracts usually reveals that they have common points, whatever the object of the joint venture may be. Some of these common features include:

- the concern of the parties to foresee a maximum of potential future opportunities and problems. Given the lack of a common entity that will be jointly managed upon an on-going basis, the parties (subject to a general ability to vary the jv contracts) have in essence to agree and foresee future developments and problems at the outset of their relationship;
- provisions on automatic modification of this or that aspect of the jv contracts and, more precisely, the financial aspects (in French, 'clauses de révision') where a change in circumstances upsets the commercial balance of the arrangements; it must be kept in mind that under French law, the courts have no right to redraft the wording of a contract;
- provisions addressing the balance of power between the joint venturers in respect of decisions concerning the joint venture;
- detailed provisions on the settlement of disputes.

2.2 Advantages

(i) *Flexibility*: Jv contracts provide great flexibility to the contractual joint venturers, avoiding the restraining effects inherent in setting up a separate legal entity (*see* for instance 4.3 below) and allowing all types of individual initiatives, for example, in respect of the supply of services, leases of property or loans.

Under French conflict of laws rules, the law governing the jv contracts may be freely chosen by the parties, subject to requirements of public policy in

---

[4] If French law governs the jv contracts, it should be noted that the courts (or the arbitrators) may modify the contractual penalties if the agreements have been partially performed, or if such penalties appear significantly excessive or insufficient to them.
[5] In French, 'contrats inommés'.

France. The same restrictions also apply in practice to public policy rules of the countries where the jv contracts are actually performed. For the purposes of this section, we will assume that French law has been chosen to govern the jv contracts.

(ii) *Absence of predetermined structure, freedom*: Contractual joint ventures do not constitute a legal category; they are not subject to any specific rules as are sales agreements, agency agreements or loans, for example.

They are not governed by any specific set of laws, but only by the French law on contracts.

Contractual joint ventures are governed by Article 1134 of the French Civil Code, which stipulates that 'legally formed agreements are the law to those who signed them', in other words, each party binds itself by contract as if it were bound by law.

Duties and obligations of the joint venturers can thus be kept to a minimum. However, there are limits to the contractual freedom due to public policy rules applicable in the actual place where they are performed and especially:

- French economic regulations (competition law, for example) applies to contractual joint ventures (*see* 5.4 below);
- similarly, joint ventures concern employees and the use of human resources can raise problems specific to labour law.

(iii) *Ease of termination*: If no specific duration is stipulated, the jv contracts may be cancelled at any time by one of the parties with proper and reasonable notice and without liability to pay the other party damages or other compensation as a result of such termination.

(iv) *Secrecy* (*see also* 2.4 (iv) below): If the parties so wish, a contractual joint venture can be far more secret than a joint venture set up as a common entity (there is no obligation to file information with the Trade and Companies Register for example).

2.3 Disadvantages

(i) Requirement that the jv contracts be very carefully drafted as there will be no legal structure *per se* to implement them. The parties thus have to agree on all aspects from the outset.

(ii) '*De facto* created partnership', possible consequences for informal cooperation schemes having the appearance of a partnership.

The absence of a predetermined legal category does involve certain difficulties, particularly *vis-à-vis* third parties who may be induced to believe that a partnership exists between the parties. Indeed, these third parties could be tempted:

- either to prove that an actual legal structure exists between the different partners, namely a '*de facto* created partnership' (in French, 'société[6] créée de fait');

- or to claim that the actions of the partners involved were unusual and created an *appearance* (in French, 'apparence') of them acting in common.

(a)   *De facto* created partnership (*see also* 3.6 below)

The qualification of a '*de facto* created partnership' is not very precise under French law.

Article 1873 of the French Civil Code, as amended by the French Act of 4th January 1978 specifies that the rules applicable to partnerships in the form of 'sociétés en participation' (*see* 3.6 below) are also applicable to '*de facto* created partnerships'.

The law does not give a precise definition since this type of partnership results from facts and circumstances related to each case, for example, the particular actions or attitudes of two or several persons, who might be deemed to be acting as 'partners'.

In order to decide if a joint venture constitutes a '*de facto* created partnership' or not, the courts will search for the existence of essential features of a partnership or corporate contract which are set forth under Article 1832 of the French Civil Code for partnerships and corporations, namely:

- the parties' intention to form a partnership or corporation (*affectio societatis*),
- the contributions by each party,
- the sharing of profits, savings and losses.

(b)   'Appearance'

In instances where third parties have entered into an agreement with one of the joint venturers because they reasonably believed that the person they were dealing with was a representative of a 'partnership' due to the circumstances and actions of such representative, they can sue the alleged partners as having acted in common and if they are merchants as being jointly and severally liable.

There is a fundamental difference between a '*de facto* created partnership' and an 'apparent partnership'.

The existence of a '*de facto* created partnership' requires evidence that the three essential factors described in (a) above are definitely present. This is not the case for an 'apparent partnership'. This last can be assessed only by third parties, according to how they reasonably perceived the behaviour of the individuals concerned even if some or all of the three above-mentioned factors were lacking. Therefore, certain evidence is required:

- evidence acceptable to the judges that the parties involved 'appeared' to be acting as 'partners'

---

[6] In French, the word 'société' is a generic term for partnerships and corporations.

- evidence that the third party was encouraged to believe that he was dealing with an 'apparent partnership.'

2.4   When to select contractual joint ventures

Contractual joint ventures generally do not include the main activities of the joint venturers (such as production or sales) but are used either for specific operations or for ancillary activities where the joint venturers need assistance. As the following examples will show, contractual joint ventures should be selected when a common entity structure is not justified because the common activities are to be carried out on a short-term or experimental basis, do not require significant financing or for confidentiality reasons.

(i) *Contractual joint ventures used for specific deals*: The classic example comprises the collaboration of independent parties for the supply of products or services, in circumstances where they agree to share profits and losses. A distinction should be made between such collaborative efforts and the award of subcontracts by a lead contractor which does not constitute a joint venture.

(ii) *Contractual joint ventures used for ancillary activities of the joint venturers*: Industrial or commercial firms (generally other than competitors) looking for synergy of efforts in a given specific field (research, collection or processing of data, marketing in specific areas, management or other services, transportation, cash management, insurance, etc.) may collaborate through a contractual joint venture.

Thus, in the field of distribution, collaboration beyond entering into a normal distribution agreement, for instance through joint entry into a new market by a producer and a seller, may allow the development of better commercial policy:

- the producer will have the advantage of controlling and developing the conditions under which its products are marketed without bearing all the costs related to such entry into a new market alone.
- the seller, for his part, will benefit from the reputation and know-how of the supplier in a more direct manner.

Likewise, through a 'piggy back arrangement' with sharing of profits, a producer can benefit from the sales organisation set up by another producer for different products and thus may attempt to enter a new market while both parties mutually benefit from the synergy thus created.

In the field of research and development, agreements are often entered into between two or several companies for the purpose of conducting common studies. Such agreements usually also take into consideration how the results of such common studies will be put to use on a joint basis.

(iii) *First step of cooperation*: For major contracts (such as supply of heavy equipment or production plants) as well as for new product development, a contractual joint venture is often the first step for potential future partners to present an offer in common or to develop a product on a joint basis. If this first step proves successful, the parties will then proceed to the second step by establishing a common entity between them.

(iv) *Special types of contractual joint ventures*: For the sake of the record, we would like to mention two types of investments in France which are in fact two other types of contractual joint ventures.

- 'Invisible' investment (in French, 'investissement deshabillé')

  (a)   It should be noted here that for reasons related to confidentiality (either to circumvent French or foreign laws or simply to avoid overreaction of competitors, clients or suppliers), investments are sometimes carried out through a set of contracts (loan agreement, supply agreement, distribution agreement, technical assistance agreement, licences to industrial property rights, etc.). The effect of such contracts is to confer a measure of control over an undertaking without the investor(s) taking an interest in the capital of the relevant undertaking. The resulting distinction is between legal and economic (and commercial) control.

  French courts may naturally decide that such contracts are void when they run contrary to French public policy, but when the object of the venture is only to avoid application of a foreign law (not involving French public policy) or to avoid reactions of third parties), the contracts will be valid under French law, if exchange control requirements (*see* 5.1 below) are met.

  (b)   In addition, when a non-resident entity enters into contracts from abroad with one or more parties for the purchase of goods in France, the processing of such goods in France and their subsequent resale, the French tax authorities tend to consider that such transactions are taxable in France as they constitute a complete cycle of activity. In such case the non-resident entity is, in essence, treated as if it had a permanent establishment in France.

  This risk, however, is mitigated when the foreign entity involved is a resident of a country which has signed a tax treaty with France, since the definition of the term 'permanent establishment' under the treaty will then prevail in any event.

- Management lease agreement (in French, 'contrat de location-gérance')

This is an agreement by which the owner of a business leases the management of this business to another party (the 'tenant manager'), for a limited period.

The tenant manager manages and operates the business at his own risk. The owner receives rent, which is usually either fixed or proportional to the turnover.

This type of agreement which is governed by French legislation (and which is often used by small-sized companies or those facing financial difficulties) may be a useful form of joint venture, if one of the joint venturers wishes to 'assign' his business temporarily to the other joint venturer.

2.5 Formation documents, key aspects

There are no specific formalities applicable to formation documents prescribed by French law. The parties will set out their respective rights and obligations contractually.

The jv contracts usually contain, *inter alia*, provisions on the following.

2.5.1 Duration

The duration may vary according to the purpose of the joint venture and the parties' agreement (*see also* 2.5.6 below).

2.5.2 Sharing of obligations

Individual obligations and common obligations should be differentiated.

Individual obligations are respectively fulfilled or implemented by each party, under each party's own responsibility. This system is set up in order to avoid the risk of creating a *de facto* partnership (*see* 2.3 above). These individual obligations for which each party is liable must be specifically laid down by contract.

Obligations for which the parties are jointly liable are theoretically implemented in common. However, joint obligations can also include those performed individually by each party, but on behalf of all the parties; in this case, the party performing the obligation receives compensation from the others.

2.5.3 Sharing of the results of the joint venture

The parties will agree upon how and in what proportion the results (profits, assets produced etc.) of the joint venture will be divided between them. In the case of research and development common examples comprise a right of first refusal to the results or an exclusive right of each party on such results.

2.5.4 Management structures

Two kinds of management structures are basically required in combination, although these are subject to great variation.

(i) *A collegiate structure of deliberation: the committee*. Committees are often known as coordinating committees (in French 'comités de coordination') or steering committees (in French 'comités de direction'), such terms conveying no special meaning, and are composed of representatives of the parties who meet to take the necessary decisions to accomplish the goals of the joint venture. The roles of such committees are detailed in the jv contracts. The committee constitutes an internal organism of the joint venture.

(ii) *An executive structure: the leader or 'chef de file'*. If a common entity has not been set up, one of the parties (the leader) must represent the other(s) in dealings with third parties.

2.5.5 Settlement of litigation

Contractual joint ventures often provide for conciliation procedures and organise them in a very precise way, sometimes successively when a previous procedure may have failed. For instance:

- first, an attempt will be made to settle disputes before the committee;
- then, in case of failure, before the senior management of each party;
- finally, in case of continued disagreement, before an expert or a court of arbitration.

2.5.6 Termination of the joint venture

This issue is a matter of negotiation between the parties.

Terminating a contractual joint venture is usually less complex than dissolution of a partnership or liquidation of a corporation.

(i) Each party is not ordinarily entitled to terminate the jv contracts 'at will' during the initial fixed term.

(ii) In contrast, each party usually does have the right to terminate the jv contracts at any time on the following grounds:

- failure of the partners to agree on a decisive issue,
- material breach or default under the jv contracts by the other party,
- insolvency of the other party,
- change in the control of the other party.

2.6 Tax aspects

2.6.1 Principles

- A contractual joint venture normally enjoys tax transparency, i.e., each joint venturer will be subject to taxation on the portion of the income which he derives from the entity.
- Income, expenses and tax benefits (including investment tax credits, interest and deductions for depreciation) are passed on directly to each joint venturer. The tax treatment of each venturer can be different depending on whether the joint venturer is a partnership which is transparent for tax purposes or a corporation subject to corporate income tax at its own level.
- Where participation in a contractual joint venture is treated as only a part of the entire commercial activity of a joint venturer, the result of that participation will be taken into account as part of the profits or losses of that entire activity.

2.6.2 VAT

A contractual joint venture is generally not subject to VAT in France, unless it has a 'permanent establishment' in France (*see* 2.6.3 below).

2.6.3 'De facto' *created partnership and 'permanent establishment'*

The French tax authorities could be tempted to qualify a contractual joint venture as a '*de facto* created partnership' (*see* 2.3.(ii) above) and as concerns foreign joint venturers, as a 'permanent establishment' in France, in order to tax the profits of the joint venture at the level of this '*de facto* created partnership' or 'permanent establishment'; all joint venturers should be wary in this respect.

2.7   Foreign involvement

See 5.1 below.

2.8   Acquisition, use of business assets and intellectual property rights

2.8.1 Acquisition and use of business assets

In practice, business assets to be used in common have to be made available by one or several of the joint venturers, who will allow the other(s) to use them. This reflects the absence of a common entity. Joint ownership does exist in France (in French, 'indivision') but requires the signature of all joint owners for any decision of transfer and is generally to be avoided.

2.8.2 For the use of industrial property rights

See 5.3 below.

2.9   Competition law considerations

See 5.4 below.

3.   JOINT VENTURES IN THE FORM OF A PARTNERSHIP

3.1   Introduction

French partnerships (in French 'sociétés de personnes'), as opposed to French corporations studied in 4, are characterised by the unlimited liability of the partners and restrictions on the assignment of partnership interest, particularly to non-partners.

French partnerships include 'ordinary' partnerships (namely the 'société civile' and the 'société en nom collectif' (*see* 3.4 below) and the 'société en participation', the existence of which is normally not disclosed to third parties (*see* 3.6 below). In addition, there are intermediary structures, including:

- the French 'association', which is a not-for-profit organisation (*see* 3.2 below);
- the French 'groupement' and especially the 'groupement d'intérêt économique' (*see* 3.3 below),
- the French 'société en commandite' (*see* 3.5 below), which is actually a hybrid type of partnership and corporation.

The rules applicable to transforming one type of partnership into another or into a corporation are complex, but generally have little effect from a tax standpoint. This section does not review the problems arising at the time of dissolution or transformation, however the following rules may be noted:

If a 'société civile', 'société en nom collectif', 'société en commandite' or a 'groupement d'intérêt économique' is changed into a corporation, this does not entail creation of a new legal entity. In addition, taxation issues, particularly capital gains, are not affected. If the profits of the current year do become immediately taxable, the other tax consequences will generally be limited and the potential capital gains will generally escape taxation.

On the other hand, if a not-for-profit organisation or a 'société en participation' is changed into a corporation, this does entail the creation of a new legal entity with heavy tax consequences.

A 'groupement d'intérêt économique' may be changed into a 'société en nom collectif', without involving the creation of a new legal entity and therefore this operation has no consequences tax-wise.

3.2   The French association

3.2.1 Introduction

The French-style not-for-profit organisation (hereinafter referred to as an 'association'), generally called 'association de la loi de 1901' from the Law governing its creation and activities, is actually a contract between two or more parties (whether individuals or legal entities, whether French or foreign) who pool their knowledge or activities to achieve an aim other than sharing of profits.

The fact that an association lacks a profit generating purpose is the main difference between associations and corporations or partnerships. Nevertheless, associations may make profits, although they cannot distribute them to their members without becoming 'de facto created partnerships' (*see* 2.3(ii) above and 3.6 below).

There are three types of French associations:

- undeclared, which have no legal entity status and are mere contractual agreements (to which the rules mentioned in 2 above apply);
- declared, which have legal entity status, but which cannot be the recipients of legacies or valuable gifts;
- declared with the title 'of public interest status' (in French, 'association déclarée d'utilité publique'), which have legal entity status and full legal capacity.

Moreover, French law restricts the right of associations to own real estate (they can only own real estate necessary to achieve their purpose).

3.2.2 Advantages

There are no specific advantages; *see*, however, 3.2.4 'When to select'.

3.2.3 Disadvantages

Associations are characterised by the fact that they are prohibited by law from distributing profits to their members.

In the event of liquidation, the assets cannot be distributed to the members, but must be transferred to another association with similar objectives. However, contributions made by members can be recovered by them if this is provided for in the Articles of Association, in the contribution agreement or pursuant to a resolution of the general meeting of the members.

3.2.4 When to select

Before the French 'groupement d'intérêt économique' was created, joint ventures other than contractual joint ventures could only take the form of corporations, partnerships (including 'sociétés en participation') or associations, and this latter form was chosen when the sharing of profits at the level of the joint venture was not the aim of the joint venturers.

This practice has been pursued, and today there are still joint venturers who choose this form, for instance when managing a research and development office or promoting the use of new products. Associations continue to hide true industrial or financial agreements, the real aim of which is the actual search for profits at a level other than that of the association itself, namely profits generated indirectly at the level of each joint venturer from the activities of the association. For instance, an association can promote the use of a new type of product on a general basis, while its members actually manufacture and sell such product separately.

3.2.5 Formation documents, key aspects

An association generally has very simple Articles of Association (copied from forms suggested by the French authorities) to which specific by-laws (in French, 'règlement intérieur') may be added, which define the relationship between the members (in French, 'sociétaires') and the association.

Formalities of incorporation for a declared association are fairly simple (filing of the Articles of Association at the Préfecture, announcement in a legal newspaper).

3.2.6 Taxation of associations

(i) *Taxation on contributions*: A flat duty (of 430 FF in 1990) is levied on contributions (except real estate contributions in kind which are subject to a tax rate of 1% of their value).

(ii) *Taxation on income*: The net income generated by an association is generally taxable at the reduced rate of 24% except for the net income generated by a business activity (as opposed to proceeds generated by its investments) which is taxable at the full corporate income tax rate, i.e., presently 34% on undistributed profits (*see* 4.6.2 below).

(iii) *VAT*: In principle, VAT is applicable to the activities of or services rendered by an association, but there are a few exceptions for certain philanthropic or non-profit activities.

(iv) *Other taxes*: An association is also subject in principle to local taxes, to French tax on salaries, to registration duties, etc., just as French commercial entities or companies.

3.3   Groupings

3.3.1 Introduction

There are two types of grouping in France (in French, 'groupements').

(i)   Temporary grouping of undertakings (in French, 'groupement momentané d'entreprises') which is used for temporary cooperation and is in fact a special type of contractual joint venture (*see* 2 above) involving the appointment of a common representative to deal with third parties.

Features of a temporary grouping of undertakings are as follows:
– The common representative has sole power to negotiate with clients.
– The common representative deals with suppliers of goods and services (this will result, generally, in economies of scale and savings in time).
– The temporary grouping of undertakings is a simple and flexible structure.

(ii)   Economic interest grouping (in French, 'groupement d'intérêt économique' – hereinafter referred to as a 'GIE').

The GIE was instituted by French Ordinance dated 23rd September 1967 and corresponds to a structure which is somewhere between an association (*see* 3.2 above) and a partnership, with legal entity status.

However, the purpose of a GIE is in principle restricted to increasing and developing the activities of its members (implementation of all means likely to facilitate or develop the business of its members and to increase or improve the results of such business).

The GIE is mostly a service entity. The object of a GIE is not to make profits *per se*, although it may make profits in the normal course of its business. There is no minimum capital requirement. The members are jointly and severally liable for the debts which a GIE may incur in the completion of its objective.

A structure similar to the French GIE and inspired by it exists at the European level. This structure is the European Economic Interest Grouping or 'EEIG' (in French, 'Groupement Européen d'Intérêt Economique' or 'GEIE'), *see* chapter 1.

3.3.2 Advantages of a GIE

- A GIE has all the advantages of a partnership and benefits from tax 'transparency'.
- It is a flexible structure with a limited object and easy to operate. Although much less complicated than a Corporation, it may be able to reach the same economic goals in many situations.
- Considering the purpose of a GIE, the French tax authorities accept that it operate on a not-for-profit basis.
- It does not have the same limitations as an EEIG (*see* 3.3.7 below).

3.3.3 Disadvantages of a GIE

- In theory, the activities and objects of a GIE are limited.
- As in any partnership, its members have joint, several and unlimited liability for all the debts of the GIE.
- Many countries do not have a similar form of partnership, and business transacted outside France by a GIE often involves problems, especially with respect to the tax rules applicable in such countries. For instance, the question often arises as to whether the GIE is to be treated as a corporation for tax purposes.

3.3.4 When to select

The temporary grouping of undertakings (*see* 3.3.1 above) is perfectly adapted to joint ventures set up for a specific purpose (such as the construction of a building) where once such purpose has been accomplished, the joint venture is dissolved. But if the cooperation of the parties is planned to last for a long period of time and is not limited to one specific purpose or transaction, a GIE is a better adapted structure due to its legal entity status. A GIE is also recommended for undertakings in the same sector of activity (or facing similar problems) and also for entities of the same group, in order to increase their efficiency by using the services of the same vehicle.

3.3.5 Formation documents, key aspects

- Temporary groupings of undertakings must follow all the rules applicable to contractual joint ventures (*see* 2 above). In particular, the jv contract(s) establishing a temporary grouping must address matters such as (i) the scope of the powers granted to the common representative; (ii) whether the members will be jointly and/or severally liable; (iii) how the common representative will account for the income and expenses on behalf of all the members and (iv) in what capacity (or on whose behalf) the common representative will present himself to third parties and draw up invoices or bills for the grouping.
- A GIE is governed by its Articles of Association and by a set of by-laws (in French, 'règlement intérieur'). These by-laws are generally not disclosed to third parties. A GIE must be registered with the Trade and Companies Register, may or may not have capital, may or may not be for a commercial purpose (*see* footnote 7 to 3.4.1 below) and may issue debentures (if all of its members are entitled to do so). Its duration and the terms and conditions for entry of new members and for withdrawal of old members may be freely determined in its Articles of Association, but withdrawal cannot be forbidden (or be subject to such strict rules that withdrawal is virtually impossible). GIEs are managed by one or several manager(s) (in French, 'administrateur(s)'), who may be either private individuals or legal entities and who bind the GIE in all business falling within the objects laid down in the Articles of Association.

Taking into account the unlimited liability of the members for the debts of the GIE, it is very advisable to limit the objects of the GIE and also to limit the powers of the manager(s). However, limits to the powers of the manager(s) are not binding on third parties, but may give rise to payment of damages by the manager(s) to the members in case of breach.

3.3.6 Taxation

- Temporary groupings of undertakings fall under the French tax system applicable to contractual joint ventures (*see* 2.6 above).
- A GIE is subject to the same tax system as partnerships (ie 'tax transparency') which are not subject to corporate income tax (*see* 3.4.6 below) as concerns taxation of profits.

Contributions in cash or in kind to a GIE are subject to a 1% registration duty.

A minimal flat registration duty of FF430 (in 1990) is applicable to transfer of shares of a GIE (and not 4.8% as for the transfer of partnerships' shares).

As far as all other taxes are concerned, a GIE is subject to the same rules as any other French legal entity, with the exception that if certain specific conditions are met, VAT may not be due on services rendered to those of its members which are already exempt from VAT.

3.3.7 The EEIG (in French, GEIE)

(See Chapter 1)

In France, an EEIG appears to have more drawbacks than advantages compared to the French-style GIE, in practice. Indeed, a French GIE may for instance:

- employ more than 500 workers,
- be a member of another French GIE.

3.4 Ordinary partnerships

3.4.1 Introduction

Under French law, there are two basic types of partnerships, namely the 'société civile', which is a civil partnership and the 'société en nom collectif' or 'SNC' which is a commercial partnership and whose members have the French legal status of a merchant (in French, 'commerçant').[7]

However, 'sociétés civiles' may be considered commercial if they carry out activities which are commercial in nature according to French law. In such cases, among other obligations, they will be subject to the accounting requirements of commercial companies, to the jurisdiction of the commercial courts and to the corporate taxation system in the same way as French corporations (*see* 4.6.2 below).

Taxwise, a 'société civile' is treated as a transparent entity not subject to corporate income tax except if it carries out activities which are commercial in nature as indicated above or if it specifically so elects.

---

[7] It would be useful here to recall the important difference under French law between civil and commercial entities.

(a) Legal entities are regarded under French law as 'commercial' i) either because they are organised under one of the commercial forms provided for by law, such as the 'société anonyme' (or 'SA') the 'société en nom collectif', the 'société à responsabilité limitée' (or 'SARL') or the 'société en commandite', regardless of their purpose or ii) irrespective of their form, if they conduct an activity or pursue a purpose of a commercial nature according to Articles 632 and 633 of the French Commercial Code (such as the purchase of property for resale, leasing of movable property, brokerage or commission agent activities, manufacturing, transportation or mining). These legal entities are thus subject to the French Commercial Code and the jurisdiction of the Commercial Courts.

(b) Other legal entities are regarded under French law as 'civil'. 'Sociétés civiles' are not subject to administrative rules applicable to commercial entities, such as some of the registration formalities with the Trade and Companies Register or requirements relating to the way their accounts must be held. In general, 'sociétés civiles' are subject to the Civil Code and the jurisdiction of the Civil Courts.

In practice, however, the rules applicable to both these types of entities are tending to become more and more similar, especially from a tax standpoint.

3.4.2 Advantages and disadvantages of a 'société civile'

(i) *Advantages*: The main advantage of a 'société civile' (assuming it is not subject to corporate income tax) is its 'tax transparency', meaning that profits and losses flow directly to its members who will each be taxed for their own share in the profits. In addition, the organisation and operation of this type of partnership is quite simple and it is managed by one or several manager(s) (in French, 'gérants') who must be approved by the members.

(ii) *Disadvantages*: The main disadvantage is the unlimited liability of the members for the debts of the 'société civile'. Such liability is not joint and several, but *pro rata* to the amount of each partner's contribution to the capital.

Moreover, transfer of partnership interests is subject to a 4.8% registration duty and to heavy formalities.

3.4.3 Advantages and disadvantages of a 'société en nom collectif'

The 'société en nom collectif' is a simple form of French commercial entity benefiting from legal entity status.

(i)   *Advantages*:

- The formalities to form and operate this type of partnership are limited to drawing up Articles of Association and registration in the Trade and Companies Register. There are no legal requirements as to a minimum level of capital.
- It is a flexible structure, benefiting from 'transparent' tax status (if it does not elect to be subject to corporate tax).

(ii)   *Disadvantages*:

- The partners are indefinitely, jointly and severally liable for the partnership's debts. Thus, the partners' absolute reciprocal trust is necessary in this case.
- The 'société en nom collectif' cannot make public issues of shares, debentures or other forms of stock.
- Transfer of interests in the partnership is subject to heavy formalities and to a 4.8% registration duty.

3.4.4 When to select

- A 'société civile' is generally chosen as a vehicle for a joint venture for real estate activities, particularly management and operation of real estate assets (such as vineyards, farms, quarries) or construction activities.
- A 'société en nom collectif' is advisable for joint ventures between a small number of partners who know each other well, trust each other completely and who wish to benefit from its 'tax transparency'.

3.4.5 Formation documents

The key documents for a 'société civile' and for a 'société en nom collectif' are their Articles of Association. In addition, collateral agreements (*see* 1.2(iii) above) and an agreement between the partners on the operation of the partnership are also frequently prepared.

The Articles of Association should deal with the scope of the powers granted to the manager(s) (in French, 'gérant(s)') , the duration of the partnership and a system for dispute resolution.

In a 'société civile' and a 'société en nom collectif' a statutory auditor is compulsory once thresholds related to the amount of turnover, number of employees and total assets have been met.

3.4.6 Taxation and accounting

- Contributions
  In principle, contributions to the capital in cash are only subject to the minimum flat registration duty of FF 430, contributions in kind are subject to a 1% registration tax (except when the partnership has elected to be subject to corporate income tax and contribution is met by an entity not ;su;bject to corporate income tax).
- Taxation of profits
  Unless corporate income tax applies (either on election by the partnership[8] or pursuant to tax law if the partnership has a commercial activity, *see* 3.4.1 above) the profits of the 'société civile' and of the 'société en nom collectif' are taxed at the level of partners only at the tax rate applicable to the category of income concerned.
- Transfer of partnership interest
  A registration duty of 4.8% is applicable as indicated above.
- Other taxes
  Like all French undertakings, the 'société civile' and the 'société en nom collectif' are subject to local taxes, business tax (in French, 'taxe professionnelle'), to French tax on salaries, to registration duties and to other miscellaneous taxes.

3.5 The 'société en commandite'

3.5.1 Introduction

A 'société en commandite' is actually a hybrid form of a partnership and corporation where capital and power are separated between:

- on the one hand, the 'commandités' (general partners), who are automatically deemed to have merchant status (in French, 'commerçants'), and

---

[8] If the 'société en nom collectif', is subject to corporate income tax, it will be taxed as a 'societe anonyme'.

have joint, several and unlimited liability for all the debts of the partnership, but have almost sole control over management;
–   on the other hand, the 'commanditaires' (limited partners), who make
    financial contributions, but whose liability is limited to the amount of
    their contributions and who do not take an active part in management.

There are two types of 'sociétés en commandite', the 'société en commandite
simple' where the limited partners are basically in the same situation as the
shareholders in an 'SARL' (*see* 4.1 below) and the 'société en commandite
par actions' where the limited partners are comparable to the shareholders
in an 'SA' (*see* 4.1 below). In practice, the 'société en commandite simple'
is seldom used, as the SARL has the advantage of being simpler to operate.
The following comments will deal only with the 'société en commandite par
actions', hereinafter referred to as an 'SCA'.

3.5.2 Advantages

–   Separation between the partner(s) in charge of management and the other
    partners acting as mere financial investors, who appoint members of a
    supervisory board (in French, 'Conseil de Surveillance'), which supervise
    the management (i.e. the general partners).
–   When listed on a stock exchange, avoidance of hostile take-over bids.

3.5.3 Disadvantages

–   The unlimited liability of the general partners for the SCA's debts.
–   Rather cumbersome to operate as in practice there is a tendency towards
    conflict between the financial interests of the limited partners and those
    of the general partners.

3.5.4 When to select

Although not often used in the past, the structure of the SCA seems the best
and soundest means for one joint venturer to have almost total control over
management when the other joint venturers prefer to only have a share in
the profits. This structure in fact has been rediscovered in recent years due
to its advantages.

3.5.5 Formation documents

Just as for other forms of partnerships, the Articles of Association and agreements between partners for the operation of the partnership are the most important documents for a joint venture in the form of an SCA.
    Two important questions to be resolved in the Articles of Association are
the rules concerning the appointment of the manager(s) and the decision-making
process noting that the SCA is managed by one or several managers (in French,

'gérants') who must be chosen from among the general partners and that the manager need not be private individuals (an SARL is often chosen).

When drawing up the Articles of Association, the partners have great freedom to set the conditions under which the managers may be appointed or dismissed (for instance by the general partners and the limited partners acting jointly or by the general partners acting by themselves).

3.5.6 Meetings

Collective decisions (outside those concerning operational management which are handled by the general partners) require the separate consultation of the general partners and limited partners:

- the general partners decide on a unanimous basis unless the Articles of Association provide otherwise (in practice there are sometimes three general partners and the Articles of Association provide for specific majority rules for some decisions, such as incorporation of subsidiaries);
- the limited partners decide in the same way as shareholders in an SA, namely two-thirds majority of the shares of the limited partners present or represented for modification of the Articles of Association, and a majority representing over 50% of such shares for other decisions. Such other decisions mainly involve approval of the accounts or, depending on the Articles of Association, decisions related to major investments or entry of new limited partners.

General partners who also hold shares normally reserved for the limited partners (this is possible but generally not recommended as it runs contrary to the spirit of this type of partnership) are entitled to vote at meetings of limited partners except in decisions appointing the members of the supervisory board.

3.6 Undisclosed entities

3.6.1 Introduction

In France, there are two types of entities which are normally undisclosed to third parties. These are:

- The 'société en participation', which is in theory the most appropriate structure for a joint venture in France, and the simplest form of partnership. The 'société en participation' may be disclosed if the shareholders so wish;
- the 'de facto created partnership' which is legally equivalent to a 'société en participation' (per Article 1873 of the French Civil Code), except that there are no Articles of Association (*see* 2.3 (ii) for the two types of *de facto* partnerships in France).

3.6.2 Advantages of a 'société en participation'

Besides all the advantages of most partnerships in France (tax 'transparency', flexible structure), it is the case that the 'société en participation' may remain secret (except to the tax authorities) which is the main advantage.

3.6.3 Disadvantages of a 'société en participation'

The fact that this type of partnership may be kept secret can nevertheless become a drawback. As the 'société en participation' does not have legal entity status, it is represented by one or more managers who will appear the owner(s) of the assets and liabilities of the partnership from the point of view of third parties; the structure therefore in a sense mis-states the underlying commercial and economic reality.

3.6.4 When to select

The 'société en participation' is mostly used (i) when one partner cannot or does not want to appear officially as such or (ii) as an initial step prior to an official joint venture or (iii) when the partners belong to the same group of companies.

De facto created partnerships are often not actually 'selected' but result from a decision of a court or the tax authorities qualifying as such an existing relationship between individuals and/or entities conducting an activity in common.

3.6.5 Formation documents

A 'société en participation' requires Articles of Association (generally short) and in practice, ancillary documents such as those relating to loans granted by one or several partners, for its formation. The Articles of Association (but not the ancillary documents) must be sent to the tax authorities and must mention, among other information, the contributions by each partner, the method adopted for sharing profits and losses and the duration of the 'société en participation'.

As mentioned above, '*de facto* created partnerships' are generally not officially formed, and there are no official formation documents.

3.6.6 Taxation

'Sociétés en participation' and '*de facto* created partnerships' are basically subject to the same taxation system as official partnerships (the 'société civile' and the 'société en nom collectif' – *see* 3.4.6 above).

3.7   Foreign involvement

See 5.1 below.

3.8   Acquisition, use of business assets and intellectual property rights

See 5.2 and 5.3 below.

3.9   Competition law considerations

See 5.4 below.

4.   JOINT VENTURES IN THE FORM OF A CORPORATION

4.1   Introduction

A jointly owned corporation is generally the standard form of cooperation used for joint ventures of any economic significance when the joint venturers have agreed to create a vehicle for such cooperation and when such joint-ventures are intended to be disclosed to the public.

The most appropriate form in France for a corporation where powers and rights can be balanced equitably between shareholders is the 'société anonyme' or 'SA', which is (except for family undertakings) the most common French form of commercial company with limited liability. In the following discussion, we will confine our study to the 'société anonyme', but some of our comments are also applicable to the French 'société à responsabilité limitée', or 'SARL'.

The SARL is a simpler form of commercial company with limited liability, but it has several drawbacks both with respect to joint ventures (impossibility to have different classes of shares) and with respect to French company law (for example, more complicated formalities with respect to transfer of shares). A SARL is thus generally not chosen as a vehicle for a joint venture.

The problems related to the dissolution and change of corporate form of a 'société anonyme' are not examined in the following developments.

4.2   Advantages

(i)   The first advantage of a corporation is its independence from the joint venturers as described in 1.3.2 above, which is indeed the case for all common entities. Thus, a corporation is taxed directly.

However, compliance with French company law, especially rules governing the management bodies of the corporation, is essential.

(ii)   *Limited liability.* Under French law, although the limited liability of the shareholders is a basic principle in a 'société anonyme' (and in a 'SARL'), the corporate veil may be pierced in two cases:

– when a corporation is incorporated for the actual purpose of circumventing the law (namely to commit an act which is unlawful under French law or public policy),

> – in the case of insolvency, where judicial proceedings can be extended by the court to the persons having '*de facto*' or '*de jure*' managed the corporation (and this is generally the case for joint venturers). It should however be noted that in this case, proof that the '*de facto*' or '*de jure*' managers were *at fault* must be provided by the plaintiff.

(iii) *Current French law.* Finally and this seems to be the most important advantage, the set of rules (resulting from French Laws and Regulations, case law and practice) applicable to the French 'société anonyme' is well known and has worked well in the past. This set of rules offers additional assurance to the joint venturers and they are dispensed from enacting their own rules.

4.3 Disadvantages

Although there are many advantages in choosing the structure of a 'société anonyme', there are certain drawbacks, such as:

(i)   incorporation formalities are intricate (for instance minimum of seven shareholders, minimum capital of FF 250,000),

(ii) it is impossible to make contributions of future work (in French, 'apports en industrie'),[9]

(iii) special Board authorisation is generally required for any transactions with an entity having the same directors as the 'société anonyme' which is in practice the case of the mother companies (and their affiliates and/or subsidiaries) and of the subsidiaries of the 'société anonyme' itself,[10]

(iv) the yearly accounts must be published and then filed with the Trade and Companies Register,

(v)   special rules are applicable to 'auto-contrôle', i.e. when a 'société anonyme' directly or indirectly holds its own shares,

(vi) appointment of a statutory auditor is mandatory, who is in practice an 'independent eye', and can only be dismissed by court order.

Nevertheless, despite the above disadvantages, the 'société anonyme' corporate structure is so well known, respected and integrated into the French economic system, that its advantages prevail over these drawbacks.

---

[9] It is impossible, for instance, to receive shares in consideration for a contribution consisting of committing oneself to placing knowledge or service at the corporation's disposal in the future, whereas this is possible in certain types of partnerships.

[10] This rule, the aim of which is to avoid 'self dealings' by directors contrary to the corporation's interest, is essential and must be kept in mind at all times but suffers an important exception regarding transactions done in the ordinary course of business at normal conditions.

4.4 When to select

(i) *Ultimate step of successful cooperation agreements.* As indicated in 1.2 above the last step of a joint venture is actual work in common by the joint venturers.

A common entity in the form of a corporation is the standard vehicle for actual work carried out openly and jointly on a day-to-day basis, especially when capital contributions are required.

A 'société anonyme' is indeed the normal form for companies, as this French corporation is allowed to take on new shareholders, to be listed on the stock exchange and is able to progress independently from its shareholders.

(ii) *Standard form of joint ventures of significance and more particularly of industrial joint ventures.* Small-scale joint ventures, for reasons related to simplification and to the lack of public notice requirements, will normally be formed through a contractual joint venture or by organising one of the types of joint venture French partnerships (most often the 'groupement d'intérêt économique – GIE' or the 'société en participation' – *see* 3.3 and 3.6 above). For large-scale joint ventures, the structures are generally unsuitable and the 'société anonyme' is more appropriate.

Supposing for instance that two foreign groups want to operate their existing plants in France on a joint basis. They would have to create a common entity to which such plants (or the shares of the companies owning such plants) can be contributed, or a common entity to manage such plants. Cooperation agreements (without creation of a legal entity) or a GIE (with a limited object) would only meet their goals half way, and a 'société en participation' would not make sense if the jointly-run operation is to be carried out openly thus such foreign groups they will choose to create a 'société anonyme'.

(iii) *First step towards a merger.* Before actually merging, two French entities generally like to have an 'engagement period' during which they are able to get to know each other better. They will often use the GIE structure or a 'société en participation' for such purpose. However, they may also wish to work together in a given field of activity (for instance export to a specific country, development and sale of a new product, cooperation on an existing product) and for such purpose may choose to incorporate a common entity in the form of a corporation, to which they will contribute part of their activity, or which will be in charge of managing part of their activity.

4.5 Formation documents

4.5.1 Introduction

(i) In all cases, whether the corporation is created by the joint venturers, or whether one or several joint venturers invest in an existing corporation of another joint venturer, there are two main documents which are required in connection with its creation, to which the collateral agreements mentioned in 1.2 (iii) above must be added. These two documents are:

- the Articles of Incorporation (in French, 'Statuts') of the corporation, which in addition to standard provisions, will include special provisions applicable to the balance of rights and powers of the joint venturers: such provisions generally relate to the four rights embodied in each share of stock, namely:
  - the right to vote,
  - the right to dividends,
  - the right to liquidation surplus,
  - the right to transfer the share.
- a Shareholders Agreement (in French, 'Protocole d'Actionnaires'), which in addition to provisions related to the initial formation of the corporation, typically includes:
  - general principles of policy,
  - procedures for cooperation,
  - preferential rights in case of share transfers (reinforcing the provisions in this respect contained in the Articles of Incorporation),
  - non-competition clauses between the partners,
  - dispute resolution provisions.

For further details, *see* 4.5.4 below.

(ii) The provisions of the Articles of Incorporation differ from those in the Shareholders Agreement as:

- the provisions of the Articles of Incorporation are public and binding on third parties and can be enforced by the courts by requiring specific performance;
- whereas the provisions of the Shareholders Agreement are not disclosed to and are thus not binding on third parties and will in principle only give rise to a claim for damages in the event of breach (and not to a claim for specific performance).

4.5.2 Preliminary questions

(i) When preparing the initial draft of the Articles of Incorporation for a 'société anonyme' or adapting those of a previously existing corporation, four preliminary questions arise relating to provisions to be included in the Articles of Incorporation on the balance of powers and rights of the joint venturers.

(a) The first question which arises is whether the share capital of the 'société anonyme' should be divided into classes of shares with special rights, each class to be allocated to a joint venturer or to its group. In practice, such allocation by class (A, B, etc.) appears to be the best method to provide protection for joint venturers who are minority shareholders, but it is not the only method:

- similar results may be achieved without allocation by class by including specific provisions in the Articles of Incorporation. For example, by requiring that directors be chosen only among persons nominated by at least 10% of the shareholders (such 10% having to propose at least

three candidates), and by having special majorities of the Board of Directors for certain types of decisions. However, in our opinion such a system is more subject to criticism and less flexible than using classes of shares;
- other methods take advantage of the possibilities offered under French law to dissociate the voting rights from the pecuniary rights embodied in the shares, such as:
  - division between bare ownership (in French, 'nue-propriété') and usufruct (in French, 'usufruit') whereby the holder of usufruct is entitled to the income from the share,
  - division of some or all of the shares into investment certificates and voting certificates,
  - creation of shares with preferred dividends and without voting rights,
  - issue of special bonds giving rights to shares through conversion, exchange, etc., under certain conditions.

However, in practice, the above systems which are sometimes used in joint ventures where there is an outside investor, do not offer the same guarantees as classes of shares and are subject to severe legal restrictions.

(b) Another question is whether or not each joint venturer (particularly when a foreigner) should establish a company or partnership through which it will hold its interest in the joint venture (a 'holding company'). The answer depends first on whether the foreign joint venturer has or will have other interests in France and would like to have them held by a French holding company, second on whether third parties will be investing in the holding company's capital, and third possibly on foreign tax considerations (*see* 4.6 below).

(c) Another question is whether the less common form of a 'société anonyme' with a 'Directoire' (Management Board) and a 'Conseil de Surveillance' (Supervisory Board) with a maximum of five members should be chosen. This system of management copied from the German system has many disadvantages primarily due to the fact it is more cumbersome, but does have the advantage of offering more independence and stability to the Management Board which freely assumes the day-to-day management of the corporation, subject only to the supervision of the Supervisory Board. Because of this advantage, some joint venturers adopt it for their common entities, upon the basis that a good Management Board may be the proper referee in case of a disagreement between the partners. In practice, we do not advise using any system where a referee could show a tendency to favour one side, and prefer to suggest systems of arbitration in case of dispute which are better able to take into consideration the points of view on all sides. And in the following section, we have only considered a 'société anonyme' with a Board of Directors.

(d) A fourth question also arises which is: should the procedure of special advantages (in French, 'procédure des avantages particuliers') be followed? This procedure involves the appointment by the court of a special auditor, who will be required to submit a report to the shareholders, and is mandatory when special advantages, such as the allocation of classes of shares with special rights (*see* 4.5.3 (ii) below), are given to a shareholder or a group of shareholders, and not to the other shareholders. In fact, this procedure can be avoided, when the special advantages are granted equally to all shareholders at the time the corporation is created or when such advantages are granted to one joint venturer after incorporation, not as a result of personal preference, but because such advantages would have been granted to any investor able to make a similar contribution to the joint venture's objectives.

(ii) *Problem of premium.* When a joint venturer enters into an existing corporation, one question arises in particular: should the entry of the said joint venturer be made through a purchase of shares from the existing shareholders or through an increase in capital, with a premium (which will take into account the difference between the net asset value of the existing corporation compared to the par value of the shares issued, or which will just be an 'entry ticket' benefiting the corporation and to be paid by the new shareholder)? The choice is in practice a matter of business strategy, as French law is rather flexible in this respect.

4.5.3 Drafting of the Articles of Incorporation

(i) *Provisions of the Articles of Incorporation*

- Special attention must be paid to the provisions on the method and type of notice for convening each meeting of the Board of Directors and of the shareholders.
- If the system of different classes of shares is chosen, the Articles of Incorporation will have to provide clearly:
  (a) who will be the first owners of the shares of each class (unless this is done at an extraordinary general meeting of shareholders),
  (b) that when a shareholder of a given class purchases shares of another class, these are immediately converted into shares of the former class,
  (c) that decisions to increase capital should also provide for issue of shares of different classes (and likewise, any decision to issue debentures convertible into shares),
  (d) under what conditions the classes of shares will be cancelled or will lose some or all of their special rights (for instance if a class represents less-than 10% of the corporation's capital),
  (e) the special rights of each class.

(ii) *Special rights of each class of shares.* Such special rights generally consist of:

(a) a special pre-emption right granted first to the shareholders of a given class, and then to the other shareholders (and then possibly even to the corporation itself for reduction of capital purposes);
(b) right to have a certain number of directors appointed respectively from among the shareholders of each class and special majority requirements for the Board of Directors for certain decisions (as the directors must

be shareholders, the best way to avoid 'treason' of a director is for the joint venturer he represents to benefit from a call option so as to be able to recover the share(s) of such director upon short notice);

(c)   right to have the Chairman of the Board (who, under French law, is the chief executive officer of the corporation) and the general manager(s)[11] appointed respectively from among the directors holding shares of given classes, and possible limitation of the powers of the Chairman of the Board and general manager(s) (for instance joint decisions may be required from the Chairman of the Board and the general manager(s) in certain cases). However, such limitations will not be binding on third parties who, when they are unaware of such limitations, may require enforcement of a contract although in violation of such limitations;

(d)   right for each class of shareholders (when there are two) to appoint one of the corporate statutory auditors (in French, 'commissaires aux comptes') when there are two;

(e)   requirement that special meetings of shareholders of each class approve any amendment to the Articles of Incorporation, and other special important decisions;

(f)   possible pre-emption rights of the shareholders of one class of shares in the event of a sale of the assets of the corporation upon liquidation (although such provision may not have full effect in the event of sale of assets by a court-appointed liquidator following insolvency);

(g)   right for each share of each class to a minimum (or given) dividend, which in exceptional cases may be based for each class of shares on the profits of one specific sector of activity of the corporation. Such right may be cumulative (namely if not allocated one year, included in the next year's payment);

(h)   provision for arbitration in case of a dispute between shareholders with generally an amicable settlement clause (French case law seems, however, to consider that arbitration agreements cannot cover disputes on the validity of the Articles of Incorporation, and Article 2060 of the French Civil Code prohibits arbitration on matters of public policy).

(iii) *Problems in drafting the Articles of Incorporation.* When drafting the above-mentioned provisions, the rules of French company law which are part of French public policy[12] must be kept in mind. Although courts seem to be rather liberal with respect to initial organisation of powers in a corporation

---

[11]   The general manager (in French 'directeur général') is an authorised representative of the corporation (he may represent it towards third parties and enter into binding agreements on its behalf). The general manager may or may not be a director. The general manager is appointed by the Board of Directors upon proposal of the Chairman of the Board. The scope of his powers is also discussed and determined by the Board of Directors (he may therefore have the same powers as the Chairman of the Board).

[12]   Public policy rules apply completely to the organisation of a French corporation and it is impossible to argue, even when the shareholders are foreigners, that only the rules of international public policy (namely attenuated French public policy rules) apply.

among the shareholders (especially in case of joint ventures where the joint venturers each own 50% of the capital), they do not appear to allow an increase of the quorum required by law in the Board of Directors and shareholders' meetings, and are in general rather strict about the enforcement of the legal rules to limit voting arrangements or to protect minority shareholders. Accordingly, the unfortunate consequence is that provisions which are often found in the Articles of Incorporation of common entities, such as, in particular, the provisions applicable to the appointment of general manager(s) (who must legally be appointed upon the proposal of the Chairman of the Board), provisions on appointment of statutory auditors upon the proposal of the holders of each class of shares, provisions on the requirement to call special meetings of shareholders of each class when general meetings of shareholders are called could be challenged in court.

4.5.4 Drafting the Shareholders Agreement

(i) *Provisions of the Shareholders Agreement.* The Shareholders Agreement normally includes:

(a)   provisions on the establishment of the corporation: contributions in kind or in cash by the joint venturers, with all the related information as to their valuation; sale of assets by the joint venturers to the corporation with the price of such sale; certain provisions contained in the Articles of Incorporation, such as the name of the corporation and the name of the first directors, the chairman and the general manager(s) of the corporation; provisions on collateral agreements between the joint venturers and the corporation, if applicable (*see* 1.2 (iii) above);

(b)   main principles of policy to be applied by the corporation towards third parties (banks or employees, for example) and towards the joint venturers (supply of goods or services to them by the corporation, dividend distribution policy, meeting the financing requirements of the corporation with, generally, commitments by the joint venturers to lend money or to give guarantees and the consequences of breach of such commitments); and principles with respect to the entry into the corporation of other shareholders and the strategy on listing the shares of the corporation on a stock exchange;

(c)   procedures of cooperation between the shareholders;

(d)   rights of pre-emption (i.e. 'first refusal') to reinforce the provisions of the Articles of Incorporation which case law tends to interpret restrictively; the provisions on pre-emption can indeed be broader in the Shareholders Agreement and, for instance, extend the right of pre-emption to all rights to shares (issued by the corporation) and to all kinds of transfers, whether direct or indirect;

(e)   non-competition provisions (*see* 5.4 below) between the joint venturers themselves and between the corporation and each joint venturer and even in some cases, limitation on the access of the directors to confidential information (know-how for instance) of the corporation;

(f)   provisions relating to problems between joint venturers, namely referral of all disputes to arbitration (according to the same rules as the arbitration clause in the Articles of Incorporation) or 'Russian Roulette' clauses (usually termed a 'ping-pong' clause in France), the mechanism of which is similar to that applicable in England (*see* chapter 8, 5.5 (vi) (a)); special attention should be paid to the possible insolvency and court-ordered liquidation of a joint venturer, and all ancillary problems related to the departure of a joint venturer, especially reimbursement of the loans the venturer may have made to the corporation, substitution of the guarantees he gave in favour of the corporation, non-competition commitments between him and the corporation, use by him of information (including technical information, patents, know-how) obtained from the corporation;

(g)   provisions applicable to duration of the Shareholders Agreement (generally the duration of the corporation) and 'force majeure' in the last respect although French law applicable to 'force majeure' is fairly elaborate, legal counsel will often advise including certain events contractually (such as strikes) which are not normally considered by the courts as events of 'force majeure';

(h)   rules relating to future development of the cooperation between the parties, such as establishing the corporation or other new joint ventures in other countries;

(i)   deposit with a third party of the shareholders' register for the corporation;

(j)   in order to facilitate direct contact between the joint venturers, appointment by each respectively of a representative in addition to the directors of the corporation (but who in some cases can also be directors);

(k)   rules on public announcement of the formation of the corporation;

(l)   if applicable, provisions on any rights of the joint venturers to assets generated by the corporation (such as intellectual property rights);

(m)   provisions on applicable law if any of the joint venturers are foreigners (this may raise a problem: the ideal is to have the same law applicable to the Articles of Incorporation and to the Shareholders Agreement, but the Articles of Incorporation are automatically subject to French law).

(ii) *Problems in drafting the Shareholders Agreement.* The three main problems in drafting the Shareholders Agreement relate to:

(a)   avoidance of prohibited voting arrangements: French law prohibits voting arrangements, especially at shareholders' meetings (a shareholder must be able to vote freely); however, a shareholder can always guarantee that certain acts will be carried out by the corporation (if this is the case and this guarantee is not met, he is then liable for damages for breach of this contractual commitment). And in practice, such guarantees (in French, 'engagements de porte fort') actually have the same results in many cases as those prohibited voting arrangements would have;

(b)   abiding by other rules of French public policy: for instance, the members of the general meeting of shareholders must have the right to dismiss directors (any agreement to the contrary being void) and the rights of minority shareholders provided for by law must be respected;

(c)   avoiding action which is detrimental to the interests of the corporation (*see* comment in 1.3.2 (ii) above).

4.6   Tax aspects

French corporations are naturally subject to the French tax system like all French entities with respect to VAT, local taxes (taxes on ownership and use of real estate, professional tax, etc.), registration duties and corporate income tax. The following developments relate only to those aspects of major importance.

4.6.1 Taxation on contributions

Cash contributions to a 'société anonyme' are subject to a flat tax of FF 430 (for 1990), while contributions in kind generally give rise to a registration duty of 1%. Special rules apply when contribution is made by individuals on legal entities not subject to corporate income tax.

4.6.2 Corporate income tax

The net profits of a French corporation are subject to corporate income tax at the rate of 34% on undistributed profits (as from 1991) and 42% on distributed profits.

Capital gains are taxable items for French corporations. A distinction should be made between short- and long-term capital gains.

Short-term capital gains are those made on assets which have been held for less than two years. Capital gains, up to depreciation actually accounted for (depreciation recapture), however, are always treated as short-term capital gains, regardless of the date of acquisition of the asset sold. Short-term capital gains are subject to the ordinary corporate income tax rate.

The long-term capital gain tax rates apply to fixed assets which have been held for more than two years. As from November 1, 1990 there exist three rates for the taxation of long term capital gains, namely 15% on intellectual property rights, 19% on other fixed assets except for land to be developed, debentures and UCITS or similar rights on which the applicable rate has been raised up to 25%.

To determine the amount of taxation of long- and short-term capital gains, capital gains and capital losses are offset against each other and only the excess of gains over losses is subject to tax. However, it is not possible to use long-term capital losses to offset short-term capital gains or normal trading profits.

4.6.3 Taxation of dividends, interest and other income

(i) *Taxation of dividends*
  (a) *Tax credit*. Residents of France who are paid dividends by a French corporation benefit from a tax credit (in French, 'avoir fiscal') equal to 50% of the dividends received. When dividends are paid to non-residents, this tax credit also applies (and can be refunded if it exceeds withholding taxes on dividends) in accordance with certain tax treaties in force between France and foreign countries. These treaties limit the benefit of the tax credit to those shareholders who do not directly or indirectly hold more than a certain percentage of the share capital of the corporation distributing the dividends (generally 10%).

  If a French corporation distributes dividends from its reserves which have not been subject to the full rate of French corporate tax, such French corporation will be obligated to make a payment to the French Tax Authorities equal to the tax credit corresponding to such distribution. This payment is known in French as the 'précompte'.

It should be noted that when a French corporation does not benefit from the tax credit, the 'précompte' paid by the French distributing corporation is reimbursed to the foreign shareholder after deduction of the withholding tax applicable on dividends.

  (b) *Withholding tax*. Dividends paid to non-residents are subject to a withholding tax (in principle 25%), the rate of which varies in accordance with applicable tax treaties (it is often decreased to 15% and sometimes to nil).
  (c) *Parent/subsidiary exemption* (in French, *'régime mère filiale'*)[13]
  Dividends paid by a French or a foreign corporation to one of its French parent companies (subject to French corporate income tax) holding in principle 10% of its capital (or less than this percentage if the equity interest is at least FF 150 million) are deducted from the parent company's total net earnings, with the exception of management expenses determined at a flat rate of 5% of total dividend income inclusive of tax credits (whether special dividend tax credit or withholding tax credit). In return for this exemption, the parent company cannot benefit from the 'avoir fiscal' attached to dividends.

  These rules are also applicable to foreign parent companies which

---

[13] A special system called 'intégration fiscale' which is even more favourable may be opted for in the case of French parent companies owning 95% of the share capital of their French entity. This optimal tax system involves complete consolidation for tax purposes of the results of the parent with those of its subsidiaries taken into consideration for consolidation purposes.

are subject to French corporate income tax through a permanent establishment in France. For this purpose, the shares of the French corporate entity distributing a dividend should of course appear on the balance sheet of the French permanent establishment of the foreign parent company.

Distributions by the French parent company do not entail the payment of the 'précompte', as the tax credit attached to dividends from French common entities may generally be offset against the applicable 'précompte'.

(ii) *Taxation of interest and other income.* Interest and other income (especially royalties) received from a French corporation is taxed at the level of the beneficiaries. However, when such beneficiaries are not residents of France, depending upon the applicable tax treaty, a French withholding tax may apply.

(iii) *Choice between interest and dividends.* This question is often raised by foreign joint venturers investing in a French corporation. The answer depends upon the specifics of each case, but certain factors should always be taken into account:

- There is no capital/borrowing ratio except when the loans are granted by the shareholders.
- French tax law places limitations on the deductibility of interest payable to shareholders:

  - rate of interest subject to a ceiling calculated by reference to the average gross interest rate of debentures issued by non-state controlled French corporations, beyond which it is not deductible,
  - maximum amount for loans by shareholders exercising the management of the corporation on a *de jure* or *de facto* basis, such maximum amount (beyond which the interest produced by the loan is not deductible) being equal to one and a half times the corporation's capital,[14]
  - requirement that the total capital of the corporation be fully paid up.

Moreover, in order to avoid double taxation of those interests (non deductible in France and taxable in the country of the shareholders), EEC regulations (convention no 90/436 CEE dated August 20, 1990) to be implemented by the EEC member states have provided for an 'adjustment' of taxation between the two states concerned.

- The rate of French withholding tax depending upon the applicable tax treaty; for foreign companies which hold more than 25% of a French corporation, the withholding rate is generally 5%;

---

[14] This 'thin capitalisation' rule is in principle not applicable when the loan is granted by an entity which, although belonging to the group of the shareholder concerned, is not itself a shareholder ensuring *de facto* or *de jure* management.

- the ratio between the rate of return of the investment in the corporation and the rate of borrowings by the foreign joint venturer concerned;
- availability of borrowings by the corporation from third parties.

4.6.4 Interest of having a holding company in France

Except for the purpose of having a holding company for investments in shares of entities outside France or if there are foreign tax-related issues of importance, in our opinion, there are no special reasons under French tax law for a foreign joint venturer investing in a French corporation to have such interest held through a French holding company, (unless third parties are to invest in the holding company's capital.

More specifically, considering the fact that the tax system allowing consolidation is available only for corporations which are at least 95% owned, this requirement will generally not be met in the case of a joint venture in the form of a common entity, so that interposing a holding company to hold this interest in the joint venture, together with other equity interests in France is probably of no tax benefit in France.

4.6.5 Cancellation of debt by joint venturers

Under French law, there are limits to the tax deductibility by shareholders of the losses resulting from the cancellation of debts owed to them by their subsidiaries. For such purpose, a distinction should be made between losses resulting from the cancellation of commercial debts which are tax deductible, and losses resulting from the cancellation of financial debts which are only tax deductible up to the amount necessary to have the subsidiary the liabilities of which exceed its assets, come back to a net worth position of nil. The following factors should be carefully considered when dealing with debt cancellation in subsidiaries: exchange control notifications, effect on the financial position of the subsidiary (debt cancellations are deemed profit at the level of the subsidiary) and effect at the level of the joint venturer concerned (who should in particular consider (i) making the debt cancellation subject to a type of French hardship clause, i.e., 'clause de retour à meilleure fortune', (ii) the assignment of the debt to another creditor for a low value or (iii) the conversion of the debt into a subordinated loan).

4.6.6 Taxation on transfer of shares

Transfer of shares of a 'société anonyme' is not subject to registration duties, unless there is a written deed of transfer signed by the seller and purchaser (or equivalent) executed in France, in which case a 1% registration duty applies with a maximum of FF 20,000 per transfer. Transfers of shares of a 'société anonyme' are ordinarily carried out through a mere transfer form signed by the seller and giving instructions to the corporation; such transfer form (which does not constitute a deed) is handed to the purchaser in exchange for the price and then remitted to the corporation by the purchaser.

The seller is naturally directly liable for capital gain tax.

4.7   Foreign involvement

See 5.1 below.

4.8   Business assets of a corporation

See 5.2 and 5.3 below.

4.9   Competition law considerations

See 5.4 below.

4.10   Conclusion

The French corporation, despite the disadvantages discussed in 4.3 and the additional uncertainties from a legal standpoint as described in 4.5.3 (iii), remains in fact the most adequate and elaborate form of joint venture currently available in France. This is not only due to the fact that it is a very familiar structure for experienced business people and practitioners, but also because this type of structure, which can provide a proper balance of rights and powers between the joint venturers, can easily be adapted to the relevant circumstances.

5.   GENERAL FRENCH LEGISLATION APPLICABLE TO ALL FORMS OF JOINT VENTURES

5.1   Foreign involvement

Although French Regulations applicable to foreign investments are currently being simplified and are on the verge of elimination as far as EEC nationals and undertakings are concerned, several sets of Regulations applicable to foreign joint venturers doing business in France must be taken into account:

(i)   Regulations applicable to 'direct foreign investments' in France, which in some cases i) require prior approval from the French Treasury Department and ii) entail certain reporting requirements. These Regulations also apply to direct investments in France made by a common entity in which a foreign party has previously directly invested as partner or shareholder.

Direct foreign investments are defined mainly as:
— the purchase, establishment or expansion of any business;
— all transactions which singly or together, concurrently or successively, enable one or more persons to obtain or increase 'control' in any French partnership or corporation engaged in industry, agriculture, commerce, finance or real estate or which enable one or more persons to expand such a partnership or corporation already under their control.

In most cases 'control' of a French company is deemed to result from an over 33⅓%[15] shareholding (capital or voting rights) by non-residents alltogether, but lesser shareholdings, depending on the circumstances (when for instance accompanied by shareholder loans, or by industrial property rights licenses granted by the investor), or mere loan contracts or guarantees can also exceptionally be considered as 'control'.

Mere contractual agreements normally are not considered as investments, unless they give rise (or are deemed to give rise) to a permanent establishment of the non-resident in France, but a management lease agreement (*see* 2.4 (iv) above) of a French partnership or corporation may be considered as a direct foreign investment in some cases.

Direct foreign investments in France may be freely made by non-residents for the purpose of creating a new partnership or corporation or for most transactions related to the development of an already existing 'direct foreign investment'.

Prior approval from the French Treasury Department remains necessary for direct foreign investments in an existing French partnership or corporation. The French Treasury Department is required to oppose the application within one month. Failure to act in this time period is deemed to be an approval of the investment. However, for foreign direct investments in France made by EEC residents, such approval relates only to control of specific aspects of the investment[16] and is automatically deemed obtained fifteen days after notification has been given to the French Treasury Department if the Treasury has not objected (or asked for further information).

Reporting requirements also apply to some direct foreign investments in France (even when prior authorisation is not required).

(ii) Exchange Control Regulations which currently mainly consist of

---

[15] Different rules apply to foreign investments in French corporations listed on the stock exchange.
[16] Mainly if the investor is actually an EEC resident or under EEC control (as defined in the French Regulations i.e. when such EEC investor is directly or indirectly controlled over 50% by individuals other than French nationals or companies having their domicile in the EEC) and if the investment is not made in undertakings involved in the fields of public authority, public policy, public health, public security, trade of weapons or ammunition or to avoid the implementation of French Laws or Regulations.

reporting requirements (for the special rules concerning industrial property rights *see* 5.3 below).

(iii)   Regulations applicable to specific fields of activity: several economic sectors, such as press, banking, insurance, transportation, agriculture, energy, arms or public 'concessions' are subject to specific governmental regulations (requiring for instance authorisations, specific provisions in the Articles of Incorporation, nationality requirements for directors or managers, etc.).

(iv)   Regulations requiring a residence permit for all foreigners residing in France and requiring, in addition, an authorisation to work in France a special foreign business licence (in French, 'carte de commerçant etranger')[17] for non-EEC nationals working in France and more generally French legislation applicable to aliens.

5.2   Business assets of the common entity

(i) *Acquisition of business assets*. The acquisition of business assets from third parties generally raises no problems, while acquisition (through contribution in kind or purchase) by a French common entity of business assets from the joint venturers raises the problem of special formalities required under French company law, especially the appointment by the Commercial Court of a contribution appraiser (in French, 'commissaire aux apports') to protect minority shareholders as well as third parties such as creditors. This also involves the problem of proper valuation acceptable to the French tax authorities, making valuation by an independent accountant very advisable, and more importantly, the problem of the fate of said assets in the event the joint venturer who contributed them withdraws from the common entity. This last problem must be addressed in the joint venture agreements.

These problems are particularly acute when the assets acquired by the common entity from a joint venturer are industrial property rights and when the purpose of the joint venture is to develop a new product through the synergy of the joint venturers. In such a case, it is often advisable to have each of the concerned joint venturers license (and not sell) the relevant industrial property rights (including trademarks, if any) to the common entity without the right to sub-license, in consideration for both a royalty and an immediate cash payment. Such cash payment will constitute a claim of the concerned joint venturer over the entity and can be used to pay up this joint venturer's subscription to the capital of the common entity. In most cases, the licence agreements should include confidentiality provisions and other clauses providing for automatic termination in case of withdrawal of the joint venturer concerned.

(ii) *Use of assets of the common entity*. This raises a problem regarding the scope of application of the non-competition arrangements between the common

---

[17] Such foreign business licence is required for the chairmen, general managers and authorised representatives of French partnerships or corporations, when non-EEC nationals.

entity and the joint venturers. Such arrangements should be detailed and include provisions on the possible departure of any of the joint venturers. Special attention should be paid to the assets and especially the trade name, the goodwill and the industrial property rights developed by the common entity and their fate in the event the common entity is liquidated. Both the shareholders agreement and the collateral agreements (*see* 1.2 (iii) above) should be very specific about such problems and should attempt to provide for proper solutions in advance.

5.3   Rules applicable to industrial property rights

Joint ventures frequently involve the sale or licence of industrial property rights (especially trademarks, know-how, patents) or copyrights between the joint venturers, and between the common entity and the joint venturers.

It is impossible to summarise all the rules applicable under French law, and we will focus on the aspects which seem the most important to us.

5.3.1 Points to be considered

Three points require careful consideration:

   (i)   The joint venturers will have to prepare an inventory of the industrial property rights (under French law this includes patents, trademarks, know-how, design rights but not copyrights) and copyrights and especially of the know-how at each partner's disposal, so that each party may determine the information he will need from his partners and which he will be authorised to use for the purpose of the joint venture or, on the contrary, the information he will have to provide and which his partners will be authorised to use.

   (ii)   The contractual documents also define the rights of the parties and the common entity to use these industrial property rights or copyrights.

   (iii)   In addition, the contractual documents should lay down the rules which shall apply to the future know-how, copyrights and other techniques or industrial property rights generated by the joint venture, as the statutory provisions of French law are insufficient in this respect.

Specific 'inventions' made outside the scope of the contractual documents or developed in connection with works or assignments conducted under related agreements, but which are made and financed by one of the parties so that these inventions do not fall within the precise field of cooperation of the venturers should be distinguished from the inventions developed and financed jointly by the parties (common inventions).

The parties will have to decide on the attribution of ownership rights (to one party or to all parties jointly) and the use of the common inventions (licence to use free of charge for the parties, decision as to whether to sub-license to third parties, etc.).

For instance, provisions covering application for trademarks, which may be filed by the parties during the performance of their contracts for products or techniques discovered in common, should also be defined.

5.3.2 Exchange control rules

Notifications

(i)   The International Transfer Division of the French Industrial Property Institute ('Institut National de la Propriété Industrielle' or INPI') must be notified of contracts for the sale, purchase and/or licence of industrial property rights between non-residents and residents by the contracting party whose domicile or head office is in France, within 20 days following signature.

(ii) On an annual basis, the contracting party residing in France must file a form with the said division of the INPI indicating the total amount of funds transferred, as well as the new developments generated in connection with the performance of the sale or licence agreement.

(iii) When the sale or licence agreement is terminated, notification is also required with indication of the termination date.

(iv) *Transfers of related funds*. Transfers of funds in connection with industrial property rights between France and foreign countries may be freely carried out, provided they are done through bank transfers and that reference is made to the notification mentioned in (i).

5.3.3 Tax considerations

See 1.4 above.

5.4   Competition law considerations

The creation of a joint venture should also be examined in terms of competition law issues.

Indeed, the creation of a joint venture may fall under the scope of application of French competition law, as well as that of EEC law.

In both cases, the issues involve considerations related to concentrations (5.4.1) and prohibited agreements and/or abusive use of a dominant market position (5.4.2).

It should be emphasised that in order to have a clear idea of the effect of a joint venture from the standpoint of competition law, *all* the agreements entered into between the parties should be considered, including:

– Articles of Incorporation of the common entity;
– all main contractual documents including Shareholders Agreements; and
– any agreements, especially collateral agreements directly or indirectly

related to the joint venture (distribution, know-how, trademark, patent agreements, etc.).

5.4.1 Concentration issue

The creation of a joint venture may, in many cases, be analysed as a concentration. This issue should therefore be taken into consideration.

(i) *French law*. The provisions of the French Ordinance dated 1st December 1986 and of the ensuing Decree for implementation provide the following guidelines:

(a)   Article 39 of the Ordinance describes concentrations as 'Any act whatsoever, in any form, which has the effect of transferring ownership or usufructary rights to all or part of the assets, rights and obligations of an undertaking or which has as its object or effect, to allow an undertaking or group of undertakings to exercise, either directly or indirectly, a decisive influence on one or several other undertakings.'

(b)   Thus, the first question to be raised is whether a joint venture, which may potentially constitute a concentration, falls under the scope of the said Ordinance as defined in Article 38, which sets two different alternative criteria in order to determine if the provisions of the Ordinance do apply:

  – the undertakings involved in the joint venture must have together made over 25 percent of the sales, purchases or other transactions on the national consumer, commodity or equivalent services market, or on a substantial part thereof;[18]

  – or achieved an aggregate turnover (before taxes) which amounts to FF 7,000,000,000, on the condition that at least two of the undertakings which are parties to the joint venture have made a turnover of at least FF 2,000,000,000.

(c)   If the joint venture falls under the scope of the Ordinance, the next question is whether the Minister of the Economy should be notified of the joint venture.

  Indeed, under French law, there is no obligation to notify the competition authorities (as opposed to certain other national laws and to the EEC Regulations on concentrations).

  It is possible to notify either a proposed joint venture or a joint venture which has been completed within the previous three months.

  The issue as to the decision to notify or not must be considered through strategical analysis depending on the information at hand, such as market shares, turnover, volume of activity and the background of the undertakings involved.

  The main interest in notifying the Minister of the Economy of the agreement is that failing a reply within a maximum period of two months

---

[18] The reference market to be considered here is limited to (i) the particular products or services in question and the products or services which may be substituted for them and (ii) the territory.

(which may be extended to six months if the Minister refers the case to the Competition Council) from the date of notification, if the Minister has not replied, the concentration is deemed approved.

Notification of the draft agreements followed by discussions and possible approval of the Ministry will naturally provide more security to the parties, permitting them to go ahead and develop their new structure.

If the parties decide not to notify and the authorities subsequently consider that the joint venture does fall within the scope of Article 38, penalties may be incurred which can amount to up to 5% of the gross turnover in France during the last financial year or, in the case of individuals, FF 10,000,000. In addition the agreement(s) between the parties may be declared void in whole or in part.

(d)   However, it must be mentioned that such security will only apply as far as concentration legislation is concerned. The same agreements may give rise to other discussions regarding prohibited agreements or dominant market position issues.

(ii) *EEC law*. EEC Regulation No. 4064/89 dated 21st December 1989 (JOCE December 30, 1989, L. 395/1) applies to all community-scale mergers as from 21st September 1990. For further clarification on this issue, please refer to the section concerning EEC Law in Chapter 1.

5.4.2 Prohibited agreements and abusive use of a dominant market position

A joint venture may constitute a prohibited agreement between undertakings (in French, 'entente') or may lead to a dominant market position and therefore to possible abusive use of such position.

These two issues must be contemplated in light of the provisions of the French Ordinance dated 1st December 1986, the Treaty of Rome and subsequent Regulations.

It should be mentioned that the wording of Articles 7 and 8 of the Ordinance (dealing with prohibited agreements and abusive use of a dominant market position) are very close to the wording of Articles 85 and 86 of the Treaty of Rome.

(i) *French law*

(a)   Article 7 of the French Ordinance dated 1st December 1986 prohibits agreements between two or more undertakings affecting or having a possible effect on competition.

Once again, the agreements do not need to be in written form to fall under the scope of application of this provision.

Jv contracts may fall under the scope of application of Article 7 in that they may constitute an instrument for determining common commercial or industrial strategies, exchanging information or restricting the entry of potential competitors on the market.

(b) Article 8 of the French Ordinance prohibits abusive use of a dominant market position and/or abusive use of a state of economic dependency.

If the first issue (dominant position) is quite familiar to French law, the second one, which concerns economic dependency was introduced into French legislation only in 1986.

Abusive use of a dominant market position often consists in imposing artificially high selling prices, practising sales refusals or applying discriminatory sales conditions either towards consumers or towards economically dependent co-contractors.

(c) Agreements or decisions prohibited pursuant to these provisions are void unless they may fit within the scope of Article 10 of the Ordinance which leads to a 'bilan économique' (overall assessment from an economic point of view) of these agreements. The analysis made for the application of Article 10 is very similar to the one under Article 85 (3) of the Treaty of Rome (*see* (ii) below).

(ii) *EEC law (see also* chapter 8). If a joint venture has activities in different EEC Member States or where it has activities limited to France but which have an effect in other EEC Member States, then the joint venture will also have to be considered in the light of Articles 85 and 86 of the Treaty of Rome as well as in the light of the national laws of the relevant states.

CHAPTER 3
German joint ventures

1. GENERAL INTRODUCTION

1.1 The term 'joint venture' has no clearly defined meaning in German business practice, and even less so, in legal practice. While some use the term in a narrow sense to denote a jointly-owned and managed company,[1] others adhere to a broader concept and include any type of formalized cooperation between independent companies.[2]

From a commercial standpoint, the following are perhaps the most widely-used arrangements to be found in German business practice that might be called joint ventures in a broader sense.[3]

i) Long-term supply arrangements

These are often coupled with some form of technical cooperation and assistance to develop or adapt existing products of one party to fit a particular purpose of the other party. This arrangement may be mutual in that each party may provide the other with its own products to complement the other party's product program.

In most cases this relationship is of a contractual nature, as the parties do not set up a joint corporate vehicle.

ii) Cooperative distribution arrangements

Where two parties' production programmes are complementary, the parties may decide to entrust distribution to one party, which will then sell its own product and those of the other party. The relationship between the parties may be a distributorship or agency.

iii) Joint development agreements

These may provide for the separate conduct of R & D activities and the subsequent exchange of results or the pooling of resources through task forces and perhaps a joint corporate entity.

---

[1] 'Gemeinschaftsunternehmen', *see Wiedemann*, Gesellschaftsrecht, Vol. 1, 1980, p. 118.
[2] *See Langefeld-Wirth*, RIW (Recht der Internationalen Wirtschaft) 1990, p. 1.
[3] For an analysis of different forms of cooperation see *Sölter/Zimmerer*, Handbuch der Unternehmenszusammenschlüsse, 1972, pp. 149–213.

Here the transition from a contractual to a corporate arrangement may be gradual.

iv) Joint project agreements[4]

Widely used in the construction industry, this agreement enables different companies to pool their forces to place a common bid for a particular project and carry out the project if the bid is successful.

In most cases a joint project agreement may either create a partnership, at least as far as the internal relationship between the parties is concerned, or provide for the formation of a joint corporate entity to act in relation to third parties.

v) Cartels[5]

Cartels are arrangements between several companies, usually of the same industry, to coordinate a certain aspect or part of their activities. Under such a scheme the participating entities might undertake one or several of the following:

- to coordinate general terms and conditions on payment and delivery;[6]
- to coordinate and combine discount policies;[7]
- to coordinate norms and specifications for third party customers or suppliers;[8]
- to coordinate prices and/or production/sales quantities,[9] usually only for the purpose of export[10] to avoid obvious domestic antitrust problems;[11]
- to coordinate production programmes to allow each member to focus on a portion of a product range while ensuring that each member, or a joint vehicle, may offer the full product range.[12]

Even though many cartel arrangements provide for some joint entity to serve as an administrative and coordination office, the cartel usually leaves its members' independence intact.

Often the members form such an entity and include this entity as a party to the cartel agreement, in particular where the entity assumes central functions of purchase or distribution.

---

[4] Projektgemeinschaft, Konsortium, Arbeitsgemeinschaft (ARGE).
[5] Kartell.
[6] Konditionenkartell.
[7] Rabattkartell.
[8] Normenkartell, Typenkartell.
[9] Preiskartell, Quotenkartell.
[10] Exportkartell.
[11] For a discussion of German antitrust aspects, *see* 7 below.
[12] Spezialisierungskartell.

vi) Joint venture companies[13]

This is the 'classic' joint venture in the narrower sense where the joint venture partners form a joint entity to absorb and continue certain of their own functions, or where they wish the joint entity to develop new activities previously not carried out by its members, or where the new entity does both.

Due to the wide variety of forms a joint venture may take, the rules applying to them are scattered over different areas of German law, including contract, partnership, corporate, antitrust, and other special disciplines.[14]

In accordance with the structure followed elsewhere in this volume, this chapter will distinguish between:

  (i)   contractual joint ventures,
 (ii)   civil law and other non-registered partnerships,
(iii)   partnership joint ventures,
 (iv)   limited partnership joint ventures, and
  (v)   joint venture companies (other than partnerships).[15]

2.   CONTRACTUAL JOINT VENTURES

2.1   Introduction

In this paragraph the term 'contractual joint venture' will be used to denote cooperation agreements between different parties that do not involve the formation of a partnership or company.

One must appreciate, however, that the proper characterisation of a cooperation project as contractual or involving the creation of a partnership is not merely a function of using a certain terminology or form of documentation but depends on the substance of the arrangement. Section 705 of the German Civil Code[16] defines as a civil law partnership[17] any agreement – irrespective of its form – by which the parties undertake to further a common purpose. By contrast, the parties to a non-partnership contract each pursue their individual purposes, albeit complementary to each other. If an agreement meets the common purpose test, the rules governing civil law, and perhaps commercial, partnerships[18] apply unless the agreement lawfully provides otherwise. In

---

[13] Gemeinschaftsunternehmen.

[14] The East German Joint Venture Regulation (Verordnung über die Gründung und Tätigkeit von Unternehmen mit ausländischer Beteiligung in der DDR, of January 25, 1990, GBl 1 p. 16) only enjoyed a short lifespan and was repealed in June, 1990 in connection with the creation of a monetary, economic, and social union between the two German states. As a result of unification, the legal ramifications for joint ventures in the Eastern part of Germany no longer differ from those in the West.

[15] In German legal terminology the term 'company' ('Gesellschaft') comprises both partnerships (non-trading and trading, general and limited) and corporations (limited liability companies and stock corporations).

[16] Bürgerliches Gesetzbuch, 'BGB'.

[17] Gesellschaft *bürgerlichen* Rechts, 'GbR'.

[18] For a discussion of civil law versus commercial partnership, *see* 3.1 and 4.1 below.

addition, the parties to the joint venture will be taxed as members of a partnership and deriving business income from a partnership, which may lead to a reallocation of income and expenses.[19]

Even if a cooperation agreement does not involve the creation of a partnership, one will have to analyse its contents to determine whether it represents some other type of contract defined in the Civil Code or the Commercial Code.[20] While German law allows the parties to tailor their agreement so as to fit their individual needs,[1] the codes set forth rules for certain standard contracts such as sales, leases, loans, or agencies. In interpreting individually drafted agreements, or whenever a novel issue not expressly contemplated by the parties needs to be resolved, German courts will look for guidance in the codified contract law. If the agreement at issue fits the characteristics of a contract defined in the code, the rules governing that type of contract will apply unless the parties otherwise agree, to the extent that the law allows them to. Thus, an agreement to cooperate in the area of distribution and marketing may constitute an agency agreement as defined in the Commercial Code[2] even if the parties never considered their relationship to be one between principal and agent. As a result, the party later found to be the agent may be entitled to severance compensation upon termination of the arrangement.[3] Therefore, in drafting a contractual joint venture agreement, the parties should

- (i) analyse their agreement to determine whether it meets the common purpose test for a partnership,
- (ii) analyse their agreement to determine whether it meets the characteristics of another type of contract defined in the law,
- (iii) check their agreement against the statutory scheme found to apply in accordance with (i) and (ii) to ensure that all relevant areas are covered and the agreement is in accordance with statutory law, and
- (iv) otherwise be as specific as possible on all key contractual issues.

Still, the line between partnership/non-partnership joint ventures and contracts of different codified types may not always be easy to draw. In German commercial and legal practice, this does not appear to have presented an obstacle to the creation of custom-made contractual joint ventures.

2.2 Advantages

Described below are a number of typical characteristics of contractual joint ventures that are usually considered as advantages over a partnership or corporate joint venture. One must appreciate that the ultimate characterisation of

---

[19] For a discussion of the tax aspects of joint ventures, *see* separate headings below.
[20] Handelsgesetzbuch, 'HGB'.
[1] BGB, Sec. 305.
[2] Handelsvertreter, HGB Secs. 84 *et seq*.
[3] HGB, Sec. 89 b.

a particular aspect as being advantageous or disadvantageous will always depend on the strategic goals of the parties looked upon in their entirety.

i) Low level of commitment

Perhaps the most striking difference between a contractual joint venture on the one hand and a partnership/corporate joint venture on the other hand is the relatively low level of commitment that a contractual joint venture implies.

- The first effect of this is psychological. For a company to form an alliance with another through a joint vehicle is usually considered as a strategic move of fundamental importance, contrary to a contractual arrangement.
- Since the contractual joint venture is usually considered as being a less far-reaching step, it can often be accomplished without the need to involve top-echelon corporate decision-makers.
- The contractual joint venture will usually require smaller financial and managerial resources to be dedicated to its implementation and ongoing operation.
- A contractual joint venture can be set up for a shorter period of time and be terminated more easily than a partnership/corporate joint venture.

ii) Continued independence of parties

Through a contractual joint venture the parties maintain their economic and legal independence. A partnership or corporate joint venture, by contrast, works to connect the joint venture partners more closely as they assign a certain part of their activity to a jointly-owned entity.

This also reflects on the joint venture partners' liability and tax position. In a contractual joint venture the partners will not usually have to answer for each other's acts and omissions, nor do they need to involve each other in their tax planning and administration.

iii) Allocation of risks

Through a contractual joint venture, each party may shift the legal or financial risks associated with a particular aspect of the project to the other party. To name an example, if the object of a joint venture is the joint distribution of both parties' product range by one party, the risk of overhiring would be with the party entrusted with distribution. By contrast, these risks will usually be shared in a partnership/corporate joint venture.

iv) Ease of formation

The documentation required to set up a contractual joint venture is usually less comprehensive than in the case of a partnership/corporate joint venture. Similarly, formal and procedural requirements are less stringent.

Thus, the formation of a joint venture company (GmbH or AG) requires notarisation of the Articles of Association and, possibly, the submission of valuation reports by independent auditors. The formation of any joint vehicle that actively engages in trading, whether general or limited partnership, GmbH or AG, must be notified to the Commercial Registry[4] and, depending on the circumstances, is more likely to require filing with the German Federal Cartel Office.[5] All of these procedures may delay the finalisation of the transaction and generate notarisation, filing, and higher advisory fees.

By contrast, a contractual joint venture can usually be formed without compliance with any formal or procedural requirements. In certain cases the – German or EEC – cartel authorities may have to be notified or requested to give their approval.[6]

v) Ease of operation

As German partnership and corporate law is less formalised than that of many other jurisdictions, the differences between operating in a contractual versus a partnership/corporate joint venture are not substantial. Thus, neither partnership law[7] nor the Act Concerning Limited Liability Companies[8] require any formal meetings to be held or documents (such as corporate minute books, stock ledgers etc.) to be kept at a certain location. Nevertheless, lacking separate constitutions, management and funding, contractual joint ventures are less formal and in consequence less prone to develop lives of their own and thus easier to control.[9]

vi) Flexibility of joint venture structure

A contractual joint venture may be easily amended, reduced or expanded in scope if the need arises to address a new situation. Such changes do not require changes in the internal workings of a separate entity nor compliance with any notification procedures.

vii) Ease of termination

As already mentioned above, a contractual joint venture is usually easier to terminate, as termination does not entail the liquidation and dissolution of a joint entity in accordance with corporate and tax law.

---

[4] Handelsregister.
[5] Bundeskartellamt, *see* 7 below.
[6] *See* para. 7.1 below.
[7] HGB, Secs 105 *et seq.*
[8] GmbH-Gesetz.
[9] Ease of operation, or the lack thereof, would certainly be a key consideration in deciding against using an AG (stock corporation) as a joint vehicle, but partnerships and GmbHs represent alternative vehicles that are much easier to administer than an AG. *See* 6.1 below.

viii) Secrecy

The formation of a contractual joint venture will usually not be published, as there is no partnership/corporate vehicle to register with the Commercial Registry. Notification and subsequent publication may be required in certain circumstances under antitrust law.[10] The termination of the contractual joint venture may be kept away from the public, unlike the dissolution of a partnership or corporation which is notified with the Commercial Registry and published in local and national papers.[11]

2.3   Disadvantages

i) Fewer synergetic effects

The parties to a contractual joint venture will probably not achieve the same level of synergy as in the case of a joint partnership or corporation. In a contractual joint venture, all parties need to maintain adequate staff in their own organisation to monitor the project. The exchange of business and technical information is more limited, and opportunities for product innovations and cost savings are less vigorously pursued than by an independent entity.

ii) Lack of external flexibility

The downside of a higher level of control by the joint venture partners and independence from one another is a lack of flexibility by the joint venture project as such. Contrary to a partnership or corporate joint venture, a contractual joint venture may not react to changes in the environment or new market conditions as easily as an independent joint venture entity, as this might require the involvement of the joint venture partners to modify the joint venture conditions.

iii) Risk of recharacterisation as a partnership or statutory type of contract

As mentioned above, an individually drafted cooperation agreement may constitute a partnership under German law, or have to be characterised as a certain type of contract defined in the law. This may present the parties with unwanted contractual or even tax consequences.

iv) Limited field of use

Fewer synergetic effects, the lack of external flexibility and, generally, the absence of a joint vehicle designed to pursue the cooperation project narrow

[10] *See* 7.2 (ii) below.
[11] *See* HGB, Secs. 143, 157 (partnership); GmbH-Gesetz, Sec. 65 (GmbH); Aktiengesetz, Secs. 263, 267, 273 (stock corporation).

the field of application of a contractual joint venture down to circumstances where the formation of a joint venture partnership or company does not, or not yet, seem appropriate.

2.4 When to select

Due to the fact that the finding of a common purpose implies the creation of a partnership,[32] the use of a contractual joint venture will most likely be confined to two-party situations, the participation of three or more parties invariably implying a common purpose.

Accordingly, the following projects may qualify for a contractual joint venture:

(i)   long-term supply and delivery arrangements,
(ii) manufacturing agreements,
(iii) joint distribution in the form of agency, distributorship or franchising,
(iv) joint research and development,
(v)   know-how licensing.

Project agreements and cartels[33] will usually constitute partnerships rather than contractual joint ventures, as in most instances they imply a common purpose and, thus, a partnership.

The conclusion of a contractual joint venture may also be a first step at the beginning of a collaboration between two parties. It would allow them initially to play down the importance of the project, both internally and externally, and to terminate it smoothly if unsuccessful or turn it into a fully-fledged partnership or corporate joint venture if successful.

In very limited circumstances a project may be structured as a contractual joint venture to avoid regulatory difficulties, in particular those stemming from antitrust restrictions, which would arise if a partnership or company were formed. Since the authorities might recharacterise the contractual joint venture as a partnership, however, the parties would need to actually restructure the substance of their cooperation and operate it in accordance with the structure to prevent it from being found to constitute a partnership.

2.5   Formation documentation, key aspects

i) Form of documentation

Contractual joint venture agreements do not require any particular form to be enforceable. Theoretically they could be entered into orally, but for obvious evidentiary reasons they should be made in writing and be as complete as reasonably possible.

[12] *See* 1 above.
[13] *See* 1 above.

Certain clauses must be laid down in writing in order to be enforceable. The most important provision in this context is Sec. 34 of the Act Against Restraints of Competition,[14] pursuant to which any agreement or resolution aiming at a restraint of competition is unenforceable *per se* if it is not laid down in writing. Thus, any clause providing for exclusivity or any non-compete clause must be clearly spelled out in the contractual documentation. Similarly, a commercial agent's post-contractual covenant not to compete requires a written document signed by the principal.[15]

It is always preferable to address all relevant issues in the main agreement. The use of side letters, if later uncovered, often gives rise to a suspicion by the authorities that the parties intended to conceal a vital part of the agreement. This is true, in particular, for agreements that may be questionable from an antitrust standpoint.

ii) Drafting style

German law and practice is rather flexible in accommodating different drafting styles, including a style influenced by the legal traditions of a foreign jurisdiction. As a general rule, German agreements are shorter than common law-style agreements. Definitions are usually drawn from the relevant code, and exceptions and qualifications based on good faith and practicability are implied. To apply foreign-style drafting techniques to a German agreement may create conflicts of interpretation and should be avoided.

iii) Issues to consider

Due to the diverse application of contractual joint ventures, little of general applicability may be said. The following areas are most likely to receive particular attention:

(a) *Characterisation of agreement*
If the agreement is modelled after a statutory type of contract (sale and purchase, agency, etc.), it should state so and name the parties accordingly ('supplier', 'agent', etc.). This will reduce the risk of the agreement later being recharacterised as a partnership or other type of arrangement.

(b) *Funding*
Since there is no joint vehicle to make contributions to, the agreement should specify which party bears the costs and expenses associated with the project such as:

– development costs if products need to be changed, including tooling and testing,
– the costs for training,

---

[14] Gesetz gegen Wettbewerbsbeschränkungen, 'GWB'.
[15] HGB, Sec. 90 a, subs. 1.

- the costs for new product listings (DIN, UL, CSA, etc.),
- marketing expenses (catalogues, fairs, etc.),
- product re-call and litigation costs.

At the same time ownership rights (e.g. regarding tooling) must be specified.

(c) *Performance thresholds (minimum sales, agreed quantities, etc.)*

If any such terms are agreed, the agreement should clearly spell out the consequences of a party's failure to meet such obligations (i.e. cause for termination, reduction of geographical area, change in prices, termination of exclusivity features, etc.).

(d) *Pricing*

If all parties to a contractual joint venture are German residents (including German subsidiaries of foreign-based groups), prices may not be quoted in currency other than Deutsche Marks unless a special exemption is obtained from the German *Bundesbank* or a block exemption applies.[16] The same is true for automatic price adjustment clauses tied to the general inflation rate.[17] If the adjustment depends on changes in the prices for similar goods or services[18] or the clause requires the parties to renegotiate prices if certain price elements have changed,[19] no approval or exemption is required.[20]

(e) *Liability*

The agreement should be specific on the consequences of breach by either party. Liability for intentional conduct may not be excluded.[1] As the German law of sales provides for an intricate scheme of remedies in the event of delivery of defective products,[2] the parties to a purchase and supply contract must ensure that their agreements on warranty liability are properly reflected. Liability to third parties, in particular in the area of product liability, must be carefully allocated between the parties and perhaps be insured against.[3]

(f) *Termination*

It is a fundamental principle of German law that any long-term agreement may be terminated by either party with immediate effect for cause,

---

[16] Währungsgesetz (Currency Act), Sec. 3, 1st sentence and Communication (Mitteilung) No. 1009/61 regarding block exemptions.

[17] Währungsgesetz, Sec. 3, 2nd sentence.

[18] So-called Spannungsklauseln.

[19] So-called Leistungsvorbehalt.

[20] BGH (Federal Supreme Court), BGHZ 14, 310; BGHZ 81, 142.

[1] BGB, Sec. 276 subs. 2.

[2] According to the BGB, the buyer's remedies for breach of implied warranty (Mangel) are reduction of purchase price (Minderung), delivery of substitute products (Nachlieferung) or rescission of the contract (Wandelung), Secs. 459, 461, 480. Damages are available only in the event of breach of express warranty (zugesicherte Eigenschaft) or fraud, Secs. 459, 463. All remedies may be lost if the defect is not notified to the seller immediately, HGB, Secs. 377, 378. The limitation period is only six months from delivery, BGB, Sec. 477.

[3] According to Sec. 13 of the Produkthaftungsgesetz (Product Liability Law), the parties to a contract may not disclaim liability to third parties. This does not prevent them from granting each other rights of indemnification.

which German law calls an 'important reason'.[4] This rule is usually reiterated in the agreement. In addition, the parties may want to define certain instances that will be deemed to present an 'important reason' *per se*, such as bankruptcy or insolvency; a change of management, shareholders or group affiliation; and certain serious acts of breach. It should be noted, however, that due to the mandatory character of the termination right for cause, a contractual list of important reasons cannot be termed exhaustive.

(g)   *Governing law, jurisdiction*

German private international law honours the parties' choice of the law that is to govern their agreement.[5] To avoid any ambiguity the parties to an international joint venture will be well-advised to include a governing law clause.

Jurisdictional clauses will likewise be upheld.[6] In technically complex joint ventures it may be advisable to agree on an arbitration clause.

2.6   Tax

Since a contractual joint venture does not create any taxable entity, each party's participation constitutes part of its regular commercial activities and is taxed accordingly.

The issue of recharacterisation for tax purposes calls for particular attention. If a contractual joint venture creates a partnership, all income derived from it and expenses incurred in connection with it will be attributed to the partnership, and profits achieved will be taxed as partnership income.[7] As a result, payments to one party, which under a contractual scheme may constitute an expense, may be recharacterised as a distribution of partnership income. In addition, the partnership may be liable for trade tax[8] based on its assets and income so recharacterised.

Therefore, a joint venture and the contractual documentation should be set up in such a way as to minimize any risk of recharacterisation.

2.7   Tax aspects of foreign involvement

If the contractual joint venture is structured so as not to imply the creation of a partnership, the foreign party will be taxed as in any cross-border trade situation. Under internal German tax law and applicable double taxation

---

[4]   'Wichtiger Grund', *see* BGB, Secs. 626 (employment), 723 (partnership); HGB, Sec. 89 a (agency).
[5]   Einführungsgesetz zum BGB (Introductory Law to the Civil Code, 'EGBGB'), Art. 27 *et seq.*
[6]   ZPO, Secs. 38, 39. In a European context see Arts. 16, 17 of the 1968 European Convention on Jurisdiction and Judgements.
[7]   Einkommen aus Gewerbebetrieb, Einkommensteuergesetz (Income Tax Code, 'EStG'), Secs. 15 *et seq.*
[8]   Gewerbesteuer, in accordance with the Gewerbesteuergesetz (Trade Tax Act). For further details, *see* 4.6, 5.6 below.

treaties, a foreign party will be taxed on income derived from a German partnership[9] and a German permanent establishment.[10] There is a particular risk of a permanent establishment being set up where the foreign party sends personnel or advisers to Germany to work on the joint venture project on a more than *ad hoc* basis or provides permanent support (i.e. accounting, counselling, software) to the other party from a German basis.

2.8 Acquisition and use of business assets and intellectual property rights

i) Business assets

In a two-party situation it will usually not be difficult to determine who holds title to assets and to include special provisions deviating from the statutory situation where appropriate.

Specific provisions are advisable where assets are jointly funded but used primarily by one party. This may apply to such items as tools, machinery, testing equipment, software, or documentation. In the absence of an agreement on the point, it will remain uncertain whether the parties hold joint or fractional title, perhaps in proportion to their respective funding shares,[11] or whether the party in possession is the sole owner. In the proper circumstances it may be useful to provide for a partial refund of expenses to the funding party if the other party retains possession of the item upon termination (premature or ordinary) of the arrangement.

ii) Intellectual property

To carry out the purposes of the joint venture, each party will often have to use intellectual property rights owned by the other, including patents, trademarks, design rights, copyright, or know-how. Even though necessary licences to the other party may be implied,[12] it is preferable to specify the rights to be licensed and the terms of the licence.

Often the joint venture is likely to generate new intellectual property rights; in some cases like joint development agreements this may be the main purpose of the joint venture. Where new intellectual property rights are created, the agreement should address all those issues not clearly resolved by statute.

Inventions made and works created by employees in connection with their employment do not automatically accrue to the employer. German law starts from the general principle that authorship is individual, not corporate.[13] To

---

[9] EStG, Secs. 15 *et seq.*
[10] Betriebstätte, Abgabenordnung (Tax Code), Sec. 12. See, *e.g.* the Convention of 26 Nov. 1964 between the Federal Republic of Germany and the United Kingdom of Great Britain and Northern Ireland for the Avoidance of Double Taxation and the Prevention of Fiscal Evasion, as amended, Art. II (1) (b), Art. III.
[11] Gemeinschaft nach Bruchteilen, BGB, Secs. 741 *et seq.*
[12] See Urheberrechtsgesetz (Copyright Act), Sec. 31 subs. 5.
[13] See Patent Act (Patentgesetz), Sec. 3; Copyright Act, Sec. 7.

bridge the gap, the Employees' Inventions Act[14] requires the employee to notify the employer of any invention or technical improvement made on the job and enables the employer to claim the invention against adequate compensation.[15] If the employer so claims the invention, all rights thereto accrue to him and he may apply for any national or foreign patent registration or other protection available.[16]

While these rules apply to inventions capable of protection under the Patent Act and the Design Rights Act,[17] they do not extend to works enjoying copyright protection.[18] While title to copyrights may not be transferred *inter vivos*, the employer will be deemed to have a royalty-free licence sufficient to exploit the work in a reasonable manner.[19] Even though this rule has been established for a long time, employer and employee often enter into a written agreement clearly delineating the employer's rights to the copyrighted work, in particular in the high-tech area.

Inventorship or authorship is a factual question to be proven by the person seeking intellectual property right protection. Where an invention is made or a work is created jointly by several individuals, all intellectual property rights vest in them jointly.[20]

On the basis of the main statutory features as described above, the joint venture agreement should address the following issues:

- It should require each party to claim all employees' inventions for the benefit of the relevant party and the joint venture.
- To avoid factual dispute over authorship, the joint venture agreement should specify the parties' respective title rights to any inventions or works made or created in relation to the object of the joint venture.
- Aside from title, the agreement should state the respective rights of exploitation to any intellectual property rights, including the right to grant licences to third parties.
- The parties' obligations as regards applications for patent or other protection, maintenance of any registrations, and actions to be taken in connection with intellectual property right litigation (including the rights to take action and the allocation of costs in connection therewith) should be spelled out in the joint venture agreement.
- Where the creation of copyrighted works is not only incidental to the employment but its main purpose (such as in the case of computer programming), both the employer and employee should make express

[14] Gesetz über Arbeitnehmererfindungen, 'ArbNErfG'.
[15] ArbNErfG, Secs. 5 *et seq.* In accordance with Sec. 11, the Federal Ministry of Labour Law has issued guidelines on the assessment of the compensation.
[16] ArbNErfG, Secs. 13, 14. The filing for national protection is even mandatory, Sec. 13 subsec. 1.
[17] Gebrauchsmustergesetz.
[18] ArbNErfG, Sec. 2; Copyright Act, Sec. 43.
[19] RG (Reichsgericht), RGZ 153, p. 1; OLG Koblenz BB 1983, p. 992; *Schaub*, Arbeitsrechtshandbuch, 6th ed., 1987, § 115 IX, p. 773.
[20] Patent Act, Sec. 3, 2nd sentence; Copyright Act, Sec. 8; ArbNErfG, Sec. 5 subs. 1, 2nd sentence, 12 subs. 2.

provision for rights to the work. The same applies to the parties to a joint venture agreement.

- The agreement should cover both the period while the cooperation continues and the period thereafter.

2.9   Conclusion

Given the broad definition of partnership under German law, the contractual joint venture will be the appropriate structure for those cooperation projects, the primary characteristic of which is the exchange between the parties of goods, services, resources, and money, rather than the contribution of such resources to a joint vehicle.

This does not mean, however, that the use of the contractual joint venture is overly limited, or that it is rarely the appropriate structure. On the contrary, due to the lower level of commitment implied, the simplicity of formation and termination, and the flexibility in choosing the appropriate structure, the contractual joint venture enjoys a wide range of applications in all areas of the economy, including manufacture, distribution, and research and development.

3.   CIVIL LAW PARTNERSHIP, SILENT PARTNERSHIP, SUBPARTICIPATION

In German commercial practice there exist some joint venture structures which go beyond a merely contractual joint venture but fall short of establishing a true company. They include the civil law partnership, the silent partnership and the subparticipation.

3.1   Civil law partnership

By definition of law the civil law partnership (Gesellschaft des bürgerlichen Rechts) is an association of partners who have agreed to further a common purpose.[1] Although the common purpose can be the conduct of a business in a broader sense of the term, most of such partnerships would then automatically qualify as a commercial partnership (OHG),[2] except mainly where:

(a)   the partnership is not registered with the Commercial Registry and its purpose, albeit commercial, is not regarded as a trade as defined by the Commercial Code;[3] or

(b)   the purpose is to establish the partnership for a special project only instead of a longer term or broader commercial purpose.

[1] Civil Code, Sec. 705.
[2] For a description of the OHG, see 4 below.
[3] Commercial Code, Sec. 1 *et seq.*

Civil partnership joint ventures will exist mainly in the following circumstances:

- joint ventures in the agricultural sector;
- professional partnerships among accountants, lawyers, architects, etc.;
- in the building industry: partnerships between contractors for the development and execution of a particular project;
- in the banking and insurance sector: syndicates for a particular financing or agreements among underwriters of bonds, rights issues or insurance risks, etc.

The civil law partnership is not a legal or taxable entity. It comes into being by an express or implied agreement between the partners to further the common purpose. The assets initially contributed by the partners or subsequently obtained in the course of the business will be owned by the partners jointly. The rules of the law governing civil law partnerships are seldom appropriate for partnerships in the commercial sector. In the absence of an agreement to the contrary among the partners, the civil law rules would for instance provide that:

(a)   all partners are joint managers of the partnership and all transactions and any other acts need each partner's consent;[4]

(b)   neither the partnership interest nor any co-ownership right to any asset is assignable;[5]

(c)   each partner may at any time terminate the partnership without giving prior notice, except where in an exceptional case the date of termination would violate legitimate interests of the partnership as a whole.[6]

Companies forming a civil law partnership for a special project will define their respective rights and responsibilities in a partnership agreement that takes into account their specific needs and the position of each individual partner. In the financial services sector, German law agreements among banking institutions (e.g. sub-underwriting agreements or agreements among managers in a bond issue) are often similar to those which the international business community employs in other jurisdictions. Contractors jointly undertaking to develop and perform a particular building project often model their agreement on a sample contract the Association of the German Building Industry has worked out for its member firms.[7]

3.2   Silent partnership

The silent partnership (stille Gesellschaft) is a joint venture structure where one of the partners is a passive investor who makes a contribution to a business anticipating an adequate return from the profits of that business, but has no

---

[4] Civil Code, Sec. 709.
[5] Civil Code, Secs. 717, 719.
[6] Civil Code, Sec. 723.
[7] So-called ARGE-Vertrag of 1971.

responsibility for or control of the management at all. The silent partnership agreement is made between the silent partner and the business itself rather than with the shareholders or partners who established it. Depending on the terms of the partnership agreement, the silent partner is sometimes in a position similar to that of a lender.

The silent partnership is easily formed by an agreement between the business and the prospective silent partner. It is not registered with the Commercial Registry. The silent partner's share in the profits is defined in the partnership agreement and is usually agreed to be a certain percentage of the annual profit up to a maximum of a certain percentage (e.g. 25%) of his contribution.

The Commercial Code[8] implies a number of terms which, in the absence of an express or implied agreement to the contrary, will govern the relationship between the business and its silent partner. Thus, the following rules will apply unless the issues have been dealt with differently in the partnership agreement:

(a) the silent partner shares not only in the profits, but also in the losses; if as a result of losses his account has been reduced below the amount of his initial contribution, he is not entitled to a distribution of profits until the losses allocated to him have been compensated by subsequent profits[9] (although he does not have any general liability vis-à-vis third parties on account of those losses);

(b) the silent partner will not have any joint title or other right to the assets of the business,[10] nor will he participate in any increase of hidden reserves during the term of the partnership;

(c) the silent partner is not entitled to control or review management decisions;

(d) the silent partnership can be terminated at any time by giving six months' prior notice, such termination to become effective at the end of a fiscal year.[11]

3.3 Subparticipation

A subparticipation (Unterbeteiligung) may be agreed between a principal partner who holds stock in a company and a subparticipant acquiring a beneficial interest in part of such stock against payment of a certain amount to be agreed.

A subparticipation is entered into by an agreement between the principal partner and the subparticipant and can relate to shares, interests or participations in any type of company or business. Usually, the subparticipation is confidential and the principal partner is not even under an obligation to disclose the subparticipation to his partners/other shareholders in the business. This

[8] Commercial Code, Sec. 230 *et seq.*
[9] Commercial Code, Sec. 231 *et seq.*
[10] Commercial Code, Sec. 230.
[11] Commercial Code, Secs. 234, 132.

structure is sometimes used where an assignment in full or in part of the stock held by the principal partner is not possible as a matter of law (e.g. because of the by-laws of the business) or would be unwise for business reasons (e.g. because the participation of a certain individual or company is not to be made known). The subparticipation structure is also employed where a stockholder intends to subscribe for further stock in connection with an increase of the capital but due to a lack of funds has to look for a co-investor.

German codified law does not contain any provision dealing specifically with subparticipations. The subparticipation is by its legal nature a form of civil law partnership and economically similar to the silent partnership. There is little of general validity that can be said about the subparticipation agreement, except that it has to tie in with the partnership/shareholders' agreement of the company itself in which the principal partner is engaged. Since the Commercial Code does not provide any rules for what it considers a typical or normal subparticipation, the agreement will have to address in as much detail as possible issues such as capital contribution, information and co-determination rights, accounting, share of profits, term and dissolution of the subparticipation agreement.

4.   PARTNERSHIP JOINT VENTURES

4.1   Introduction

If the joint venture partners wish to establish a joint company rather than create a merely contractual relationship, the commercial partnership (offene Handelsgesellschaft, abbreviated as OHG) is one of the vehicles to be considered. This form is eligible to two or more partners jointly operating a business which the Commercial Code recognizes as a trade.[12] It is regulated by the Commercial Code.[13]

The OHG is not a separate legal entity. The owner of the business and its assets is the group of individuals, companies or corporations who are the partners of the partnership. In general, the law does not consider the OHG as an entity distinct from its partners. Since the OHG does not afford a 'corporate veil' the law looks to the identity of its individual partners. This also applies in the context of income taxation and this tax aspect may sometimes be the main incentive for selecting an OHG structure.

On the other hand, the law recognizes that a business cannot be successful unless it can act and be perceived as a quasi-independent body. The Commercial Code therefore facilitates the operation of an OHG in a way which makes the lack of separate legal personality less noticeable in the conduct of the

---

[12] Commercial Code, Sec. 1 *et seq.*
[13] Commercial Code, Sec. 105 *et seq.*

business. First, the OHG is registered with the Commercial Registry under its own firm name and will trade under that name. Second, the OHG may under its firm name obtain legal rights and incur liabilities, be assigned title to tangible or intangible assets and even be registered as owner of property in the land register.[14]

One of the most important features of the OHG is the joint and several liability of its partners for all its debts and liabilities.[15] A creditor is entitled to recover not only against assets held under the firm name of the OHG, but also against the private property of all partners.

The OHG is tailored for partners who are all in full control of the management of the business. It does not have an independent board of directors and management functions are performed by the partners themselves. Unless otherwise provided in the partnership agreement and published by the Commercial Registry, each individual partner can act for the OHG and contract on its behalf.

This management structure along with the unlimited liability of all the partners limits the use of the partnership structure as a commercial joint venture. However, the tax transparency may in certain scenarios outweigh these disadvantages.

4.2 Advantages

i) Ease of formation

In brief terms, the OHG is established by the partners agreeing to operate a business jointly. If this business is a trade within the meaning of the Commercial Code[16] and the understanding of the partners is that the joint venture shall not only deal with one particular project,[17] the operation automatically qualifies as an OHG. The establishment of the OHG then has to be notified to the Commercial Registry, but it can already start trading while the registration is pending or even before the notification has been submitted.

Unlike the formation of a GmbH,[18] the arrangement between the partners does not have to be reflected in a notarised document and there is not even a legal requirement of a written partnership agreement. It may happen that the partners thus unintentionally create a partnership. In the absence of a partnership agreement specifying the rights and duties of the partners, their

---

[14] Commercial Code, Sec. 124.
[15] Commercial Code, Sec. 128.
[16] Commercial Code, Sec. 1 *et seq.*
[17] As would be the case in an underwriting consortium, a syndicate of banks for a particular financing or a partnership of contractors in the construction industry for the development of a particular site. If such a special purpose company is established, it will usually qualify as a civil law partnership, even if it pursues a commercial business, *see* 3.1 above.
[18] *See* 6.5 below.

relationship *inter se* would be governed by the Commercial Code. It is true to say, though, that no experienced company or individual will carelessly make such an arrangement without negotiating with the other partner(s) the details of a written partnership agreement. In nearly every case at least some of the rules of the Commercial Code on the internal structure of the OHG would be inappropriate and need to be rebutted by contrary agreement between the partners. Issues that the partnership agreement will typically address are discussed further below.[19]

ii) Flexibility

In view of the personal liability of all partners the law is not concerned about contributions or preservation of capital, allocation or distribution of profits and similar matters. Moreover the law assumes that all partners are businessmen or companies rather than unsophisticated investors and that they have equal rights between them unless a partner gave up a certain position or right in the partnership agreement; accordingly, there are no mandatory regulations for the protection of holders of minority interests which would complicate the management or the decision-making process. The partners are free to determine the internal structure so that it matches their specific needs.

iii) Ease of variation

If the partners feel that the capitalisation, management structure or some other issue has to be adapted to unforeseen or changed circumstances, they can easily amend the partnership agreement. There are no formalities to be observed. This is also true for accepting new partners or splitting up with existing ones.

iv) Secrecy

The Commercial Registry will list the OHG under its firm name. It will also show the names and addresses of all partners.[20] Since all subsequent changes in the names and addresses of the partners also have to be notified to the Registrar, it is easy for the public to ascertain their identity. Unlike joint venture companies in the form of a GmbH[1] the partnership agreement does not have to be submitted to the Registrar and the public thus has no access to information on the internal organisation and structure of the OHG or the allocation of rights and responsibilities to the individual partners.

---

[19] *See* 4.5 below.
[20] Commercial Code, Sec. 106.
[1] *See* 6 below.

4.3 Disadvantages

i) Liability to third parties

Each partner is jointly and severally liable for all liabilities of the OHG, whether incurred by contract, quasi-contract, tort, product liability, or otherwise.[2] Even if the partner leaves the OHG, his unlimited liability to existing creditors will survive.[3]

ii) Unanimity required for resolutions

The OHG is treated as a 'personalistic' rather than a 'capitalistic' company. Any resolution of the partners therefore requires a unanimous vote of all partners concerned, except where the partnership agreement allows for certain issues to be resolved by a majority of the partners.[4] Individual partners may thus find themselves in a position where they can effectively veto an amendment of the partnership agreement or other resolutions to be taken. Similarly, subject to the terms of the partnership agreement, each partner has the right to veto any course of action which another partner is trying to pursue or any step he is going to take in the management of the company.[5] Especially in a joint venture with several partners the position of one individual partner may be stronger than is beneficial to the joint venture as a whole.

iii) Lack of independent management

The responsibility for managing the OHG lies with the partners themselves.[6] The OHG does not appoint any directors. This is sometimes a distinct disadvantage where the partners would otherwise prefer a non-partner to be the top manager and decision-maker. The only way to mitigate this problem is to grant one or more employees far-reaching proxies to act for the OHG. On the other hand, such employees would still remain one tier below the partners to whom they have to report and they are not members of a board.

iv) No transferability of partnership interest

The interest in the OHG is not assignable without the consent of all other partners. Although this may be appropriate for a joint venture in most instances, it will not in others and the partnership agreement would have to specify to what extent a partner can transfer his interest freely to any or only particular transferees identified in the agreement.

[2] Commercial Code, Sec. 128 *et seq.*
[3] According to Commercial Code Sec. 159 the claim of a creditor will become time-barred five years after the partner has been struck off the Commercial Registry.
[4] Commercial Code, Sec. 119.
[5] Commercial Code, Sec. 115.
[6] Commercial Code, Sec. 125.

4.4   When to select

The OHG is usually not the preferred choice of partners who are searching for the most beneficial structure of a joint venture. The unlimited personal liability of the partners of the OHG together with the other disadvantages mentioned in 4.3 mostly dictate the selection of a GmbH in cases where a joint venture is to be established. The main reason why an OHG structure may still be chosen is tax. The benefit of tax transparency for income tax purposes which the OHG affords[7] sometimes outweighs the disadvantages of the OHG structure. It should be added that tax transparency is also achieved by the limited partnership. Thus, if tax transparency is desirable under the circumstances, the joint venture can be structured as a particular type of limited partnership which combines tax transparency with a limitation of liability of most or even all the partners.[8]

4.5   Formation documentation, key aspects

The partnership is usually formed by an agreement in writing. In practice these agreements vary from very short agreements (mainly where two individuals establish a joint venture for which the implied terms of the Commercial Code are appropriate) to extremely long and elaborate ones (mainly where the concept of the proposed partnership differs from the concept underlying the rules of the Commercial Code). Issues to be addressed include the following:

i) Firm name

The partners have to agree on the name under which the OHG will be trading. The firm name has to include the name of at least one of the partners.[9] The choice is also restricted by several rules of the Commercial Code designed to avoid misleading the public about the business purpose or size of the company or causing confusion due to the similarity of the name with that of preexisting businesses.

ii) Contributions of the partners

In contrast to a corporate structure such as the GmbH, the partnership does not have a stated capital. The partnership agreement would simply state what contribution each individual partner has to make. The contribution may have to be made by a cash payment or in kind, for example by transferring title to certain property, supplying machinery or assigning industrial property rights or know-how. The partner may even be released from any obligation to

---

[7] *See* 4.6 (i).
[8] *See* 4 below, particularly for a discussion of the GmbH & Co. KG structure.
[9] Commercial Code, Sec. 19.

contribute to the establishment of the OHG. Such a release is sometimes agreed in favour of a partner who at the same time undertakes the main responsibility for the active management of the company.

iii) Management

In the absence of express or implied agreement to the contrary, each individual partner has the full right to act for the OHG and thus obligate not only the OHG and himself, but all his partners, too.[10] This authority is only qualified by the right of each of the other partners to veto any future transaction or step which he disapproves.[11] Such a management structure is often inappropriate and the law allows the partners to adopt a different system by agreement.

The partnership agreement will also address the question whether to notify the Commercial Registry of any restriction of a right of a partner to represent and bind the company. Unless registered with the Commercial Registry, any such restriction to which a partner may be subject according to the partnership agreement would be ineffective as against third parties.[12]

iv) Quorum and voting rights

Partners' meetings are held to adopt a new strategy, to take decisions about acts or transactions which go beyond the normal conduct of the business of that particular company, to accept new partners or to approve an assignment of an interest in the partnership, to dissolve the company or to vote on other matters which according to the partnership agreement are reserved to the decision of the partners. These resolutions need a unanimous vote of all partners.[13] The partners will have to consider whether this is appropriate for their joint venture or whether the partnership agreement should impose less strict requirements. Sometimes power is conferred upon one of the partners to determine certain issues alone or, in the case of a multi-partner joint venture, the partnership agreement may allow majority votes.

v) Allocation of profits and losses

According to the implied terms of the Commercial Code, profits and losses are shared equally by the partners.[14] The agreement should specify whether that is intended by the partners and it should also provide to what extent drawings are allowed without the consent of the other partners.

---

[10] Commercial Code, Sec. 114.
[11] Commercial Code, Sec. 115.
[12] Commercial Code, Secs. 125, 15.
[13] Commercial Code, Sec. 119.
[14] Commercial Code, Sec. 121.

vi) Termination/dissolution

A carefully drafted agreement will address the issues of term and dissolution and the procedure of winding-up the partnership. According to the Commercial Code[15] the OHG is dissolved upon the expiry of the agreed term, upon a resolution of the partners to dissolve, in case of bankruptcy of the OHG, in the event of a death or bankruptcy of a partner, if a partner or his creditor as successor has terminated by giving six months' notice[16] and if a court declares the OHG dissolved as a result of a so-called important reason.[17] The partnership agreement may modify or expand these grounds for dissolution and, even more importantly, may contain a clause that, instead of winding-up the partnership, one of the partners has the option to carry on the business on his own and to pay compensation to the others according to a specified formula. The partners will also frequently agree that in the event the court finds a serious breach of the partnership agreement by one of the partners, the aggrieved partner has a right to expel the partner who committed the breach.

4.6   Tax

i) Taxation of income

The OHG is not a taxable entity for income tax purposes. If the partners are individuals their share of the profits is a part of their overall business income to be taxed under the Income Tax Act.[18] If a partner is a corporation, the profit achieved as partner of the OHG is part of the corporations's income and subject to corporate income tax.[19] Any capital gain from sale of a partnership interest is also normal business income, but in most cases subject to a preferential tax rate.

In the event that the OHG suffered trading losses, each partner will be able to offset the part of the losses attributable to himself against income from other sources. It is partly this effect of tax transparency which may induce the joint venture partners to select a partnership structure if, e.g. in the establishment of a joint research and development centre, they anticipate losses for more than a start-up period.

The taxation procedure is such that the tax office at the partnership's place of business determines each year's results and allocates them to the partners in accordance with their individual share.[20] This determination will then be binding on all parties concerned[1] and will be taken into account by the tax

[15] Sec. 131.
[16] Secs. 132, 135.
[17] Which mostly will have been a severe breach of the partnership agreement by one of the partners, Commercial Code, Sec. 133.
[18] Einkommensteuergesetz, Sec. 15 subs. 1 no. 2.
[19] Körperschaftsteuer.
[20] Public Levies Act (Abgabenordnung), Sec. 180 subs. 1 no. 2 a, Sec. 179 subs. 2.
[1] Public Levies Act, Sec. 182.

office in subsequently assessing the taxes payable by the respective partner on the basis of his overall income.

ii) Capital Tax

Tax transparency also applies for purposes of capital tax. The tax authorities will assess a so-called unitary value of the business assets and attribute it to the partners according to their percentage of ownership.

iii) Trade tax, VAT, land transfer tax

German trade tax is briefly described elsewhere in this chapter.[2] With regard to this tax the partnership is regarded as a taxable entity and it is the OHG itself which owes the tax. The same applies for VAT and land transfer tax.

4.7 Foreign investment

There are no regulations restricting foreign nationals from participating as partners in a German OHG. As a result of the tax transparency the foreign partner will be treated as if maintaining an enterprise in Germany[3] and his profits will be taxed at a rate of 46%. The foreign investor will have to consider mainly whether the relevant tax convention grants tax relief by allowing a credit against taxes in his country of residence[4] and whether it would be more beneficial to hold the partnership interest through a German subsidiary.

4.8 Acquisition/use of business assets and intellectual property rights

Title to assets and industrial property rights may either vest in the partnership, i.e. the partners jointly, or in one of the partners. In the latter case the partnership will use these assets or rights under a tenancy agreement, a lease, a licence or a similar arrangement.

Often enough, partners undertake to make available to the OHG certain assets as their contribution to the partnership. The partnership agreement should then specify whether a transfer of title (contribution *quoad dominium*) or a cost-free licence or similar arrangement is intended which would only enable the OHG to use this asset free of charge (contribution *quoad usum*). The law assumes that a transfer of title was meant to take place if the asset is 'consumable', i.e. if it is usually specified by reference to a number, measure-

---

[2] Para. 6.6 (ii).
[3] This is usually confirmed by the relevant tax treaty, *see* e.g. Art. III (2) of the Convention between the Federal Republic of Germany and the United Kingdom for the Avoidance of Double Taxation of 26th November 1964.
[4] For the UK, *see* the British-German Tax Convention, Art. XVIII.

ment or weight, or if the value of the asset has been assessed by an estimate of the partners.[5]

4.9   Competition law considerations

During the term of his participation the partner is subject to a non-competition obligation, unless released from this obligation by the other partners.[6] The rationale behind this implied non-competition obligation is that the Commercial Code assumes that each partner is actively involved in running the business. For certain qualifications to this rule under antitrust laws and a broader discussion of competition law, the reader is referred to 7 below.

4.10   Conclusion

Owing mainly to the lack of limited liability, the partnership joint venture structure is seldom employed, and if so mainly to enjoy potential benefits of tax transparency. Even so, an understanding of the OHG is required for appreciating its sister, the limited partnership (KG). While also affording a 'look-through' structure for income tax purposes, the KG avoids some of the disadvantages of the OHG structure.

5.   LIMITED PARTNERSHIPS

5.1   Introduction

The limited partnership (Kommanditgesellschaft, abbreviated as KG) is a common type of company in German commercial practice. The KG is in many ways similar to the normal commercial partnership (OHG).[7] In regulating the KG the Commercial Code contains a block reference to the rules on the OHG and only lists certain exceptions where the law of the limited partnership differs from that of the OHG.[8]

The main distinction between the limited and the full partnership is that the limited partnership not only has general, but also limited partners. The general partner has the same position as a partner in an OHG. He is exposed to an unlimited personal liability for all obligations of the KG and at the same time is responsible for the management. By contrast, the limited partner has to make a capital contribution to the KG, but his liability is limited to the amount of this contribution.[9] Although he may have to share in losses

---

[5] Civil Code, Sec. 706.
[6] Commercial Code, Sec. 112.
[7] Described in 4 above.
[8] Commercial Code, Sec. 161 *et seq.*
[9] Commercial Code, Sec. 171.

in excess of his contribution, he is never obliged to cover such losses by making further contributions.[10] In keeping with his limited liability he is not entitled to or responsible for the management of the company.[11]

The KG can have individuals or corporations as partners, or a combination of both. This permits the establishment of a special KG structure which is frequently employed in West Germany, the GmbH & Co. KG. Typically, two partners will first establish a limited liability company (GmbH) with a very thin capitalisation. As a second step the GmbH will participate in a newly established KG with the GmbH taking on the role of the general partner and the GmbH's shareholders being the limited partners. Both shareholders/ partners thus hold two interests: a share in the GmbH and an interest as limited partner in the KG. In effect, both partners avoid any personal liability as only the GmbH acts as general partner. The courts have acknowledged that this is not an unlawful avoidance structure, even if the GmbH has few funds available and may have been founded only with the statutory minimum capital of currently DM 50,000.

5.2 Advantages

The KG enjoys practically all of the advantages of an OHG.

If the KG is established as a GmbH & Co. KG, two companies have to be formed and this slightly dilutes the ease with which the OHG is formed and handled. Besides, certain information about the internal structure may be more difficult to keep secret because the articles of association of the GmbH would have to be filed with the Commercial Registry and are available for inspection by the public. On the other hand these differences are fairly insignificant and by far outweighed by the advantages which the GmbH & Co. KG often provides in comparison to an OHG or even a 'normal' limited partnership (KG).

5.3 Disadvantages

The KG shares with the partnership the disadvantages of the partnership structure.[12] The principle disadvantage of the personal liability of the partners is only mitigated by the fact that it only applies to the partner(s) who act(s) as general partner(s).

If a special purpose corporation such as a GmbH is used to serve as general partner, the risk related to the personal liability of the partners can be completely avoided. The courts will only in very rare circumstances pierce the corporate veil and allow an enforcement of claims against shareholders of a corporate general partner of the KG.

[10] Commercial Code, Sec. 167 subs. 2.
[11] Commercial Code, Secs. 164, 170.
[12] *See* 4.3 above.

The GmbH & Co. KG also solves a management problem which may other-wise come up in the OHG and KG alike.[13] The limited partners have no right to participate in the management of the company, save only for a right to veto any steps which would go beyond the usual conduct of the business.[14] Management responsibility thus lies with the GmbH being the general partner. As regards the GmbH itself, its shareholders (typically identical with the limited partners of the KG) may adopt an internal and management structure which is adequate for the particular joint venture business. In contrast to the 'normal' KG they can appoint a non-partner chief executive officer of the GmbH who will then act for the GmbH and, at the same time, the GmbH & Co. KG which the GmbH as its general partner is representing.[15]

5.4   When to select

The KG may be selected in the rare cases where one partner is prepared to take the risk of personal liability as a means of credit support or for some other reason and wishes to take on the management of the joint venture. At the same time the other partners must agree to take a back seat by giving up day-to-day management responsibility or control whilst having the advan-tage of limited liability.

Upon an analysis of the alternatives, very often the GmbH & Co. KG will prove to be better suited. For all practical purposes it functions like a GmbH, but offers tax transparency which will be an advantage, e.g. if it is anticipated that the joint venture will incur trading losses for a couple of years.

5.5   Formation documentation, key aspects

The documentation establishing the KG is similar to that establishing the OHG. Certain differences are of course due to the fact that the limited partner in several respects has a position which is distinct from that of a partner of the OHG or the general partner of the KG. Apart from limiting the limited partner's liability to the amount of his contribution as specified in the partnership agree-ment and subsequently notified to the Commercial Registry, the Commercial Code implies certain terms regarding the rights and obligations of limited partners which need to be altered by the agreement if inappropriate under the circumstances. If, for example, a limited partner is meant to enjoy the right to take part in, supervise or control the management of the KG, the partnership agreement would have to confer such rights on him.

In the event that a GmbH & Co. KG is formed, the documentation for the KG must tie in with that for the GmbH which is to be general partner. Typically the percentage interests of the limited partners in the KG will

---

[13] *See* 4.3 (iii).
[14] Commercial Code, Sec. 164.
[15] For a discussion of the internal structure of a GmbH, *see* 6.5 (iii) (a) below.

correspond to the amounts of stock they hold in the GmbH. Since the GmbH controls the management of the joint venture while nearly all the assets and rights are vested in the KG, it is imperative to ensure that shares in the GmbH can only be assigned together with the pertaining KG interest and vice versa.

5.6 Tax

Taxwise, the KG and all its partners, whether general or limited, are in the same position as with an OHG.[16]

Tax authorities also recognise a GmbH & Co. KG as a true limited partnership even if the general partner-GmbH is endowed only with the minimum capital and as a result of its structure the GmbH & Co. KG operates more or less exactly as a GmbH. There are only few exceptional cases where individual limited partners had such a weak and inferior position in the partnership agreement and the company practice that they were found not to be entrepreneurs and owners of the business in spite of the general rule of tax transparency.[17]

In order to be able to attribute 100% of the profits and losses to limited partners, the partnership agreement often specifies that the GmbH is excluded from joint ownership in the assets of the KG and does not share in the profits or losses of the business. It will then only be entitled to a management fee in consideration of its duties as general partner of the KG.

5.7 Foreign investment

In respect of possible foreign investment the same considerations apply as in the context of an OHG.[18]

5.8 Acquisition/use of business assets and intellectual property rights

Since here again limited partnerships are just a special form of partnership, see the statements in 4.8 above.

5.9 Competition law considerations

The limited partner is not subject to a non-competition obligation.[19] This reflects his subordinate position within the company and the fact that he is not involved in its management. Although the limited partner is thus not bound

---

[16] *See* 4.6 above.
[17] The test to be applied and the relevant factors were laid down by the Federal Supreme Tax Court in a judgment of 30th July 1975, Bundessteuerblatt 1975 part II p. 818 *et seq.*
[18] *See* 4.7 above.
[19] Commercial Code, Sec. 165.

by a non-competition obligation in strict legal terms it is generally assumed that he has a duty to be loyal to his fellow partners and to act in good faith to further the business of the KG. This imposes on him a duty which the court will try to define more precisely in view of the individual partner's rights and obligations under the partnership agreement and the strength of his position among his partners. The scope of this duty may be found to be similar to that of a non-competition obligation and the partners are well advised to specify in the partnership agreement whether and to what extent the limited partner is supposed to refrain from establishing, participating in financing or otherwise supporting a competing business. The partners may allow the limited partner to compete with the KG or, notwithstanding the restrictions of antitrust law,[20] may impose upon him a non-competition obligation which is equivalent to that of the general partner.

5.10   Conclusion

The limited partnership structure is used fairly often, by comparison with the full partnership (OHG) joint venture. Its most common form is the GmbH & Co. KG which is employed where the partners want to operate through a joint venture corporation and at the same time enjoy tax transparency.

6.   JOINT VENTURE COMPANIES

6.1   Introduction

The motives for establishing a joint venture company ('jvc') in Germany do not differ from those in other advanced economies. A jvc provides a permanent basis for pooling the resources of the partners, thereby enabling the individual partners to decentralise certain functions or to enter into a new field of activity that requires the combined efforts of several participants. Often the foreign investor may want to join forces with partners based in Germany to overcome more easily cultural and language barriers and benefit from market familiarity and existing customer contacts.[1]

German corporate law offers two types of companies that may serve as a jvc:

    (i)   The *GmbH* (Gesellschaft mit beschränkter Haftung, or limited liability company); and

    (ii) the *AG* (Aktiengesellschaft, or stock corporation).

The form of company most often selected for joint ventures with foreign participation is the GmbH. Originally designed primarily for small family-owned

---

[20]   *See* 7 below.

[1]   *See Schaub*, Gemeinschaftsunternehmen, in *Sölter/Zimmerer*, Handbuch der Unternehmenszusammenschlüsse, 1972, pp. 181–2.

businesses, the law on GmbHs provides maximum flexibility as regards capitalisation, management, and internal decision-making procedure while ensuring
the limited liability of its shareholders. By contrast, the law governing AGs
is much less permissive, prescribing mostly mandatory rules on corporate structure and procedures while allowing for various sources of outside financing.
The AG, therefore, is the ideal vehicle for a large publicly-held company while
the GmbH is primarily used for small- to medium-sized businesses with a small
number of shareholders.

The discussion of the jvc, therefore, will focus on the GmbH. Variations
to be observed when dealing with an AG will be indicated where appropriate.

6.2   Advantages

The relative advantages and disadvantages of forming a jvc, as opposed to
using a contractual or partnership joint venture, are to a large extent the mirror
image of the advantages and disadvantages of those types of joint venture.
It will, therefore, suffice to highlight the key characteristics of a jvc that may
be considered advantageous in the usual circumstances. For a detailed discussion, the reader should refer to 2.2 and 2.3 above.

i) High level of commitment

By forming a jvc, all partners make a clear statement of commitment to each
other and to the public.

- To form a jvc involves the dedication of considerable managerial and
  financial resources to the joint project and requires high-level corporate
  approval, all of which is viewed by the other partners as an indication
  of a serious commitment.
- The formation of a jvc must be publicised and often requires the involvement of regulatory authorities.[2] The ensuing publicity cannot be easily
  retracted.
- To operate a jvc jointly in the market place, perhaps under a joint corporate name, creates a joint market presence, which is difficult to terminate.

ii) Clarity of structure

The existence of a separate legal entity presents a clear structure which facilitates
external operations and internal procedures of the jvc.

- All transactions of the jvc create rights and obligations only of the jvc
  and not individual partners.
- The jvc being a separate legal entity, it is easy to determine who holds
  title to business and intellectual property rights.

---

[2] For details *see* 6.5 and 7 below.

- The jvc provides a clear structure for the determination of joint venture policy, referring the decision-making process to the procedures prescribed for management, board and shareholders.
- A jvc constitutes a profit centre which allows each partner to isolate the chances and risks, including liability, associated with, as well as the profits generated by, its investment in the jvc.

iii) Transferability of shares

This aspect will usually *not* constitute a decisive criterion in selecting a jvc. In German corporate practice, the transferability of GmbH shares is usually restricted in a way similar to partnerships to take account of the personalistic character of the jvc.[3]

6.3   Disadvantages

i) Lack of flexibility

The downside of having a clear structure is the lack of flexibility in shaping joint venture policy. Decision-making procedures may delay urgent responses to a changed market situation. The increased level of commitment and permanence of the involvement creates the need to reach compromises among the joint venture partners, which may dilute the individual partner's intentions.

ii) Difficulty of integration

Contrary to a contractual joint venture, a jvc develops more of a life of its own. The internal culture of the jvc may differ from that of the individual partners. This may create frictions and frustrations between the jvc and its partners/shareholders.

For other potential advantages and disadvantages, the reader should refer to 2.2 and 2.3, above.

6.4   When to select

Like in most other Western markets, the formation of a German jvc will be the preferred choice where the partners have identified long-term opportunities that need to be actively pursued by an independent entity, where the entity must employ dedicated staff and resources to achieve its goals, the partners are each willing and capable to contribute a part of those resources, and each partner wishes to share in the value created by the business. Contrary to many joint venture partnerships, the jvc will usually become involved in more than

---

[3] For details *see* 6.5 (iii) (c) below.

one project. Contrary to a contractual joint venture, all partners must be willing to remain actively involved in all aspects of the jvc's activities and share in the chances and risks of the entire operation.

The wide range of possible applications makes it difficult to name typical situations where a jvc may be selected. Aside from those situations that are likely to be similar in all Western countries, the following sets of circumstances may perhaps be found more frequently in Germany than elsewhere:

(i)   Many German family-owned businesses have outgrown their founders and require additional funding to finance further expansion and access to new markets. Instead of an outright sale, many company owners prefer to take in a strong corporate partner with whom to run the business as a joint venture, perhaps for a limited time until the owners are willing to part with their remaining shareholding.

(ii) To set up a joint venture structure may be a good solution for a German family-owned business that will not be taken over by the next generation of family members. Running the company as a joint venture allows for a smoother transition both from a managerial and market stand-point.

(iii) Even though in Germany there are virtually no areas of industry where foreign ownership is restricted, it may be advisable in the appropriate circumstances to team up with German partners as a means of entering certain local markets (such as construction) or to obtain important government contracts (such as in the area of telecommunications or defence).

6.5   Formation documentation, key aspects

i) Form of documentation in general

Like in Anglo-American legal practice, the use of a general joint venture agree-ment setting forth the principal points of agreement on the jvc and basic policy issues has also become standard German practice. To this main document, entitled 'Basic Policy Agreement', 'Cooperation Agreement' or simply 'Joint Venture Agreement',[4] drafts of the jvc's Articles of Association and all ancil-lary agreements between the jvc and individual shareholders are attached as exhibits.

Even though the basic documentation is similar, the weight of the Articles of Association as compared to that of the joint venture agreement is not the same as in many other jurisdictions, as the Articles of Association of a GmbH cover much more substance than their foreign, in particular Anglo-American, counterparts.

There are several reasons for this. Besides stating the minimum contents

---

[4] Grundsatzvereinbarung, Vereinbarung über Zusammenarbeit, Joint-Venture-Vereinbarung. The term 'Shareholders Agreement' is normally understood to cover only the exercise of voting rights.

of GmbH Articles,[5] many provisions of the GmbH-Gesetz state that a certain rule applies 'unless otherwise set forth in the Articles of Association'.[6] This may concern such fundamental issues as the transferability of shares, the distribution of dividends, or the termination of the GmbH.[7] By dealing with such items in the Articles, the shareholders exercise the contractual freedom granted to them by law.

This method also provides greater protection to the shareholders. The alternative solution would be to make these issues the subject of a shareholders' voting agreement,[8] which could also be contained in the joint venture agreement. Yet this would only give a personal claim against the party to the voting agreement to cast his vote in a certain way, which still needs to be enforced, perhaps with the court's help, before becoming effective. By including a provision on the issue in the Articles, the provision becomes an element of the GmbH's constitution and binds all shareholders, including successors-in-law, as a matter of corporate instead of contract law.

To name an example, a GmbH is liquidated upon a resolution of the shareholders[9] or in the events stated in the Articles of Association.[10] This gives the shareholders the choice to either make a voting agreement and define certain events in which they are required to vote for the liquidation, or to list those events in the Articles of Association. For the reasons stated, the latter solution reflects standard German corporate practice.

Statutory requirements regarding form also largely influence the format of joint venture documentation. While shareholders' voting agreements or a joint venture agreement are enforceable if they are made in writing, many documents regarding the structure of the jvc and rights to shares are enforceable only if notarised before a German notary. This is true, in particular, for the Articles of Association of a GmbH[11] and agreements regarding the sale and transfer of GmbH shares, including acquisition, put and call rights, and purchase options.[12] While the Articles of Association are deposited with the Commercial Registry and available to the public,[13] agreements regarding shares are not.[14] Therefore, agreements regarding rights to shares of the jvc are usually dealt with in separate – notarised – documents.

Outside these policy and secrecy considerations, there are no fixed rules on how to allocate the various issues between the joint venture agreement, the Articles of Association, and additional documents or separate agreements.

---

[5] Name, registered seat, object, amount of stated capital, amount of shares subscribed for by each shareholder. GmbHG, Sec. 3 subs. 1.
[6] Cf. GmbHG, Secs. 5 subs. 2, 3; 6 subs. 3; 15 subs. 5; 17 subs. 3, 6; 29 subs. 1, 3; 34 subs. 1, 2; 38 subs. 2; 45; 52 subs. 1; 60 subs. 2.
[7] GmbHG, Secs. 15 subs. 5; 29; 60.
[8] 'Stimmbindungsvertrag'; such agreements are generally enforceable.
[9] GmbHG, Sec. 60 subs. 1 no. 1.
[10] GmbHG, Sec. 60 subs. 2.
[11] GmbHG, Sec. 2. The same applies to the by-laws (Satzung) of an AG. AktG, Sec. 23.
[12] GmbHG, Sec. 15. No notarisation is required for the sale and share of stock in an AG.
[13] Copies are made available to any outside party against a small handling fee upon request.
[14] This also applies to the transfer of title to GmbH shares and accounts for the fact that there is no method to evidence title to GmbH shares with ultimate certainty.

The structure described below is perhaps the most common method of documenting the joint venture.

ii) Joint venture agreements

The following is a list and description of issues usually covered in the joint venture agreement:

(a) *Object of agreement*. The first clause will contain a general description of the joint venture project, including the goals of the joint venture partners, the substantive area of cooperation, the territory to which the cooperation extends, and the main features of the parties' respective contributions to the jvc and the project as a whole.

(b) *Joint venture company*. The joint venture agreement will contain general rules on the formation[15] of the jvc, including its corporate form (GmbH, Ag, or other), its capitalisation, the relevant equity participation of the shareholders, and other initial funding. A draft of the Articles of Association of the jvc will be attached as an exhibit.

Even though German corporate law is very flexible as regards variations on shareholders' rights, the creation of different classes of GmbH shares or shareholders is uncommon in German jvcs. Usually, differences are due only to a different capital participation. Occasionally the number of voting rights for a certain shareholder is set below the nominal capital participation, in particular to avoid difficulties stemming from merger control.[16] If any such restrictions are agreed, they will be set forth in detail in the Articles of Association and not in the joint venture agreement.

(c) *Management*. While the general management structure will be described in the Articles of Association, the joint venture agreement should state the agreements between the joint venture partners on the number of managing directors and rights of appointment. The joint venture agreement may name certain individuals who will act during the start-up phase and grant future rights of appointment exercisable once the start-up phase has been completed.

If the jvc initially requires certain managerial support from one or several shareholders other than board representation, the joint venture agreement should state the relevant details.

(d) *Agreements between jvc and individual shareholders*. One of the most important parts of the joint venture agreement deals with the ongoing commercial relationship between the jvc and each of the joint venture partners. Agreements to be concluded between the jvc and the joint venture partners (or companies affiliated with them) may deal with

- the licensing of intellectual property rights and know-how to the jvc,
- the leasing of office space or plant to the jvc,
- training and technical assistance to be provided to the jvc and its staff,

---

[15] If the jvc already exists, the transaction will resemble a common sale and purchase agreement and adoption of revised Articles for the jvc.
[16] *See* 7.2 (i) below.

- the supply of raw materials, components, or finished products to the jvc,
- the provision of services to the jvc in the area of accounting or managerial assistance,
- the distribution by the joint venture partners of the products manufactured by the jvc,
- the subcontracting of certain orders obtained by a joint venture partner to the jvc.

The terms and conditions governing these transactions will often be laid down in separate agreements, drafts of which are attached to the joint venture agreement. This is particularly advisable where the agreement will later be submitted to third parties or governmental authorities who are not to be given access to internal agreements between the joint venture partners, or where the side agreement is monitored and performed by lower-level staff who need not become involved in basic joint venture policy.

(e) *Future financing.* The joint venture agreement should state the principles governing future financing of the jvc, in particular

- the procedure for determining financing needs and the selection of the financing method (outside versus shareholders' financing, debt versus equity financing),
- the obligation of the joint venture partners as regards the provision of funding beyond the initial capitalisation,
- the obligations of the joint venture partners to provide collateral to secure outside financing,
- the consequences of a joint venture partner's failure to participate in providing additional funding, in particular where his relevant equity share may fall below the original share.

Financing issues may be partially covered by the Articles of Association, notably in connection with the distribution of dividends.

(f) *Distribution of dividends.* According to the GmbH-Gesetz, unless the Articles of Association of a GmbH or a shareholders' resolution provide otherwise, each shareholder is entitled to a portion of the annual profits proportionate to his shareholding.[17] Since this rule is usually inappropriate for the purposes of the jvc, the joint venture agreement often deviates from the statutory principle, either granting the shareholders power to resolve freely on the distribution of profits, or requiring all or part of the profits to be retained. Other common clauses call for the allocation of the entire profits to reserves, or of a portion of profits to reserves, or require profits to be retained until a certain debt/equity ratio is achieved, or reserves reach a certain percentage of the stated capital.[18]

Since the distribution of profits may be dealt with in the Articles of

[17] GmbHG, Sec. 29.
[18] Note that the AktG calls for the creation of a statutory reserve up to 10% of the statutory capital, AktG, Sec. 150. This model is often applied to a GmbH by shareholders' agreement.

Association, the shareholders may decide to deal with all or certain aspects of the issue in the Articles instead of the joint venture agreement.

(g) *Non-competition covenant.* The joint venture agreement should delineate the substantive and geographical area within which the partners undertake not to compete with the jvc. The validity of no-compete clauses must be tested primarily against antitrust law.[19] The outer boundaries defined by civil law are rather liberal, invalidating non-competition covenants only if they are excessive and contrary to good morals.

(h) *Termination.* While for the reasons explained above[20] the events of termination of the jvc are usually stated in the Articles of Association, the consequences thereof for the joint venture cooperation must be laid down in the joint venture agreement. In a two-party situation it may be possible to give the leaving shareholder a right to request the return of his initial contribution (such as a certain business), yet due to the enormous practical difficulties some kind of financial arrangement will be a more practical solution. If the joint venture has more than two partners, the joint venture agreement may provide for a private auction among the joint venture partners of the sale of all or part of the joint venture assets.

In addition to the liquidation of the jvc, the joint venture agreement must address the termination consequences for all ancillary agreements. In most cases cross-termination clauses will be appropriate. The survival of an ancillary agreement must also be dealt with in the event that the joint venture partner with whom the agreement is entered into ceases to be a shareholder of the jvc. Again, proper termination clauses in the relevant agreement will have to address this situation.

(i) *Governing law, jurisdiction.* In determining the governing law, the entire joint venture must be viewed in context. As the Articles of Association of the jvc will naturally be subject to German law, it is advisable to subject the joint venture agreement also to German law to avoid conflicts and discrepancies. Ancillary agreements such as a supply or licence agreement between the jvc and individual partners need not necessarily be governed by the law of the main agreement, but if not, all cross-references, in particular cross-default or cross-termination clauses, must be checked carefully to avoid conflicts.

Arbitration clauses will most likely be the preferred solution for jurisdiction over the international joint venture disputes. If the arbitration proceeding is conducted in Germany, the arbitration clause should call for an *ad hoc* arbitration panel or refer the matter to a permanent institution such as the German Arbitration Committee.[1]

If all agreements, including ancillary agreements, call for resolution of disputes by arbitration, a separate arbitration agreement should be entered into by all parties, including the jvc itself.

(j) *Miscellaneous.* The jvc may also contain additional clauses customary

[19] *See* 7.3 below.
[20] *See* 6.2 (i).
[1] Deutscher Ausschuss für Schiedsgerichtswesen.

in international agreements such as confidentiality, severability (if desired), prevailing language, etc.

(k) *Validity*. As the Articles of Association of the jvc (and perhaps other agreements) require notarisation, a written joint venture agreement remains unenforceable until notarisation of the respective documents.[2] As a reminder to the parties it is useful to include a clause reiterating this principle. Unenforceability pending notarisation may be avoided by notarising the entire joint venture agreement, including all exhibits.

iii) Articles of Association

Besides such standard items as name, registered seat, purpose, stated capital and fiscal year,[3] the Articles of Association may cover the following.

(a) *Internal structure*. The jvc's management structure and functions of the shareholders' meeting are governed by the Articles of Association.

The principal and mandatory bodies of a GmbH are the management, consisting of one or several managing directors, and the shareholders' meeting. The management is subject to the control, supervision and directions of the shareholders' meeting, which may issue general or specific directives to the management if it deems advisable. In addition, the shareholders' meeting has power to decide on the fundamental questions concerning the company, including capitalisation, appointment of managing directors, application of profits, sale of business, change of Articles, and liquidation.[4]

The GmbH-Gesetz allows for flexibility in structuring the internal affairs of a GmbH in that additional bodies may be established and vested with powers of management and policy-making. Since the law requires that each AG has a supervisory board,[5] GmbHs often follow this model in providing for the establishment of such a board. A supervisory board of the AG type is appointed by the shareholders' meeting and charged with supervising the management. Members of the management may not be members of the supervisory board, and in all affairs concerning the relationship between the management and the company, the company is represented by the supervisory board. Thus, the supervisory board is, so to speak, a permanent committee of the shareholders' meeting, to convene more than once a year depending on the requirements of the business. Contrary to the basic two-tier structure of a GmbH, instalment of a supervisory board allows a more personal representation of the shareholders, as the members of the board are appointed personally and are replaced only at the end of their term.

The rules on additional bodies within a GmbH are more liberal than in the case of an AG. Thus, the duties and functions of the supervisory board

---

[2] This follows from BGB, Sec. 139, invalidating an agreement entirely if a portion of the agreement is invalid. Whether execution of the joint venture agreement abroad avoids the problem under private international law remains controversial.
[3] GmbHG, Sec. 3; AktG, Sec. 23.
[4] For details, *see* 6.5 (iii) (b) below.
[5] Aufsichtsrat.

may be reduced to an advisory function, which often takes the form of a break-
fast round, giving management and board members the opportunity to convene
informally and discuss the affairs of the company, or be expanded to assume
most of the functions and responsibilities of the shareholders' meeting.

The three-tier management system (management, advisory/supervisory
board, shareholders' meeting) may be employed to resolve disputes within the
management. The Articles, or rules of procedure[6] issued in accordance with
the Articles, may require the management to bring controversies first before
the board, and if the issue cannot be resolved there, before the shareholders'
meeting. This procedure may induce the management to resolve the controversy
before it reaches the shareholders' meeting.

(b) *Quorum and minority protection.* In dealing with the issues of quorum
for the shareholders' or advisory board meetings, the Articles will have to
consider the statutory framework for majority decisions and the protection
of minority shareholders' rights.

A number of provisions in the GmbH-Gesetz require a majority of 75%
of the votes cast in the shareholders' meeting for the adoption of certain
decisions. Thus, the holder of more than 25% may effectively block these
decisions. These provisions, to which the courts have added other circumstances, include

- amendments to the Articles of Association,[7]
- increase of the stated capital, as this requires an amendment of the Articles,
- liquidation of the company,[8]
- change of corporate form,[9]
- merger with an AG,[10]
- transfer of all the assets to a third party.[11]

As these provisions do not address the day-to-day operations of the GmbH,
the Articles of Association of a jvc should include a list of transactions that
management may not carry out without the shareholders' approval. These may
include real estate transactions, decisions regarding financing, important contracts, compensation policies, operational changes, transactions with shareholders, and the adoption of the annual budget. If a board assumes the
supervisory functions of the shareholders' meeting, such approval powers
should be vested in the board.

(c) *Transferability of shares.* According to Sec. 15 of the GmbH-Gesetz, the
Articles of Association may require the consent of the shareholders for any

---

[6] 'Geschäftsordnung'. Rules of procedure may include provisions on assignment of responsibilities,
management, meetings, procedures for such meetings, reporting etc.
[7] GmbHG, Sec. 53 subs. 2.
[8] GmbHG, Sec. 60.
[9] Umwandlungsgesetz, Sec. 24.
[10] AktG, Sec. 355.
[11] This rule has been created by the courts.

valid transfer or other disposition of shares or tie the transfer to other conditions. This grants considerable flexibility in keeping unwanted parties out of the jvc. In accordance with this section, the Articles may provide for any number of restrictions on share transfers such as:

- an outright shareholders' consent requirement,
- a requirement of the consent of a certain majority of shareholders,
- rights of pre-emption,[12]
- rights of first refusal,[13]
- a combination of the foregoing.

The Articles may add qualifications or exceptions to the transfer restrictions to meet the specific needs of the parties involved.

(d) *Forced shareholders' change.* Most GmbH Articles of Association allow the expulsion of a shareholder from the company in certain serious circumstances such as:

- insolvency or bankruptcy of that shareholder,
- garnishment of a shareholder's share by creditors,
- breach of an essential obligation or contract,
- change of control or group affiliation of the shareholder, or
- other important reasons (cause).

The way to achieve this is the redemption of shares (Einziehung) by the shareholders' resolution.[14] As a result of the redemption, the share is destroyed, and the shareholder no longer holds any interest in the company.

In order for the clause not to be overreaching, the Articles must provide for a fair redemption procedure and adequate compensation. Instead of redeeming the shares the Articles may authorise the shareholders to request the transfer of the share to a party nominated by the shareholders, such transfer being subject to the same rules as regards cause, procedure, and compensation.

(e) *Pre-agreed shareholders' change.* The Articles may provide for instances where one shareholder may acquire the shares of another by way of option rights, or mutual acquisition and sales rights (put and call), or for those less orthodox procedures which have become common in international joint venture practice such as 'Russian Roulette', etc.

One should bear in mind that in the case of a GmbH all such arrangements require notarisation before a German notary. If the shareholders deem such schemes to be of a sensitive nature not designed to become public knowledge, they should be kept outside the Articles and referred to separate notarial documents.

---

[12] Vorkaufsrecht, BGB, Sec. 504 *et seq.*, giving the beneficiary the opportunity to acquire the shares in question on the terms and conditions agreed with a third party.
[13] Andienungsrecht (not covered by statute), requiring the shareholder to offer the shares first to his co-shareholder(s) on certain conditions before selling them to others.
[14] GmbHG, Sec. 34.

(f) *Termination.* As mentioned above, termination of the jvc being a key aspect of its constitution, it is usually dealt with in the Articles of Association.[15] Termination may be the result of events such as

- the expiry of the jvc's term,
- the giving of notice of termination by a shareholder, which may be possible at will or for cause,
- if notice requires cause, the breach by another party of an important obligation or contract (which may be an ancillary contract), another party's bankruptcy or insolvency, or the failure to reach agreement on a vital joint venture policy issue, may be defined as causes for termination.

As regards termination consequences, the Articles may allow the remaining parties to continue the jvc and buy out the party who gave notice. If a buy-out is possible, the Articles should address the method of calculating the compensation.

(g) *Accounting, profit distribution.* Since the implementation in German commercial and corporate law of the various EEC directives regarding the preparation, auditing and publication of corporate financials,[16] the Articles of Association may deal with this area rather cursorily, referring details to the law.

Instead of dealing with financing and profit distribution in the joint venture agreement, appropriate provisions may be inserted in the Articles of Association.[17]

6.6 Tax

i) Corporate Income Tax

German resident corporations such as GmbHs and AGs are subject to corporate income tax[18] on their entire income irrespective of the source from which it is derived. According to this principle, any capital gain is subject to corporate income tax.

The taxable income of corporations is largely influenced by the rules on the depreciation and writing-down of its assets:

- movable assets may be depreciated over their useful life according to certain recognized charts;
- buildings, but not real estate, may be depreciated over a period of usually 25 years;
- goodwill acquired through a specific transaction (and not created within the company) may be depreciated over 15 years.

---

[15] *See* 2.5 (i) above.
[16] HGB, Sec. 238 *et seq.*
[17] *See* 6.5 (ii) (e), (f) above.
[18] Körperschaftsteuer, governed by the Körperschaftsteuergesetz (KStG).

Interest paid by the company on loans taken is deductible as a business expense. This also applies to interest paid to shareholders on shareholders' loans, provided that the payment does not constitute a constructive dividend because of thin capitalisation. As a rule of thumb, the German tax authorities require a 9 to 1 debt to equity ratio and will usually not disallow the deductibility of interest payments if this ratio is maintained.

The taxable income of a resident corporation, determined on an accrual basis, is taxed at 50% if retained and at 36% if distributed. Double taxation of corporate profits at the company's and the shareholder's level is avoided in that the 36% tax paid by the corporation is first added to the shareholder's income in calculating the applicable tax rate and then deducted from the tax payable. This tax credit is not available to foreign shareholders.

ii) Trade tax

German businesses, irrespective of their corporate form and including resident corporations, are subject to trade tax.[19] This is a local tax, consisting of a tax on net worth[20] at a rate of up to 1%, and a profit tax[1] at a rate of up to 20%. All trade tax is deductible for income tax purposes, resulting in an additional net tax burden of *ca.* 10%.

6.7   Acquisition and use of business assets and intellectual property rights

The jvc being a separate legal entity, it will either obtain title to business assets and intellectual property rights, or use such rights by virtue of agreements with third parties or individual shareholders.

Agreements between the jvc and individual shareholders covering such issues are often part of the basic joint venture documentation.[2] If they are to be added later, the Articles of Association should require a certain majority vote to avoid dealings between the jvc and the relevant shareholder that are not at arm's length.[3]

7.   COMPETITION LAW CONSIDERATIONS

As the reader of this chapter will most likely be interested in jvs in which both a German and a non-German enterprise take part, the competition law considerations should start with an evaluation of EEC competition law. This is important due to the supremacy of EEC law over national law. An individual exemption granted by the Commission of the EEC, for instance, would leave

[19] Gewerbesteuer, governed by the Gewerbesteuergesetz (GewStG).
[20] Gewerbekapitalsteuer.
[1] Gewerbeertragsteuer.
[2] *See* 6.5 (ii) above.
[3] Cf. 6.5 (iii) (b).

no room for an investigation by the German Cartel Authority, the 'Bundeskartellamt' (Federal Cartel Office, or 'FCO') as far as the general 'cartel' provisions are concerned. With regard to merger control, the newly introduced EEC merger control will have priority over national merger control with regard to large mergers (combined annual sales of the 'merging enterprise' of 5 bn ECU or more). Merger tests differ from German law. German merger control may thus still be applicable.

The treatment of jvs in German competition law is an extremely complex and difficult matter. Jvs are subject to the general prohibition of restraints of competition, and – if a jvc is formed – may also be subject to merger control, which applies different criteria. This chapter can only give a very general summary of the most important aspects. Thus, it will be useful to make use of specialized monographs[4] and commentaries and to make an in-depth examination of the relevant provisions with regard to any particular jv.

7.1 Assessment of jvs under German law

The German Gesetz gegen Wettbewerbsbeschränkungen (Act against Restraints of Competition – 'ARC') contains several provisions which may be relevant for joint ventures. German antitrust law is based on the 'effects doctrine', thus the ARC applies to all restraints of competition which have a noticeable effect on competition in the territory of the Federal Republic of Germany, irrespective of where the underlying agreement is concluded or the restraints of competition are caused.[5]

As has been shown above, jvs may cover a variety of activities relating to cooperations, coordination of certain activities, or concentrations, in particular, the forming of joint venture companies under joint control. German competition law does not contain an exhaustive provision governing all the possible forms of jvs, and the ARC does not provide a single definition of a jv for the purposes of competition law. One of the provisions on merger control in the ARC contains a definition of a joint venture company, but that does not provide an exhaustive definition of jvs, nor does it indicate under what circumstances a jv would be considered as effecting restraints on competition.

In general, the ARC broadly distinguishes between restraints of competition by means of a 'Kartell' (either in the form of agreements, or of coordinated behaviour, or resolutions of associations of companies) on the one hand, and 'mergers' or concentrations on the other hand. As a rule, a cooperation or coordination of activities which does not entail the forming of a joint venture company would be tested only under the 'Kartell'-related provisions of the ARC (Sec. 1 *et seq.*), whereas the forming of a joint venture company operating entirely independently in the market will be considered, first and foremost, under the merger control provisions of the ARC (Sec. 23 *et seq.*). However,

---

[4] *See*, for instance, *Wiedemann*, Gemeinschaftsunternehmen im deutschen Kartellrecht (1981).
[5] Sec. 98 (2) ARC.

it is always important to look at the particular circumstances of the individual case, since the application of the rules on merger control does not exclude the application of the general provisions of the ARC, and vice versa. Thus, if a jvc is formed, and the forming of the joint venture is not to be prohibited under the provisions of merger control (since no position of market dominance is created or strengthened), the jv may still be considered as serving to coordinate the market behaviour of the companies participating in the jv, which would be a restraint of competition that may be prohibited under section 1 of the ARC.

7.2   The application of merger control rules to jvs

In all cases in which the jv partners are combining or establishing an entire business rather than a mere cooperation in specific activities, the jv will be concentrative in nature and be subject to the merger control provisions (Sec. 23 *et seq.* ARC) if it meets the 'merger' (or concentration) test, irrespective of the form of the jv (partnership, GmbH etc.).[6]

i) Definition of a 'merger' for purposes of merger control

Sec. 23 ARC contains six definitions of what constitutes a 'merger' for the purposes of merger control. These comprise, *inter alia*, the acquisition of 25% or more of the shares or voting rights in another enterprise.[7] Sec. 23 (2) No. 2, 4th sentence reads as follows:

> An acquisition of shares is also deemed to be a merger insofar as the acquiring party is provided either by means of agreement, statutes, articles of incorporation or resolution with the legal status of a shareholder of a stock corporation holding more than 25 percent of the voting capital.

Participation in a (general or limited) partnership usually falls under that definition (which, in practical terms, looks at a blocking veto), as unanimous consent is required by law, unless otherwise provided in the joint venture agreement.

The transfer of a substantial part of the assets is also deemed to be a 'merger'.[8]

Thus, the formation of the jv company by two partners with e.g. a 50/50 or a 60/40 participation ratio will always be considered a 'merger' *between the parent company and the jv.*

Furthermore, Sec. 23 para. (2) no. 2 3rd sentence ARC provides:

---

[6] Sec. 23 (2) ARC contains several merger tests, of which two are of particular importance for jvs. However, it may be necessary to check whether the jv falls under one of the other definitions of a merger in Sec. 23.

[7] Sec. 23 (2) No. 2 ARC. It is important to note that there is a 'merger' where 25% (or 50% or a majority) threshold is reached, including shares already held. Furthermore, all shares held by companies which form part of a group of enterprises are counted when determining whether the thresholds are reached.

[8] Sec. 23 (2) No. 1 ARC. For instance, a single petrol station would be considered a 'substantial part of the assets' of a mineral oil group which owns several hundred stations.

Where several enterprises, simultaneously or successively, acquire shares in another enterprise reaching the threshold specified hereinbefore, this shall be deemed to constitute a merger between the participating enterprises (joint venture) in respect of those markets in which the other enterprise is active.

Therefore, the transaction by means of which a jvc is formed is considered not only as a merger between the jv company and the individual jv shareholder, but is also deemed to be a concentration (merger) *between the different jv partners* (always provided they hold at least 25% of the shares or voting rights in the jv company). The same applies if one or more companies acquire 25% or more of the shares in an existing company (if at least one other company still holds 25% or more of the shares).

If five or more companies form a jvc with each company having less than 25% of the shares or voting rights, this may nonetheless constitute a 'merger' under the catch-all clauses of Sec. 23 (2) no. 5, in particular if the statutes provide each shareholder with a blocking veto, or if joint control by several shareholders is found to exist.

ii) Notification requirements

If the jv meets the 'merger' test, notification requirements may apply. A distinction is made between *pre-merger*[9] and *post-merger*[10] notification requirements. The most important difference between the two is that in case of a pre-merger notification requirement, there is a strict *prohibition* on completion of the envisaged transaction prior to having obtained clearance from the FCO.

Pre-merger notification of the jv is required where

- one of the participating enterprises has annual sales of *two* billion DM or more, or
- two of the participating enterprises have annual sales of *one* billion DM or more.[11]

The jv is subject to *post-merger* notification where the combined annual sales of all enterprises participating in the merger exceed 500 million DM.[12]

Where the combined total (worldwide) sales of all participating enterprises was below DM 500 million in the last completed business year, the merger control provisions do not apply, and the jv cannot be prohibited under the merger control provisions.

It is important to note that the sales thresholds in the merger control provisions are determined by reference to the total (worldwide) sales of the enterprises directly participating in the jv as well as the total sales of all affiliated enterprises which are either controlled by a participating enterprise, or which

[9] Sec. 24 a ARC.
[10] Sec. 23 (1) ARC.
[11] Sec. 24 a (1) ARC.
[12] Sec. 23 (1) ARC.

are part of the group to which the participating enterprise belongs.[13] Often, this corresponds to the consolidated sales figures of the groups of enterprises involved.

iii) Timing considerations

After notification, the FCO may prohibit the transaction within certain limitation periods:

- after the pre-merger notification, the FCO has one month to communicate to the parties that it intends to carry out an investigation of the case; if this period elapses without such a 'month-letter' from the FCO, the merger may be completed and can no longer be prohibited;
- if the FCO investigates the merger and sends the letter to the parties, it has up to four months (from the date of notification) to issue a prohibition order. If it does not do so within this limitation period, the merger may be completed and can no longer be prohibited;
- in case of post-merger notification, the FCO has one year to investigate (and prohibit) the transaction.

Even if the jv is subject to a post-merger notification only, the parties may wish to submit a voluntary pre-merger notification to have the merger cleared in advance and to avoid the risk that it will be prohibited after its completion. In this case the pre-merger timing rules apply.

In pre-merger notification cases, if a 'merger' does not cause substantive problems, or once such problems have been solved, the FCO will normally issue a 'no prohibition' letter clearing the merger. Upon receipt of such a letter, the merger may be completed henceforth (the parties do not have to wait until the limitation period has elapsed). Once cleared, or after the time periods have elapsed, the merger can no longer be prohibited (unless the parties have provided misleading information to the FCO).

Where a transaction was subject to pre-merger notification, it is also necessary to notify the completion of the transaction, but this post-merger notification is a formality (only for statistical reasons); it does not allow the FCO to prohibit the transaction.

iv) Substantive test: market dominance

Under the *substantive merger control provisions*, a jv must be prohibited where it creates or strengthens a market dominating position.[14] If the parties prove that despite the creation or strengthening of a market dominating position, the jv at the same time leads to improvements in competitive conditions (in

---

[13] Special rules exist for banks, insurance companies and publishers. For sales revenues from re-sale of goods, only 75% are taken into account for determining the sales threshold, Sec. 23 (1) ARC.
[14] Sec. 24 (1) ARC.

the same or another market) which *outweigh the negative impact* of market dominance, the merger will not be prohibited.

Market dominance is assessed by reference to the relevant market for a specific product (or commercial services) within a specified geographical area (normally the whole of the territory of the Federal Republic of Germany). Market dominance exists where an enterprise is without a competitor, or not exposed to substantial competition, or if it has a superior market position *vis-à-vis* its competitors. The latter is determined according to a variety of factors, including market share, financial resources, up- and downstream integration, etc.[15] Market shares and financial resources are very important. In case of market share, it is not the mere size of the market share in itself which could give rise to a finding of market dominance, but rather the difference in market share between the enterprise concerned and the next follower in the market.

v) Presumptions of market dominance

The ARC (also) contains certain presumptions of market dominance.[16] They are all based on certain *market share* thresholds. According to Sec. 22 (3), no's. 1 and 2, it is presumed that

- a *single* enterprise is market dominating if it has a market share of at least 33.33%, and total sales of at least 250 million DM,

or

- three or fewer enterprises are market dominating, if they have a combined market share of at least 50%, or
- five or fewer enterprises are market dominating, if they have a combined market share of at least 66.67%,
  provided that each of the enterprises had total sales of at least 100 million DM in the last completed business year prior to the merger.

Where the combined market share for several enterprises is looked at, the FCO looks at those companies which have the highest individual market share. If the market shares of the 'top three' or 'top five' enterprises reach fifty percent or two-thirds, respectively, it is presumed that they are market dominating, provided that there is no substantial competition and that they have a superior market position in relation to the competitors which do not form part of the 'top three' or 'top five'.[17] This presumption somewhat facilitates the findings of market domination, but still leaves the burden of proof with the FCO with regard to the absence of substantial competition or the existence of a superior market position.

For the purposes of merger control, there is also a stricter and unqualified

---

[15] Sec. 22 (1) No. 2 ARC.
[16] For instance, a market share of one third for a single enterprise; cf. Sec. 22 (3), 23 (a) ARC.
[17] BGH WuW/E 1824, 1828 ('Tonolli/Blei- und Silberhütte Braubach').

presumption that a market dominating position exists where three (or fewer) enterprises have a combined market share of at least 50%, or five (or fewer) enterprises have a combined market share of at least two-thirds, if each of the enterprises in the oligopoly group has had at least 150 million DM total sales in the last completed business year, and the enterprises participating in the merger – generally the jv partners and the jvc – reach a market share of more than 15%.[18]

The importance of this latter presumption is that the enterprises participating in the merger have the burden of proof that the merger will leave the competitive conditions among the oligopolists untouched so that there will be substantial competition within the oligopoly, or that the oligopolists in relationship to the other competitors outside the oligopoly have no superior market position.

vi) Other criteria for application of merger control to jvs

In general, a jv will be treated as 'concentrative' rather than 'cooperative' and be investigated under the merger control provisions where the jv is a complete undertaking established on a long-term basis and with its own commercial policy.[19] In cases in which the jv partners form the jvc with the aim of also pursuing their own genuine business interests, the jv may be subject to scrutiny under the cartel prohibition, in particular where the jv partners interfere with the jv's business decisions, rather than restricting themselves to a 'stewardship function' of a shareholder. In cases where the jv is active in an upstream or downstream market and relies to a great extent on the jv partners for its sales (or supplies), the jv will be considered to be of a 'cooperative' nature so that the jv – apart from having to comply with merger control notification requirements – is subject to scrutiny under the cartel prohibition.[20] Spillover or group effects must be avoided if the jv is to be considered entirely concentrative, and thus subject only to the merger control provisions.

For instance, a 'partial merger', e.g. the forming of a jv for joint production (or sales) by two competitors, which had a market share of 25–30% and were not exposed to outside competition prior to the transaction, would most likely be prohibited by the FCO.

7.3   The application of 'cartel prohibition' to jvs

Jvs may also be caught by the cartel prohibition. Sec. 1 para. (1) ARC reads as follows:

> Agreements made for a common purpose by enterprises or associations of enterprises and decisions of associations of enterprises shall be null and void, insofar as they are likely to influence, by restraining competition, production or market conditions

[18] Sec. 23 a (2) of the Act.
[19] Cf. order of the Federal Supreme Court ('BGH') of 1 October 1985, WuW/E 2169 *et seq.* ('Mischwerke').
[20] Loc. cit.

with respect to trade in goods or commercial services. This shall apply only insofar as this Act does not provide otherwise.

The substantive test for a restraint of competition is, basically, whether an enterprise, by means of the agreement, is restricted in its entrepreneurial freedom to select and use instruments of competition,[1] such as taking investment decisions, fixing prices, rebates and business conditions, although other elements such as size, variety and quality of supply and demand, as well as different forms and channels for distribution are taken into account.[2] In all cases, it is relevant whether the restraint of competition is the foreseeable consequence of the agreement, irrespective of whether or not this is the actual result. Thus, the main question is whether a restraint of competition is to be expected as a result of the agreement, assuming the parties follow their typical entrepreneurial behaviour. If due to unexpected developments, competition is in fact restrained at some later stage, this fact would not lead to a finding that the agreement is contrary to Sec. 1 ARC, if it was indeed not to be expected.

The restraint of competition must be *noticeable*, i.e. it must have some *external effect* influencing the conditions in the relevant market.[3]

Apart from agreements, concerted practices which have the same effect would be contrary to Sec. 25 (1) ARC, but this seems to be rare in case of jvs, as an agreement (no form being required in many cases, *see* 2.5 above) will be the basis of a jv in virtually all cases.

Agreements which are thus prohibited under Sec. 1 ARC are void, unless they are specifically exempted by other provisions of the ARC. The list of provisions exempting certain agreements from the prohibition under Sec. 1 includes the following, which may be relevant for jvs:

- Agreements serving to rationalize economic activities, if they are likely to increase substantially the efficiency or productivity of the participating enterprises from a technical, economic or organizational point of view, thereby improving the satisfaction of demand; the rationalization effect must be adequate in relation to the restraint of competition therewith.[4]
- Agreements establishing uniform methods for specification of services or for price break-downs in the economic sectors, if they do not fix prices or components of prices;[5]
- Agreements whose object is the rationalization of economic activities by means of specialisation, provided that substantial competition continues to exist in that market;[6]
- Agreements whose object is the rationalization of economic activities by means of cooperation promoting the efficiency of small- and medium-

---

[1] Cf. BGH WuW/E 1339, 1342 ('Aluminium-Halbzeug').
[2] Cf. Wiedemann, loc. cit., p. 174.
[3] Cf. Wiedemann, loc. cit., p. 178 *et seq.*
[4] 'Rationalisierungskartelle', Sec. 5 (3) ARC.
[5] Sec. 5 (4) ARC.
[6] 'Spezialisierungskartelle', Sec. 5 a ARC.

sized enterprises, provided that competition on the market is not substantially impaired.[7]

In some cases, the exemption is automatic and subject only to a control of misuses, whereas in other cases, the parties have to apply for the exemption which is then individually granted by the FCO where all the requirements are met.

In any case, the parties must notify the agreement in order to benefit from the exemption. Basic elements of the agreement are registered, and certain elements are published.[8]

Jvs which would not be prohibited by the ARC would include, for instance, a jv by two competitors to carry out a complex R&D project, if neither of the jv partners could have carried out the project itself (provided that each jv partner may exploit the result independently); or a jv for joint production, if sales are carried out by the jv partners independently; or a joint purchasing organisation.

7.4   Other provisions of the ARC which may be relevant to jvs

The ARC also refers to various other types of agreements. Agreements by means of which the parties agree on re-sale price maintenance are void,[9] except if they relate to books, newspapers or magazines.[10]

Exclusive dealing agreements are not forbidden, but subject to a supervision by the FCO to avoid misuses, Sec. 18 ARC. Such agreements must be in writing.

There are special rules concerning licensing agreements and know-how agreements in Sec. 20 and 21 ARC, respectively.

---

[7]   'Mittelstandskartelle', Sec. 5 b ARC.
[8]   Sec. 9, 10 ARC.
[9]   Sec. 15 ARC.
[10] Sec. 16 ARC.

CHAPTER 4
Italian joint ventures

1. GENERAL INTRODUCTION

The expression 'joint venture' which is often used in Italy in its English form has an economic rather than legal connotation. The usual meaning attached to the expression is the conduct of a business enterprise jointly by two or more parties or, in more general terms, the pooling together by two or more parties of resources, having an economic value, for the purpose of achieving a commercial objective.

The legal instruments available under the Italian legal system for realizing a joint venture can be identified in the following main categories: Participations; Partnerships; Joint Venture Companies; and Consortia (Internal and External).

2. CONTRACTUAL JOINT VENTURES

'Contractual joint ventures', or 'cooperation agreements', are the simplest form of arrangements structured by two or more parties to achieve a common end. Arrangements of this sort are generally considered as 'internal consortia' in Italy; and a discussion of them therefore appears as a sub-point of S 6 below concerning Consortia.

3. PARTICIPATIONS

3.1 Introduction

'Associazione in Partecipazione' (Participation Agreement) is defined by statute as a contract whereby a party (the operator) grants to another party (the participant) a participation in the profits of his enterprise or of one or more transactions in return for a specified contribution.[1] The contribution made by the participant (either, cash, intellectual property rights or any kind of tangible assets) causes the operator to acquire full title to such contribution. In the event that the contract provides for the restitution of the items contributed (upon termination of the contract) the participant will have an unsecured claim for such restitution.

[1] Article 2549 of the Civil Code.

The participant, unless otherwise agreed, participates in the losses of the enterprise (or of the business transaction in relation to which the contract has been concluded) in the same proportion in which he participates in the profits, but the losses to which such party is subject cannot exceed the value of his contribution.[2]

3.2   Advantages

The advantages connected with this type of structure are: (i) the fact that there is no obligation to make known to third parties the details of the constitution of the joint venture and (ii) that since a company cannot be a member of a partnership (not even as a limited liability partner) the structure can be used by a company whenever the formation of a joint venture company is not desirable.

3.3   Disadvantages

The main disadvantages are: (i) management powers are vested only in the operator, (ii) transfer taxes have to be paid in relation to the contribution of certain types of assets and (iii) the risk that if the operator for any reason goes bankrupt, the assets (including those contributed by the participant) will be considered part of the estate of the operator for the purposes of the liquidation pursuant to bankruptcy law.

3.4   When to select

The participation type of joint venture is advisable when there is no need or desire to create a jointly owned enterprise and when the participant is not interested in exercising any management power.

3.5   Formation documentation, key aspects

(a) Formation

The formation involves merely the execution of a contract indicating the parties, the contribution, the purpose of the joint venture and its duration, the criteria for sharing the profits and losses (if losses are shared) and the criteria for the winding up of the joint venture (including, typically, the restitution of the participant's contribution to the participant).

The contract may need to be in the form of a notarized deed when certain assets (for example, real estate) are contributed by the participant.[3]

---

[2] Article 2553 of the Civil Code.
[3] Articles 1350 and 2643 of the Civil Code.

(b) Liability

Only the operator is liable for the obligations assumed in connection with the conduct of the business of the joint venture. The participant undertakes responsibility only *vis-à-vis* the operator and only with respect to the contribution which he promised to make pursuant to the joint venture agreement.

(c) Management

The management of the enterprise or transaction is undertaken by the operator. Therefore, only the operator can enter into contracts, undertake obligations and assume responsibilities *vis-à-vis* third parties.

The participation agreement structure has been used quite often in connection with joint ventures in the field of hydrocarbon research since legislation in force up until 1967 did not permit joint ownership of research permits. In this type of arrangement, the participant contributed the major part of the technological and financial means necessary for the carrying out of the research work. In order to afford such party effective control over the management of the enterprise, the participation agreement provided that the participant would be granted (by the operator) a power of attorney. This had the effect of reversing the management responsibility, the participant becoming the agent of the operator.[4]

The participation agreement will typically specify the manner and extent of supervision that will be exercised by the participant over the enterprise or the progress of the transaction. In all cases, the participant has the right to obtain an accounting report on the business activity of the joint venture. Where the activity extends beyond a year, the participant will be entitled to such a report upon an annual basis.[5]

Unless otherwise agreed upon, the operator cannot grant participations in the same enterprise or in the same transaction to other persons without the consent of the participant.[6]

(d) Dissolution

Dissolution, save where it is by mutual consent, will typically occur upon the expiry of the contract term or upon the bankruptcy of the operator. Dissolution may also occur as a result of a material breach of contract.

(e) Transferability of interests

Due to the contractual and essentially 'personal' nature of this joint venture, the transferability of interests is not a normal feature. As a general rule, a contract may be assigned only with the consent of the parties thereto. Clearly,

---

[4] Article 1388 of the Civil Code.
[5] Article 2552 of the Civil Code.
[6] Article 2550 of the Civil Code.

when the parties to the participation agreement are corporate entities, the transfer of their interests can be achieved through a transfer of the controlling interest in the corporate entity. However, such a change in control of a joint venture is often made in the contract as a ground for the automatic dissolution of the joint venture by the other party(ies).

3.6   Taxes

Since the ownership of the business and the responsibility for its conduct is vested exclusively with the operator, any taxable income produced by the joint venture is included in the taxable income of the operator.[7] The latter, however, will attribute to the participant the agreed share of profits before taxes and the payment thus made is treated as a tax deductible item for the operator.[8]

With respect to the participant:

(i)   if the participant is engaged in a business (as an individual, partnership or corporate entity), the share of the profit received from the operator will be treated as taxable business income;[9] if the participant is a partnership, the shares of income will be imputed *pro quota* to the partners;[10]

(ii) if the participant is an individual or a non-commercial entity the profit share received will constitute capital income; the same treatment will apply to the difference between the value of contributions originally made by the participant and the value of them upon their re-assignment to the participant upon the expiry or earlier dissolution of the agreement;[11] if the participant is an individual and his contribution consisted solely of rendering personal services, the profit share will constitute income from independent work.[12]

Transfer taxes may be due in relation to the transfer (or 'contribution') of assets by the participant pursuant to the participation agreement.[13]

3.7   Foreign involvement

Under Italian law, foreigners enjoy the civil rights attributed to national citizens on condition of reciprocity and subject to the provisions contained in special statutes.[14] Subject to the above, there are no particular problems in relation

---

[7] Article 51 of D.P.R. no. 917 of December 22, 1986 ('Consolidated Income Tax Code').
[8] Article 62 no. 4 of Consolidated Income Tax Code.
[9] Article 51 of Consolidated Income Tax Code.
[10] Article 5 of Consolidated Income Tax Code.
[11] Article 41 no. 1(f) of Consolidated Income Tax Code.
[12] Article 49 no. 2(c) of Consolidated Income Tax Code.
[13] Article 2 of D.P.R. no. 131 of April 26, 1986.
[14] The principle of reciprocity in essence requires that foreign states afford Italian nationals the same rights as their own nationals. *See also* Article 16 of Provisions on the Law in General.

to the participation by a non-Italian in an Italian joint venture whatever the legal form of such joint venture may be.

3.8 Acquisition use of business assets and intellectual property rights

The structure of the Participation Agreement contemplates that the operator is the master of the business both in terms of management responsibility and in terms of ownership. Consequently, any business asset acquired during the life of the joint venture will become the property of the operator. This applies also to any intellectual property right which may be acquired and/or developed during the life of the joint venture.

3.9 Competition Law

See 7 below.

3.10 Conclusion

The participation agreement is best suited to business ventures which can be brought to completion rapidly. Here, the advantages, such as ease of formation and termination and secrecy, could outweigh the principal disadvantage of this type of structure, the lack of an independent legal entity.

The recent evolution of this type of contract seems to point towards its use as a financial instrument for investing money in a business venture.[15]

4. PARTNERSHIPS

4.1 Introduction

(a) Partnerships

The general definition of 'partnership' includes the following types of organizations specifically regulated by the Italian civil code:[16] the civil company ('societa' semplice'), the general partnership ('societa' in nome collettivo') and the limited partnership ('societa' in accomandita' semplice'). (The societa'

---

[15] Participation agreements (under which the participants had contributed money) which contemplate their transferability by the participant through endorsement of the contractual document pursuant to Article 1407 of the Civil Code, were deemed to constitute 'transferable securities' for the purpose of the control exercised by 'CONSOB' (the Italian National Securities Agency) on the securities market.
[16] Article 2249 of the Civil Code.

semplice is not usable in commercial activities and therefore will not be analysed here.)

Two important features are common in Italian law to all types of partnerships: (i) a partnership (as distinct from a company) has no 'legal personality' (although as a practical matter the consequences of lacking legal personality may be slight) and (ii) under a recent decision of the Italian Court of Cassation,[17] companies *cannot* be members of any partnership, not even as limited partners of a limited liability partnership. At least for the time being, the partnership structure is unavailable for any joint venture in which one of the members is a company.

(b) General partnership

The general partnership is a business association where all the members enter into legal relationships with third parties.[18] The members are jointly and severally liable (without limit) for all of the partnership's liabilities to its creditors. The partnership must act under a business name which shall include the name of one or more partners with an indication of the partnership relationship, i.e. inclusion after the name of the words (or more often an abbreviation): 'societa in nome collettivo' (*see* 4.1(a) above).[19]

(c) Limited partnership

The limited partnership is a form of business association which has some features of the general partnership and others of the limited liability company.[20]

The limited partnership has two kinds of members: general partners, whose position is similar to that of the members of a general partnership; and limited partners, whose liability is limited to the amount of capital contribution made to the partnership. The partnership operates under a business name (or firm name) which must include the name of at least one of the general partners and an indication of the 'limited' status of the partnership.[1]

Although (as indicated above) a partnership has no legal personality, it can nevertheless: (i) acquire rights (including realty); (ii) undertake obligations; and (iii) sue and be sued, always acting through the partner(s) who have the authority to represent the partnership pursuant to its Articles of Association.

From a strictly legal point of view, the rights acquired and the obligations undertaken by the partnership are also the rights and obligations of the partners themselves, but, by the creation of the partnership, the law allows the establishment of what is called an 'autonomia patrimoniale' i.e. an autonomy of the

---

[17] Decision no. 5636 of October 17, 1988.
[18] Article 2291 of the Civil Code.
[19] Article 2292 of the Civil Code.
[20] Article 2313 of the Civil Code.
[1] Article 2314 of the Civil Code and *see* 4(i)(b) above.

assets used in the business of the partnership vis a vis any other assets owned by a partner.[2] The autonomy in question causes the liability of individual partners towards creditors of the partnership to be in measure limited,[3] but does not affect the principle of transparency. In fact, if the partnership is declared bankrupt all the general partners will also be declared bankrupt. However, in the event that a general partner is declared bankrupt in relation to business activities which are distinct from those of the partnership, the partnership itself will not be affected but the individual's bankruptcy will automatically entitle his other partners to expel him from the partnership.[4]

4.2 Advantages

The most notable advantage is the tax transparency which allows an individual to be able to set off against other taxable income his share of partnership losses, and to have his share of profits taxed at scaled rates (that reflect his overall liability to tax) rather than at a fixed rate as would apply to a company.

4.3 Disadvantages

The main disadvantage of the partnership structure in relation to a joint venture is that companies cannot be partners. In addition, a partnership cannot be a member of another partnership except when the members of the former are also members of the latter.

The process of formation of a partnership is similar to that of a company and, as in the case of a company, there is no secrecy.[5] The unlimited liability of partners (save limited partners (*see* 4.1(c) above) is a clear disadvantage. The difficulty of transferring an interest in a partnership is often cited as a disadvantage, although there is an argument that the 'difficulty' suits the highly personal nature of a joint venture and in particular, the selection of a joint venture partner.

4.4 When to select

Because of the availability of tax transparency, the partnership should be selected as a joint venture vehicle when the venturers are individuals (as distinct

---

[2] Articles 2293, 2270, 2271, 2304, 2305 of the Civil Code.
[3] See Section 4.5 (d) below.
[4] Article 2288 of the Civil Code.
[5] See paragraph 4.5 below.

from companies) and the aforementioned tax advantage outweighs the disadvantage of lack of limitation of liability.

4.5   Formation documentation, key aspects

(a) Formation

The formation of both a general partnership and a limited liability partnership takes place through the execution before a notary public of the Articles of Association which shall contain the following elements:

  (i)   particulars of the partners (for limited partnership also an indication of the general partners and the limited partners);
  (ii)   the business name, object, legal address and duration of the partnership;
  (iii) the value of each partner's contribution to the capital of the partnership and the rules for sharing profits and losses among the partners;
  (iv)   the names of those partners who will have the power to manage and represent the partnership.

A copy of the Articles of Association (as well as any subsequent amendment) must be filed with the office of the Register of Enterprises in whose district the headquarters of the partnership are located. Failure to effect such filing causes any limitation in the powers of operation of the partnership not to be binding upon third parties.[6] A failure to file the Articles of Association would thus mean that the partnership could not argue that a given act was *ultra vires* and that a third party had constructive notice of such fact.

(b) Members

The partnership structure for a joint venture has traditionally been used by individuals.

In some cases (prior to the recent decision of the Court of Cassation)[7] the structure of the limited partnership was used also by companies (as limited partners) seeking certain tax advantages.

(c) Competition

A partner cannot exercise an activity in competition with that of the partnership for his own account or for the account of others without the consent of the other partners.[8] The breach of the non-competition provision gives the partnership the right to claim damages and may cause the removal from the partnership

---

[6] Article 2297 of the Civil Code.
[7] Decision no. 5636 of October 17, 1988.
[8] Article 2301 of the Civil Code.

of the partner in breach. The formation of a partnership may give rise to more general domestic competition law problems, *see also* section 7 below.

(d) Liability

The creditors of a partnership cannot demand payment from individual partners (i.e. general partners) until after the exhaustion of remedies against the partnership's assets and, as long as the partnership is in existence, a personal creditor of a partner cannot demand liquidation of the share of the partner who is his debtor.

(e) Management

The Articles of Association usually set forth the rules for the administration of the partnership. If no such rules are established, each partner is deemed to have full management powers; in such a case, rules are set forth by the law for resolving any conflict.[9]

In a limited partnership, if a limited partner performs general management functions (in breach of the provisions of law which prevent him from doing so), he becomes liable as a general partner and can be removed from the partnership.[10]

(f) Dissolution

Dissolution may take place by mutual consent, the attainment of the object for which the partnership was formed, the expiry of its term, or as a result of the bankruptcy of the partnership. In addition to the above, dissolution may occur with respect to the general partnership when no more than one member remains, unless a plurality of members is re-established within six months, and with respect to the limited partnership when only general partners or only limited partners are left, unless within six months any partnership deficiency is remedied.

An individual partner's interest in the partnership will typically expire in the event of such partner's death, bankruptcy, withdrawal or removal. Specific provisions are set forth by the civil code in relation to such events.[11]

Upon dissolution by reason of a departing partner, the person who has so ceased to be a partner (or his heirs in case of his death) is entitled to receive from the other partners an amount of money equal to the value of his share. The 'liquidation' of the share is made on the basis of a financial statement of the partnership as of the date on which the dissolution occurred. Payment is to be made within a certain period of time.[12]

[9] Articles 2293, 2266 and 2267 of the Civil Code.
[10] Article 2320 of the Civil Code.
[11] Articles 2293, 2284, 2285, 2286, 2287 and 2288 of the Civil Code.
[12] Article 2289 of the Civil Code.

(g) Transferability of the interest

As a practical matter, a partner cannot transfer his interest without the consent of the other partners. Even in the case of the death of a partner, the surviving partners have no obligation to continue the partnership with the heirs of the deceased. In essence, the transfer of an interest is not contemplated by law. In practice a 'transfer' is achieved by the withdrawal of the transferor and the joining of the partnership by the transferee as a new partner (subject to the consent of all other partners).

An exception is made in a limited liability partnership where a limited partner's interest can be transferred in case of his death. In all other cases, such a transfer would become effective *vis-à-vis* the partnership only with the consent of the partners representing the majority of the partnership's capital unless the Articles of Association provided otherwise.[13]

4.6   Taxes

A partnership is treated as an independent tax entity with respect to local income tax (ILOR) and VAT.[14] With respect to national income tax, there is a tax transparency since the taxable income realized by a partnership is attributed to the partners in proportion to their respective shares in the partnership.[15]

The shares of a partnership are determined by the Articles of Association. The law prohibits use of a 'leonine clause' whereby one or more partners are excluded from any participation in the profits or losses. The partnership must prepare an inventory, a profit and loss account and balance sheet each year, which must be submitted by the managers to the partners for their approval. The annual accounts are used as a base for the annual tax return which is filed by the partnership for the purpose of (i) paying the ILOR and (ii) determining any taxable income attributable to the partners.

4.7   Foreign involvement

See statement under 3.7 above.

4.8   Acquisition/use of business assets and intellectual property rights

At the time a partnership is formed, assets and intellectual property rights of the partners can be contributed by them to the partnership either outright

---

[13] Article 2322 of the Civil Code.
[14] Article 116 of Consolidated Income Tax Code and Article 1 of D.P.R. no. 633 of October 26, 1972.
[15] Article 5 no. 1 of Consolidated Income Tax Code.

by a transfer of title or by means of a licence. Alternatively, the partnership can 'use' assets and/or intellectual property rights belonging to one of the partners on the basis of a licence or lease.

The assets and/or intellectual property rights which are acquired or developed directly by the partnership during its life would be regarded as property of the partnership in accordance with the principle of the 'autonomia patrimoniale'.[16]

4.9   Competition law

See 7 below.

4.10   Conclusion

The fact that the partnership structure cannot be used in a joint venture in which a company participates, coupled with the fact than an absolute limitation of liability cannot be established, means that the partnership is suitable only for minor joint ventures in which individuals are participating.

5.   JOINT VENTURE COMPANIES

5.1   Introduction

The joint venture company ('jvc') is a common joint venture structure in Italy formed typically in one of these ways:

   (i)   where the shareholders of an existing company (individuals or corporate undertakings) agree with one or more third parties that the latter will join the (existing) company by acquiring an equity interest in it either through a purchase of existing shares or a subscription for new shares (the consideration can take the form of cash or assets, including shares in the third parties);

   (ii)   where two or more individuals or corporate undertakings agree to form a jvc (again, the consideration for the shares in the newly formed company can take the form of cash or assets including shares in the capital of the founders); and

   (iii)   where two existing companies agree to merge either through the formation of a new company or the consolidation of one of them into the other.

Jvcs are generally either SpAs or Srls. The 'Societa' in Accomandita' per Azioni' is rarely used. In a 'Societa' in Accomandita' per Azioni, the participation

---

[16]   *See* 4.1(c) above.

of the members is represented by shares (as in the case of a SpA) but two categories of shareholders exist: one with limited liability and one with unlimited liability. The management powers are attributed by operation of law to the shareholders with unlimited liability. The 'Societa' in Accomandita' per Azioni' is not suitable for use as a jvc vehicle where all the joint venturers are corporate entities since it is questionable whether a limited liability company can assume 'unlimited liability' as a shareholder in another company.

As to the choice between a SpA and a Srl, the following major differences between the two types of company may play an important role. The minimum capital of an Srl (Lire 20,000,000) is considerably lower than that of an SpA (Lire 200,000,000). The shares of a SpA are represented by share certificates which can circulate as negotiable instruments whereas no share certificates are issued by a Srl. Restrictions upon the transfer of shares can be more stringent in a Srl and only shares of a SpA can be listed on a stock exchange.[17] A Srl cannot issue debentures.[18]

5.2   Advantages

The main advantage of the jvc structure, in addition to the familiarity which the joint venturers are likely to have with the general legal, financial and tax requirements of this type of business structure, is the limitation of liability of the jvc's members coupled with their ability to participate, through the organs of the company, in the day-to-day management of the venture.

Another important advantage is that the interest in the joint venture is represented by a share of capital. Notwithstanding the fact that the inability freely to dispose of the interest seems to be an almost inherent feature in a jvc, the advantage nevertheless remains that when the interest is to be disposed of permissably, the existance of a 'share' structure greatly facilitates such process.

5.3   Disadvantages

A disadvantage is the lack of secrecy concerning the affairs of the jvc. In addition to the initial deed of incorporation and bye-laws (together with any subsequent amendments), certain information, such as the annual accounts and reports by the directors and internal auditors, the names of the directors (and their powers) and the name of the internal auditors become matters of public record, since all the foregoing must be filed with the office of the Register of Enterprises.

---

[17] The shares of an SpA are represented by stock certificates which constitute negotiable instruments. The shares of an Srl are represented by an agreed percentage of ownership or 'ideal quota'. The ideal quota is recorded in the Srl's quotaholders' book but no certificate is issued in respect thereof.

[18] Article 2486 of the Civil Code.

However, such 'lack of secrecy' does not differ very much from the position relating to a partnership except for the requirement that the jvc's annual accounts be published. A SpA must have a board of auditors. This board will prepare a report on the balance sheet to be filed at the office of the Register of Enterprises. A Srl must likewise publish its accounts; when its issued capital reaches 100 million lira it must have a board of auditors.

5.4 When to select

The jvc structure is to be selected in all cases where the joint venture is aimed at establishing a jointly owned and managed business entity which is to be independent of the joint venturers and capable of autonomous growth and development.

5.5 Formation documentation, key aspects

(a) Formation – joint venture agreement

A joint venture agreement would usually deal with the following major points:

(i) identification of any assets (and liabilities) to be contributed by the parties (together with appropriate representations and warranties);

(ii) undertakings as to any future financial requirements of the jvc (future capital injections or the providing of shareholders' guarantees for borrowings by the jvc);

(iii) provisions relating to the majority required for passing shareholders' resolutions or resolutions of the board of directors and limitations on the transferability of shares. These matters are usually also included in the byelaws of the jvc, the text of which is agreed upon by the joint venturers. The byelaws are typically an exhibit to the joint venture agreement.

(iv) the transfer of shares: *see* 5.5(g) below.

(v) other matters relating to the commercial objective of the joint venture such as licences for the use of intellectual property rights and service or supply agreements.

(b) Formation – jvc

In the event that the joint venture structure involves the creation of a new company, the formation process requires the execution of a notarised deed of incorporation of which the byelaws of the company will form an integral part. The deed requires court approval[19] and must be filed with the office

---

[19] Articles 2330 and 2475 of the Civil Code.

of the Register of Enterprises in whose district the headquarters of the jvc are located. In practice, the formation process is not much different from the one required for the formation of a general partnership or a limited partnership. Thirty per cent of the capital must be paid in immediately by the shareholders.[20]

In the case of the joint venture agreement where the parties subscribe for new shares (instead of forming a new company) the process is equally complex. A shareholders' resolution will be required for the issue of new shares (the minutes of which must be drawn up by a notary public) and such resolution (which is technically considered as an amendment to the existing dead of incorporation) must be approved by the court and filed with the office of the Register of Enterprises. A merger would be even more complex since the shareholders' resolutions of both companies would be subject to court approval and registration with the office of the Register of Enterprises. As a rule, the merger cannot be effected prior to the expiry of a two-month period from the date of registration of the resolutions, during which period the creditors of the companies could raise objections to the merger.

(c) Management

Provisions for the 'management' of a jvc cannot be entirely dealt with by the joint venture agreement because the effect of that agreement will be limited to the venturers *inter se*, and will not apply to third parties. The byelaws will therefore have pre-emptive, independent relevance *vis-à-vis* third parties. In fact, if the joint venture agreement were to regulate the activities of the jvc such that, for example, the consent of all the venturers was required for certain specified actions, but a parallel valid provision were not contained in the bylaws, then, while any action taken in breach of the joint venture agreement might give rise to an action for damages between the joint venturers, the action taken by the jvc, being in compliance with its by-laws, would nevertheless be valid and binding.[1]

The management of a jvc is to be dealt with at two levels: at board level and at shareholders' meeting level.

The byelaws of a jvc would therefore provide for the majority required for passing resolutions (i) at special meetings of the shareholders (which address, *inter alia*, changes to the objects, increases of capital, the issue of debentures, winding-up and amendments to the byelaws), and (ii) at ordinary meetings of the shareholders (which address *inter alia*, the appointment of directors and internal auditors, the approval of the annual accounts and the declaration of dividends).

The byelaws would also provide for the majority required for passing certain board resolutions such as those dealing with major financial matters, establishing mortgages and pledges on the company's assets, disposing of all or substan-

---

[20] Articles 2329 n. 2 and 2475 of the Civil Code; this applies to both Srls and SpAs.
[1] Articles 2377, 2388, 2486 and 2487 of the Civil Code.

tially all of the assets, certain capital investments and the granting of guarantees for obligations of third parties.

The byelaws also typically contain provisions providing for the election of directors such that each joint venturer can secure a representation on the board of directors of the jvc that is proportional to his equity interest in the jvc.

Recourse to the use of different classes of share is not frequent. As a general rule, each share must give the right to vote and no share can be issued with weighted or multiple voting rights. Shares with limited voting rights can be issued but not in excess of one half of the capital. In any event such shares will have voting rights in relation to special shareholders' meetings and must be *preferred* in any distribution of the company's profits and in any reimbursement of capital upon a dissolution of the company.[2]

(d) Deadlock

Provisions in the byelaws concerning the majority required for shareholders' resolutions leaves unresolved the difficulty that a deadlock between the shareholders may cause the dissolution of the company by operation of law.[3] The problem exists not only in a fifty-fifty joint venture, but also (at least from a theoretical point of view) in a jvc with several shareholders. In fact, the device of the 'voting agreement' may prove not to be effective both because no specific performance would be afforded and because a voting agreement may be considered null and void.[4] The device of a blank proxy cannot likewise be used since it is specifically forbidden by law.[5]

In fifty-fifty jvcs the deadlock problem has occasionally been dealt with by transferring (from the inception of the joint venture) full title to a few shares to a reputed corporate third party (trusted by both joint venturers) which by casting its vote in the event of deadlock between the parties assumes the role of an independent arbitrator.

Another possible solution to the deadlock problem, thus avoiding the dissolution of the jvc by operation of law, is the use of a buy-sell agreement which becomes effective upon the occurrence of a deadlock between the parties. Under such an arrangement, either party is entitled to make an offer for the purchase of the other party's shares. If the offeree does not accept such offer he will be obliged to purchase the offeror's shares at the price stated to him in the original offer.

(e) Competition

A non-competition covenant preventing the members of a jvc from competing with the activities of the jvc is generally desirable not only for the time the

---

[2] Article 2351 of the Civil Code.
[3] Article 2448 no. 3 of the Civil Code.
[4] See 'I Sindacati di voto: realta' e prospettive' by Bruno Visentini in Rivista delle Societa', 1988, 1.
[5] Articles 2372 and 2486 of the Civil Code.

jvc is in operation but also in the event that the joint venture is terminated without the jvc being dissolved. For a consideration of the competition law issues arising from the use of non-competition clauses in a joint venture agreement, *see* 7 below.

(f) Dissolution

The dissolution of a jvc will typically be triggered upon the occurrence of one of the following events:

- (i)   the expiry of the term for which the jvc has been formed, the adoption of a valid resolution for early termination, the attainment of the objective of the jvc or the realisation that the objective cannot be attained;
- (ii) the bankruptcy of the jvc;
- (iii) the reduction (because of losses) of the capital below the legal minimum, except when the said capital has been reconstituted or a reorganization of the company has occurred;[6]
- (iv) a deadlock (i.e. a failure to agree) between the parties at the level of the shareholders' meeting.[7]

Whenever an event triggering dissolution occurs, the directors must refrain from undertaking new business transactions. If they fail to do so, they will assume (in relation to said transactions) personal liability jointly and severally with the company. A shareholders' meeting must be called in order to undertake the liquidation of the jvc.

(g) Transferability of interest

Limitations to the right to transfer an interest in a jvc are a frequent feature in joint venture agreements and are a direct consequence of the fact that the 'identity' of a shareholder is often critical in a joint venture context.

The problem is twofold since one of the joint venturers can either transfer his interest in the jvc or, when a corporate entity, cause, without effecting such a transfer, his 'identity' to change as a consequence of a takeover by a third party.

Joint venture agreements frequently contain provisions to the effect that if one of the parties (that is a corporate entity) ceases to be owned or controlled by its existing shareholders, it will be obliged to sell its shares in the jvc to the other shareholders of the jvc at an agreed price. The covenant will be valid and enforceable to the extent that when the event occurs, the shares are still owned by the party that has undertaken the obligation to sell. Therefore, in addition to the above provisions of the joint venture agreement, the byelaws

---

[6]   Articles 2448 no. 4 and 2497 of the Civil Code.
[7]   Articles 2448 no. 3 and 2497 of the Civil Code.

of the jvc will typically contain provisions which prevent a shareholder from disposing of his shares without first offering them to the other existing shareholders.

Special complexity arises in cases where the shareholders of the jvc are individuals (rather than corporate entities) and the identity of a shareholder is deemed to be essential to the joint venture, such as in the case of a service company (e.g. an advertising agency). In such a case, the legal form selected for the jvc may be that of 'Srl' since the limitations upon the transferability of shares can be more stringent.[8] In particular, the bye-laws can provide that no transfer of shares is permissible without the consent of the shareholders in general meeting and also that the shares are not transferable by inheritance.

5.6   Taxes

A jvc is subject (as any other Italian company) to the normal rules for the taxation of corporate entities; in particular, it is subject to corporate income tax (IRPEG) at the rate of 36% and to local income tax (ILOR) at the rate of 16.2%. ILOR is deductible for purposes of IRPEG, with the result that the effective tax rate is 46.368%.

ILOR is payable on the taxable income of each fiscal year (fixed deductions from it are allowed for the purposes of determining the ILOR taxable base) and cannot be offset against losses of previous years. IRPEG is payable on the taxable income (from which the ILOR payable is deducted) and the offsetting against previous losses is permitted (the loss carry forward is permitted for five years).

On dividends paid by a company to a recipient who is subject to income tax in Italy, a tax credit is attributed equal to 9/16ths of such dividends. A 10% withholding tax applied by the company paying the dividend is treated as paid 'on account' of the income tax due by the recipient.

The withholding tax (at the source) applied to a recipient who is not an Italian tax payer (in the absence of a tax treaty between Italy and the country of which the recipient is a resident regulating the matter differently) is much higher (presently 32.4 per cent). The recipient is entitled to a reimbursement of up to two thirds of the tax withheld if he proves that he has paid income tax abroad on the same dividends.

5.7   Foreign involvement

See 3.7 above.

---

[8] Article 2479 of the Civil Code.

5.8   Acquisition/use of business assets and intellectual property rights

At the time a joint venture company is formed assets (including intellectual property rights) owned by one of the joint venturers can be contributed to the company in return for shares. Such contributions in kind, however, must be made at a value determined through an appraisal by a court-appointed expert.[9]

The requirement for an appraisal by a court-appointed expert applies also when a company, within two years from its formation, acquires from its founders, members or directors assets at a price higher than 10% of the company's capital.

With respect to intellectual property rights the granting to the jvc of a right to 'use' (i.e. a licence) is more frequent than an outright contribution in kind (or transfer of 'title'). When the rights in question become the property of the jvc such property will be subject to liquidation along with all other company assets, in the event of the company's bankruptcy.

5.9   Competition law

See 7 below.

5.10   Conclusion

The jvc is in practice the structure used most frequently not only because it allows the joint venturers to limit their risk to what they contribute into the jvc, but also because it is often the type of structure most familiar to them.

6.   CONSORTIA

6.1   Introduction

(a) General

A consortium is defined by statute[10] as 'a contract by which two or more entrepreneurs establish a joint organization for the purposes of regulating or conducting specified aspects of their respective activities'. The essential elements of a consortium are: (i) the establishment of a joint organization; (ii) the determination of rules to regulate the relationship between the members and the conduct of their respective enterprises; and (iii) the agreement upon a common business purpose.

---

[9] Article 2343 of the Civil Code.
[10] Article 2602 of the Civil Code.

Italian law distinguishes between an 'internal consortium' and an 'external consortium'.[11] The former does not engage in activities with third parties, whilst the 'external consortium' is organized as a 'veil' between its members and third parties. The external consortium can also be organized as a company. It is known in such cases as an 'incorporated consortium' and will be subject to the rules governing SpAs and Srls (*see* 5 above).[12] The specific features of the internal and external consortium shall be examined in this section.

(b) 'Internal consortium'

Although the internal consortium appears as an independent entity, as a matter of law it is no more than a contract between the signatories. It does not, in particular, involve the creation of a separate legal entity capable of acting as a profit centre and contracting with third parties. It follows that this structure falls generally into the category of co-operation agreements and is best suited to the achievement of mutual objectives not requiring relationships with third parties.

(c) 'External consortium'

The external consortium is capable of contracting with third parties and undertaking obligations. For such purpose, in 1976 the legislature amended some of the provisions of the Civil Code and specifically limited the liability of the external consortium to its fund.[13] Though no doubt exists that the external consortium enjoys limited liability, it is still debated whether or not the external consortium is a legal entity distinct from its members.

6.2 Advantages

Both internal and external consortia enjoy the advantage of ease of formation and management. The internal consortium, moreover, as it does not need to be registered or otherwise disclosed, enjoys total confidentiality.

6.3 Disadvantages

The major disadvantage of the internal and external consortia lies in the fact that there is no legal entity clearly distinct from its members. Moreover, lacking any mandatory minimum capitalization requirement and, in practice, the consortium fund being of limited amount, this structure is not widely used and is distrusted by creditors and third parties.

[11] Articles 2602 and 2612 of the Civil Code.
[12] Article 2615ter of the Civil Code.
[13] Article 2615 of the Civil Code.

6.4   When to select

The consortium structure, either internal or external, is selected when two or more parties intend to achieve a common end (for instance to regulate competition between them or to undertake major contracts by using a relatively simple form of management that offers absolute confidentiality as to its constitution and method of operation).

6.5   Formation documentation

6.5.1 Internal consortium

(a) *Formation*. The establishment of an internal consortium requires an agreement in writing, under penalty of nullity, which must indicate: (i) the object and duration; and (ii) the obligations undertaken and the contributions owed by the members.

The contract should also set forth the conditions for the admission of new members because the consortium falls into the category of agreements mandatorily open to the participation of other parties having the required qualifications.[14] Lastly, the contract can also, but need not necessarily, provide for: (i) the establishment of an office for the consortium, if there is to be one; (ii) the duties and powers of the management bodies of the consortium; (iii) the conditions for withdrawal of consortium members; and (iv) the varying grounds for termination of the consortium arrangements, for example, material breach, bankruptcy and the change of control of a consortium member.

The execution of the agreement does not require any specific formality or filing with any public authority.

Any amendment to the contract must be in writing, under penalty of nullity.[15] Unless otherwise agreed, the contract cannot be amended without the consent of all the members.[16]

(b) *Members*. The parties entering into the contract, or subsequently admitted to the internal consortium, thereby becoming members, must be entrepreneurs, i.e. individuals or entities who upon a continuing basis engage (for profit) in the production and trade of goods and services.[17] The contract may also require that the members possess other specific qualifications.

Unless otherwise agreed in the contract, in the event that a member transfers his business, the transferee will automatically become a member of the internal consortium.

(c) *Object*. The internal consortium, though not widely used, is generally regarded as a suitable structure to regulate competition between the members such that they increase and/or improve their capability to produce and trade

---

[14] Article 2603 no. 5 of the Civil Code.
[15] Article 2607 of the Civil Code.
[16] Article 2607 of the Civil Code.
[17] Article 2602 of the Civil Code.

goods and services. However, such objective will always be subject to domestic and EC antitrust regulations.[18]

As a result of amendments made in 1976 to the section of the Civil Code regarding consortia,[19] the internal consortium can also carry out activities for the exclusive mutual benefit of its members (for example, marketing research, quality control and joint research and development). In such cases the internal consortium will not have any dealings with third parties.

(d) *Members' obligations and contributions.* The obligations of the members derive directly from the objectives of the internal consortium as set out in the contract. In the event that the prime aim of the internal consortium is to regulate or limit competition between its members, the obligations of the members are negative. In other cases, the members may be required to provide the joint organization with the necessary means for the attainment of its objectives. Monetary contributions may also be required but they will not constitute any form of equity or endowment fund. In some instances the secondment of personnel and office space are required from the members.

(e) *Management.* As the management structures of the internal consortium are totally governed by the contract, the consortium can be operated in a relatively informal and flexible manner. General meetings of the members, a board of directors and a managing director or an executive committee are often provided for by the contract which will also set forth the rules for the appointment and functioning of such bodies.

The directors will be responsible *vis-à-vis* the members in the same way and to the same extent and manner as agents are responsible to their principals. When the directors deal with third parties, they are deemed to be agents of the members and not the internal consortium.

The law specifically provides that the individual or body who has management responsibilities in an internal consortium is authorized to inspect the members' activities and to verify their compliance with the consortium's rules.[20]

(f) *Liability.* As the consortium is not a legal entity and cannot own property or contract with third parties, each member is liable for his own acts and omissions.

If the contract requires that a member or members conduct activities for the mutual benefit of all members, it is expected that the contract will also provide for an indemnification procedure under which the member acting for the consortium and incurring a liability will be adequately protected.

(g) *Duration.* The duration of the internal consortium is ten years, unless otherwise provided in the contract.[1]

Typical causes for dissolution of an internal consortium are:

(i)   expiration of the term established for its duration;

---

[18] *See* 7 below.
[19] Law no. 377 of May 10, 1976 substantially amended Articles from 2602 through 2615 of the Civil Code.
[20] Article 2605 of the Civil Code.
[1] Article 2604 of the Civil Code.

(ii)   attainment of its objective or realisation that the objective cannot be achieved;

(iii)   unanimous consent of the members or consent of the majority of the members if there is a just cause for termination; and

(iv)   other causes set forth in the contract for example, material breach, bankruptcy or a change of control.

Upon the occurrence of any such triggering event, the internal consortium will be unable to carry on operating and its assets, after payment of debts, will be allocated to its members in proportion to their respective contributions.

6.5.2 External consortium

(a) *Formation.* The contract must be formed in the same manner and must set out the same elements as indicated for internal consortia.[2] In addition, the law requires that an excerpt of the contract must be filed with the office of the Register of Enterprises in whose district the headquarters of the consortium are located within thirty days of its execution.[3] The excerpt must indicate:

(i)   the name and object of the consortium and the location of its office;

(ii)   the names of the members;

(iii) the duration of the consortium;

(iv)   the persons who are entrusted with the presidency, the management and the representation of the consortium and their respective powers; and

(v)   the manner in which the consortium's fund is established and the provisions relating to dissolution.

Upon filing of the excerpt of the contract, the external consortium, without any further requirement or approval by a court, will be registered and fully operative.

(b) *Members.* The members must be entrepreneurs (*see* 6.5.1(b) above) and the contract may require that they possess other specific qualifications. Unlike the internal consortium, the names of the members must be published by filing the excerpt of the contract with the office of the Register of Enterprises.

(c) *Object.* The establishment of the external consortium gives rise to a structure capable of carrying out activities with third parties. It is up to the members to set out the specific object of the consortium. As external consortia are largely used by companies seeking to submit one or more joint tender(s) for a large contract, typical objects of the external consortium are the preparation of offers and the coordination of the activities subsequent to the award of contract.

(d) *Members' obligations and contributions.* In contrast with an internal consortium, a common fund must be established through the contributions of the members.[4] However, no statutory minimum is required. For the duration

---

[2] Article 2602 of the Civil Code.
[3] Article 2612 of the Civil Code.
[4] Article 2614 of the Civil Code.

of the consortium, the fund is an independent asset as against the members and their creditors.[5]

(e) *Management*. The law specifically requires the establishment of certain management structures.[6] In particular, a chairman must be appointed. Usually, a board of directors and one or more managing directors are also appointed. The names and the respective powers of all officers must be publicized by filing the relevant excerpt from the contract with the office of the Register of Enterprises.

The external consortium can be represented *vis-à-vis* third parties by any individual so appointed and authorized by the contract. However, the external consortium can be sued in the name of the chairman even though the legal representation of the external consortium had been granted other officers.[7]

(f) *Liability*. The external consortium enjoys limited liability. It is worth mentioning that under the relevant provisions of the Civil Code, before the 1976 amendment, individuals acting for the consortium had personal liability. The relevant provision of the Civil Code now in force[8] specifically provides that an individual duly authorized and acting for an external consortium is not personally liable for the obligations assumed by the external consortium. Third parties, accordingly, can only enforce their claims against the consortium's fund.

The consortium is capable of forming contractual relations with third parties in one of two ways: either for itself as a consortium or upon behalf of one or more individual corporate members (in the last case the consortium acts as a type of agent). It is generally believed that the revision to the Civil Code (outlined above) recognizes this distinction.

In the first case (i.e. where the consortium contracts on behalf of the consortium), the liability of the consortium and its members will be limited to the consortium fund, as in a corporation. In the second case (where the consortium contracts upon behalf of one or more individual members), the individual member or members for whom the obligation was assumed will be jointly liable with the consortium fund. The creditor, therefore, can enforce his claim against the consortium fund and the assets of those individual members involved. If one or more such individual members is insolvent, the claim must be internally divided among the remaining individual members concerned, in proportion to their respective shares.[9]

(g) *Duration*. The position is the same as with internal consortia.

(h) *Financial statements*. Mainly for the protection of third parties, the law requires that the annual financial statements of the external consortium be published and filed with the office of the Register of Enterprises.[10]

---

[5] Article 2614 of the Civil Code.
[6] Articles 2612 no. 4 and 2613 of the Civil Code.
[7] Article 2613 of the Civil Code.
[8] Article 2615 of the Civil Code.
[9] Article 2615 last paragraph of the Civil Code.
[10] Article 2615bis of the Civil Code.

The statements must be prepared in accordance with accounting principles applicable to Italian companies.

(i) *Temporary association of enterprises.* The temporary association of enterprises may be considered a special category of external consortium.

Temporary associations of enterprises are governed by law No. 584 of August 8, 1977 which implemented in Italy EC directives concerning public procurement contracts.

Law 584 has made it possible for two or more entrepreneurs to enter into a temporary contractual association in order to bid for and undertake large public sector construction and supplies contracts. Pursuant to such law, the entrepreneurs can jointly authorize by means of a power of attorney one of their member (the main contractor) to act on their behalf and, therefore, bid for the contract and deal with the public authority. The power of attorney, once granted, cannot be revoked until all the obligations deriving from the contract have been satisfied. All the entrepreneurs are jointly and severally liable for the performance of the contract.

6.6 Taxes

6.6.1 Internal consortium

The internal consortium is not a taxable entity for the purposes of income taxes (corporate or personal) and is, therefore, tax transparent. If a member carries out activities (such as marketing or joint research) for the benefit of all other members and receives a consideration for such services from a third party, then the consideration would be shared between the consortium members and would be treated as part of their respective taxable income.

6.6.2 External consortium

External consortia are taxable entities for the purposes of corporate income tax and local income tax.[11]

A distinction must be made between 'commercial activities' and 'non-commercial activities'.

If the external consortium engages in commercial activities as its exclusive or main purpose, it is subject to the rules for the taxation of business enterprises set out in 5.6 above. However, if it does not engage in such activities, it is treated as a 'non-commercial entity'. In such case:

(i) business income, if any, is determined and taxed separately from other items of income (for example, income from land, income from capital and miscellaneous income); and

(ii) the services rendered by the consortium to its members are not considered commercial activities if rendered in accordance with the consti-

[11] Articles 87 and 116 of Consolidated Income Tax Code.

tutional purpose of the consortium, and if compensated by fees not exceeding the attributable costs.

The commercial nature of external consortia is still under debate; the case law and Tax Authorities tend to favour 'commercial' characterization of the consortia if their members are business entities.

6.7 Foreign involvement

A foreign entrepreneur can become a member of a consortium established in Italy. It will need to consider whether the terms of the relevant double tax treaty make it advantageous to participate through an Italian subsidiary.

6.8 Acquisition/use of business assets and intellectual property

Any business assets acquired by an external consortium during its life will become part of the common fund.[12] This applies also to any intellectual property rights which may be acquired and/or developed by the external consortium. As regards the internal consortium, all assets and intellectual property rights remain the property of individual members.

6.9 Competition law

See 7 below.

6.10 Conclusion

The consortium structure, in the form of an external consortium, is a viable structure for a joint venture between Italian and foreign entrepreneurs, individuals or corporations, whose business objective contemplates tendering for and entering into large contracts, whether private or public.

7 COMPETITION LAW

The Italian Competition Law ('Rules for the protection of competition and the market')[13] in essence reproduces at domestic (as distinct from EC) level the EC competition rules as set forth in Articles 85 and 86 of the Treaty of Rome.[14] In addition, the competition law contains merger control provisions.

---

[12] Article 2614 of the Civil Code.
[13] Law no. 287 of October 10, 1990.
[14] Article 1.4 provides that the principles of EC competition law are to be applied in the interpretation of the provisions of domestic competition law.

In particular, competition law:

(a)   prohibits all agreements whose object or effect is to impede, restrict or distort in a substantial manner competition within the domestic market or a significant part of it;

(b)   prohibits the abuse of a dominant position within the domestic market or a significant part of it;

(c)   establishes certain merger control procedures in relation to the acquisition of the control of a business enterprise, or the merger of two existing enterprises or the formation (by two undertakings) of a common enterprise through the formation of a new company.[15]

Since in theory any joint venture agreement might have as its effect (if not as its object) the restriction or distortion of competition, a scrutiny of its contents from such perspective must always be made. Agreements that infringe Italian domestic competition law are automatically null and void. In addition, the parties will be liable to the imposition of fines.

The competition law provides that the agency in charge of the application of the competition law ('the Authority') can authorize, under certain circumstances, and for a limited period of time, the implementation of agreements that fall subject to the basic prohibition outlined in (a) above.[16] Moreover, the parties can notify the Authority of their 'agreement' and if no formal proceedings are started by the Authority within 120 days, such proceedings can no longer be started.[17]

With respect to the merger control provisions of the competition law, the parties are obliged to give the Authority advance notice of any transaction where: (i) the total cumulative sales of the undertakings concerned exceed in the domestic market Lire 500 billion; or (ii) the total sales of the target enterprise in the domestic market exceeds Lire 50 billion. The Authority can prohibit the 'merger', or if the 'merger' has already been put into effect can impose fines and/or order the taking of all measures necessary to restore competition.[18]

---

[15]   Note that in Italian the text of the competition law uses the word 'societa'' (which corresponds to the English word 'company'), however, in Italian, 'partnerships' are also called 'societa'' (*see* 4.1(a)).

[16]   The process parallels 'exemption' under Article 85(3) EC Treaty.

[17]   The process parallels the 'opposition procedure' employed in a number of EC directives.

[18]   The competition law entered into force on October 14, 1990. Regulations and circulars are being issued in order to serve as a guidance for the practical application of the law.

CHAPTER 5

Joint ventures in the Netherlands

1. GENERAL INTRODUCTION

The Netherlands has no legal body of law specifically dedicated to joint ventures. Instead many areas of law, in particular those relating to the structure of cooperations, partnership law, company law, tax and competition law must be applied to the large number of commercial relations that fall under the description of 'joint ventures'.

The most commonly used definition of a joint venture in the Netherlands is: 'a form of cooperation of several undertakings that remain independent ... which cooperation takes place in a collective, completely separate, undertaking, by way of contribution of know-how and participation in financing'.[1]

Before establishing a joint venture the parties must agree upon the aims of the joint venture. Such aims should include the selection of the form or 'structure' of the joint venture (for example, a purely contractual cooperation, a partnership under a specific name, a limited partnership or a joint company).

The essential aspects of a joint venture might be said to comprise:

   (i)   the cooperation of partners who remain economically independent;
   (ii)   the creation of a separate undertaking in which the cooperation will be centred and through which its activities will be performed;
   (iii)   the contribution of know-how (the total knowledge and experience that each undertaking has concerning the functions to be fulfilled in the joint undertaking).[2]

It is important to distinguish joint ventures from other forms of commercial cooperation, such as mergers and acquisitions, various forms of cartel, licence and franchise agreements where the cooperation does not give rise to a separate undertaking.[3]

The following would not be regarded as joint ventures (in the strict sense) in The Netherlands, because, as stated, they do not give rise to a separate undertaking that has been set up by the joint venturers:

---

[1] 'Joint Ventures', dissertation, Dr H. W. van Hilten, Kluwer, Deventer, 1968, p. 58. 'Joint Ventures en het Recht', M. R. Bloemsma, in: TVVS, 1960, p. 188.
[2] W. J. Slagter, Compendium van het Ondernemingsrecht, Kluwer, 5e druk, 1990, p. 437 *et seq.*
[3] M. R. Bloemsma, op. cit., *see* note 1, *supra.*

(i)   long-term supply contracts;
(ii) agency agreements pursuant to which typically the agent sells the principal's products in return for a commission;[4]
(iii) distribution agreements pursuant to which the distributor sells the manufacturer's products in its own name and for its own account;
(iv) licence agreements pursuant to which the licensor licences the right to use patents, know-how, trademarks or copyrights to the licensee; and
(v)   various forms of manufacturing agreement.

A typical example of a joint venture would be a joint undertaking set up by an American undertaking and a Dutch undertaking in The Netherlands. The cooperation would involve and draw upon the technical and commercial resources of both joint venturers. The joint undertaking would manufacture a product and would subsequently market and sell it. In the example the American partner would bring in marketing methods, patents and knowledge of manufacturing. The Dutch partner would supply raw materials or components, knowledge of the market and a distribution network.

In general a commercial undertaking has the following six functions: technical, commercial, financial, personnel, administrative and public relations. Of these functions joint venture partners will usually contribute the first three, i.e. technical, commercial and financial resources.

In this chapter attention will be focused upon the joint venture structures utilised most frequently in The Netherlands. They will be addressed in the following order:

– Pure contractual joint ventures;
– Civil partnerships without legal personality;
– Limited partnership joint ventures;
– Joint venture companies ('jvcs').

2.   CONTRACTUAL JOINT VENTURES

2.1   Introduction

A pure contractual joint venture may be the express intention of the parties and may be reflected in an agreement between them, however in many cases it will automatically give rise to the creation of a partnership. Civil partnerships

---

[4] The Act on Agency protects the agent; article 74a–74S D Commercial C, *compare also* EEC Council Directive 86/653 of 18.12.1986 on the coordination of the laws of the Member States relating to self-employed commercial agents, OJ no. L382/17.

are described in the Dutch Civil Code (hereafter referred to as 'D Civil C').[5] As soon as there is a joint purpose and an intention to divide profits, a partnership will have been created. Only if both parties continue to pursue their individual purposes (albeit that they might be complementary), will the arrangements remain a pure contractual joint venture.

There are no specific requirements concerning the creation of a partnership. It is possible to create a partnership by oral agreement. As can be seen from the above it is possible (indeed easy) to create a partnership accidentally.[6]

Pure contractual joint ventures are rare in The Netherlands. As soon as there is a joint purpose and a contribution by both partners and a division of profits a partnership will have been created. For this reason this section on contractual joint ventures will be kept short.

2.2 Advantages

(i) *Flexibility of formation*: No rigorous formalities are required for the formation of contractual joint ventures given the lack of an independent entity and a specific body of governing law.

(ii) *Ease of operation*: There is no independent entity to manage and no registration must be made in the Trade Register. In fact, the only substantial requirement for the operation of a contractual joint venture is compliance with the terms of the originating contract.

(iii) *No joint liability*: Under Dutch law each member will be liable solely for his own acts and omissions. This is, of course, subject to the proviso that a partnership has not been created accidentally.

(iv) *Ease of termination*: General contract law applies here. The contract will be governed by the general principle of good faith, which is laid down in articles 1374 and 1375 D Civil C.[7] These articles confirm in general that agreements must be executed and interpreted in accordance with good faith and fairness. If something is not exactly prescribed in an agreement 'good faith and fairness' should fill in what the obligations of the parties are. This

---

[5] Article 1655 D Civil C reads as follows:

A partnership is an agreement wherein two or more persons undertake to contribute something to a joint enterprise with the aim of sharing the profits resulting therefrom.

A partnership is an agreement between two or more persons to work together for the purpose of securing an economic advantage for all the partners, and to do so by means of the contribution of each of the partners.

Compare also Asser Maeyer, Maatschap, vennootschap onder firma, commanditaire vennootschap, 1989, pp. 47, 52–6 and 65–6. It is commented here that the element of profits should not be read too strictly.

See also Dutch Supreme Court June 24, 1932, Netherlands Jurisprudence 1932, p. 1586 and Dutch Supreme Court January 10, 1968, Netherlands Jurisprudence 1968, 134.

[6] *See for example* Asser Maeyer, 1989, p. 39; the joint use of a tractor to save costs can amount to a partnership.

[7] Article 1374 (3) and 1375 D Civil C reads as follow:

1374 (3): Agreements must be performed in good faith.

1375: Agreements are binding not only as to their express provisions, but also as to whatever, in accordance with the nature of the agreement, is required by fairness, custom or the law.

also applies if the term of notice and the conditions of termination are not spelled out exactly. This means that a party terminating should both afford the other party reasonable notice and try to limit the damage that he will suffer as a result of the termination. The joint ownership of property rarely gives rise to a problem on termination. Normally in contractual joint ventures the parties will not contribute any assets outright to the joint venture, remaining instead sole owners of any assets employed.

2.3   Disadvantage

Accidental creation of a partnership: The definition of a civil partnership is broad, namely, 'when two or more parties agree to contribute to a joint enterprise with the aim of dividing the profits' (article 1655 D Civil C). The fact that a partnership could have been created accidentally, potentially gives rise to serious consequences. Assets brought into the enterprise could be deemed to constitute partnership property and be jointly owned. With respect to liability, the joint venturers would find themselves liable (unintentionally) for each other's acts and omissions upon a joint and several basis.

2.4   When to select

The use of the pure contractual joint venture is quite rare. In view of the dangers of accidentally creating a partnership its use must be limited to situations where there is no intention to generate profits, for example, in the case of joint research and development, or the joint manufacturing of a component part for or by the joint venturers in their respective undertakings.

2.5   Documentation, key aspects

No formalities are required by Dutch law for the creation of a contractual joint venture.

(i) *Contribution*: Each party would typically make available certain machinery, personnel or intellectual property rights. Assets are not contributed outright, a reflection of the lack of a separate legal entity.

(ii) *No joint liability to third parties*: In a case where each party was responsible for certain elements of the joint venture's activities, it would typically be agreed that each party would indemnify the other party from third party claims to the extent that the indemnifying party had been responsible for the act or omission giving rise to the claim.

(iii) *Terminating the joint venture*: A party would only be entitled to terminate the agreement after providing the other party(s) with a reasonable period of notice. As described in 2.2 above, parties are bound by the general provisions as to good faith set out in articles 1374 and 1375 D Civil C.

(iv) *Termination of the joint venture with immediate effect*: The occurrence of certain events will typically entitle a party to terminate the joint venture agreement with immediate effect. Such grounds include:

(a) Bankruptcy, moratorium (the staying of all creditors by court order, '*surséance van betaling*')[8] or comparable events;
(b) An unremedied and material breach of contract; or
(c) A change of control of one of the parties.

2.6 Tax

In this paragraph the tax aspects of the joint venture will be dealt with upon the assumption that the arrangements will not qualify as a partnership.

2.6.1 Corporate income tax

Each party to the joint venture agreement will be taxable for its own profits.

In the case of a company that is resident in The Netherlands, its joint venture profits will form part of its worldwide taxable income in The Netherlands.[9]

In a joint venture between two (or more) resident companies:

each party may set-off its portion of joint expenses against its profits deriving from the joint venture; and
each party may be able to set off its profits (and/or losses) deriving from the joint venture against its profits and/or losses deriving from other activities.

A non-resident company will only be subject to Netherlands corporate income tax on profits out of Dutch sources. In the case of a non-resident company, a distinction should be made between:

(a) a non-resident company in a tax treaty situation;
(b) a non-resident company in a non-tax treaty situation.

2.6.2 (a) above

Since most of the Dutch treaties are to a large extent similar to the OECD-1977 model convention, it can be said that in general such non-resident companies are subject to Dutch corporate income tax only when the joint venture results in the existence of a permanent establishment in The Netherlands. Both for treaty purposes and for national law purposes one can in general deduce the

---

[8] Bankruptcy or insolvency has the same meaning as in most other countries. '*Surséance van betaling*' is a situation described in the Dutch Bankruptcy Code, where the Court stays all creditors while the business may proceed under the supervision of a receiver appointed by the Court.
[9] Article 7 CITA.

meaning of the term 'permanent establishment' from the commentary on article 5 of the OECD model convention of 1977.

2.6.3 (b) above

Again, the establishment (or not) of a permanent establishment in The Netherlands will, as under (*a*) above, dictate whether a non-resident party to a joint venture will become liable to Dutch corporate income tax. Moreover a non-resident company in a non-tax treaty state is in principle liable to be taxed where it receives profits out of a profit sharing arrangement.[10]

In the event that no Dutch corporate income tax liability arises, the joint venture results will in principle be taxable in the state of residence of the joint venture parties.

2.6.4 VAT

Each joint venture party will remain liable to account for VAT when it provides services or delivers goods in The Netherlands as part of its obligations within the context of the joint venture.

2.7   Conclusion

The use of contractual joint ventures remains limited since it will be treated as a partnership as soon as its perceived object is to create joint ownership and/or joint profits.

3.   PARTNERSHIP JOINT VENTURES

3.1   Introduction

The rules governing partnerships are set out in articles 1655 to 1698 of the D Civil C. The definition of a partnership in article 1655 is 'an agreement wherein two or more persons undertake to contribute something to a joint enterprise with the aim of sharing the profits resulting therefrom.[11]

There are no specific formal requirements for the creation of a partnership. It is, therefore, possible to create a partnership by oral agreement. As discussed

---

[10] Article 49.1.b.3e ITA (the Dutch Corporate Income Tax Act refers to the Income Tax Act with respect to the relevant taxable sources of foreign tax payers and the method to calculate the taxable profit of an enterprise).

[11] *See* note 5, *supra*.

in 2 above, a partnership can be created accidentally. Generally (and from a practical standpoint this is the recommended approach) parties lay down their relationship in a written contract.[12]

Often a distinction is made between public partnerships and silent partnerships. A public partnership is a partnership which participates in legal transactions under a distinct name and whose partnership status is clearly recognisable to third parties. A silent partnership is the reverse, no partnership name is used and third parties will be unaware that they are dealing with a partnership.

Two specific statutorily defined forms of partnership – the vennootschap onder firma or 'VOF' and the limited partnership ('commanditaire vennootschap' or 'CV') – are described in articles 15 through 35 of the D Commercial C. A translation of these articles of the D Commercial C is provided at the end of this chapter as *Exhibit A*. As partnerships, the VOF and CV are also governed by the articles of the D Civil C that apply generally to partnerships. However, in the event of conflict between the two sets of articles, the D Commercial C provisions will take precedence. The key distinction between a VOF and a limited partnership on the one hand and an ordinary partnership on the other is to be found in the manner and extent of individual partners' liabilities. Under a VOF, each partner is jointly and severally liable for the acts and omissions of all other partners. The same applies to the general partners in a limited partnership. Under an ordinary partnership, the liability of a partner for the acts and omissions of other partners, is limited to the amount of his capital contribution. There is jurisprudence to the effect that where a partner is solely responsible for damage to the partnership, his liability might, in such circumstances, be unlimited although the point is subject to some debate (see further 3.3(i) below).

A VOF is defined in article 16 D Commercial C as 'a partnership entered into for the purpose of doing business under a common name'. If a partnership conducting a commercial business does so under a common name, it will be treated as a VOF. The D Commercial C states that a notarial or private deed is a requirement for the foundation of a VOF (article 22 D Commercial C). Both the Trade Register Act and the D Commercial C require that a VOF be registered in the Trade Register. Its partners must also be registered. A VOF is obliged to prepare and keep books of account.[13] The context and layout of accounts is not subject to regulation and publication is not required.[14]

In the text that follows, the ordinary partnership and the VOF will be considered together. Both ordinary partnerships and VOFs may have separate bank accounts, control jointly owned assets and may sue or be sued in their

---

[12] Asser Maeyer, 1989, p. 66.
[13] *See* article 23 D Commercial C and article 6 of the Trade Register Act (registration) and article 16 D Commercial C (bookkeeping).
[14] But note the adoption of Directive 90/605 EEC extending the scope of the Fourth and Seventh Company Law Directives to partnerships and limited partnerships where all the partners comprise companies already subject to the Fourth and Seventh Company Law Directives.

own name.[15] Neither will have income tax directly assessed against it. Neither structure, as a matter of law, is regarded as a separate legal entity.[16]

In contrast to a company, property belonging to a VOF or an ordinary partnership is treated as belonging to the partners jointly. In addition, each partner performs a dual role: binding other partners in the capacity of agent while also being bound by the acts of the other partners in the capacity of principal.

3.2   Advantages

(i) *Ease of formation:* A partnership is created as soon as there is an agreement by two or more parties to participate in a joint operation for profit (article 1661 D Civil C).[17] The fact that the D Civil C does not establish formalities for the creation of a partnership is generally seen as an advantage of the partnership form over the jvc. This ease of formation, however, often means that the parties create a partnership without intending to do so. As the following summary of the principal features of Dutch partnership law makes clear, this will confer upon the parties' relationship and conduct a number of important legal consequences.[18] It is clearly possible that the parties may be unaware of such consequences or that they do not match their commercial objectives. The 'ease of formation' of a partnership under Dutch law must be seen in such context.

In the absence of an express or implied agreement to the contrary, all partners will be entitled to share in the profits of the partnership according to the proportion of their contribution to the partnership's capital (article 1670 D Civil C).[19] Every partner is, unless specified to the contrary, deemed able to represent the partnership and, therefore, to bind the other partners (provided his actions are in connection with the business of the partnership). Each partner is obliged to indemnify the other partners for any damage he causes to the interests of his partners (article 1667 D Civil C).[20] Each partner is obliged to contribute everything he promises to contribute to the partnership. If he undertakes to contribute all his working capacity, he assumes an obligation to report and

---

[15] Provided however that all the partners are named in the writ in the case of a partnership without a specific name.

[16] Asser Maeyer, 1989, p. 23.

[17] Article 1661 D Civil C reads as follows: A partnership comes into existence at the time of the agreement if no other time is provided for therein.

[18] Asser Maeyer, 1989, p. 93–102.

[19] Article 1670 D Civil C reads as follows: If the share of each partner in the profits and losses of the partnership is not determined in the partnership agreement, the share of each shall be proportionate to his contribution to the partnership.

[20] Article 1667 D Civil C reads as follows: Each partner is obliged to compensate the partnership for all damage which he has wrongfully caused to the partnership, and is not entitled to set off the amount of such damage against profits he has brought into the partnership in other matters through his labour and industry.

give full disclosure to the other partners about his activities (article 1664 D Civil C).[1]

(ii) *No mandatory law*: The Dutch law concerning partnerships (articles 1655 *et. seq.* D Civil C) includes very few restrictions. For example, there are no prescribed or mandatory methods of management and control.

(iii) *Termination*: A Dutch partnership can be terminated in a variety of ways. It follows from (ii) above (the absence of mandatory law) that the process of termination (in contrast, for example, to a jvc) is not subject to complex rules and procedures. Termination is regulated in articles 1683–89 of the D Civil C.[2] If it has been agreed that the partnership is to last only for a limited time, the partnership will automatically terminate at the end of the prescribed period. In addition, the attainment (or the impossibility of attainment) of the objective of a partnership, the termination of the partnership agreement by one of the partners, or the death of one of the partners will bring an end to the partnership. It is important to note that termination of the partnership agreement on notice can only be accomplished upon providing the remaining partners with a "reasonable period" of notice. Furthermore, such termination must be in good faith.

Termination by one of the partners or termination resulting from the death of one of the partners will cause the partnership to be dissolved. This is in most cases undesirable for the other partners. It is in practice generally agreed that if one of the parties dies, or terminates for cause, the partnership may continue. This can be accomplished by including a so-called 'continuation' clause (voortzettingsbeding) in the partnership agreement. A 'continuation' clause (voortzettingsbeding) confirms that the remaining partners will continue the partnership. A 'remaining' clause (verblijvensbeding) confirms that the other partners will assume the liabilities of the partnership. The 'assumption' clause (toescheidingsbeding) confirms that the other partners will assume the rights and obligations of the outgoing or deceased partner.[3]

(iv) *Secrecy, limited requirement of publicity*: Although partnerships as such do not have to register with the Trade Register, the registration of business enterprises is required. Thus, a partnership which conducts a business must be registered. A professional practice is not considered a business enterprise, so that e.g. law and accounting firms are not required to register. VOFs (and CVs, as well as corporations), on the other hand, are required to register, both in their own right and, in appropriate cases, as entities carrying on a business.

Each partner engaged in the partnership's business must be registered.[4] A VOF must be registered in accordance with article 23 D Commercial C

---

[1] Dutch Supreme Court, March 25, 1977, Netherlands Jurisprudence 1977, 488; Asser/Maeyer 1989, p. 80.
[2] Article 1689 of the D Civil C reads as follows: The rules governing the division of decendants' estates, the manner of division and the obligations arising therefrom among the co-heirs are also applicable to the division among partners.
[3] Asser/Maeyer, 1989, p. 289.
[4] *See* article 5 paragraph 1 Trade Register Act and Asser/Maeyer, 1989, p. 73.

and article 6 of the Trade Register Act. Importantly, the capitalisation and audited accounts of a partnership need not be filed in the Trade Register, but only the facts mentioned in article 5 paragraph 1 of the Trade Register Act.[5] Therefore, the partnership is subject to less publicity than a jvc which, *inter alia*, must file its annual accounts.[6]

If a partnership has more than 100 employees, it will have to show its accounts to the works council.

(v) *Foreign participation*: The tax-transparency of a partnership can make it an attractive joint venture structure for a collaboration involving a foreign participant.

3.3 Disadvantages

(i) *Liability to third parties (externally)*: Each of the partners is jointly and severally liable for all of the partnership's and 1680 liabilities, *pro rata* his capital contribution to the partnership (article 1679 D Civil C).[7,8] This presumption can be avoided if it is expressly agreed that a different division of liability will apply (article 1680 D Civil C).[8] If a partner has acted alone to incur a liability, there is a danger that he will be held fully liable. This last point is controversial, most legal commentators asserting that the partner will only be liable *pro rata* part[9] while lower courts have tended to impose full liability on the partner.[10] It is safest to take the stricter position of the lower courts and assume that a partner acting alone will incur full liability.

---

[5] Article 5 paragraph 1 of the Trade Register Act reads as follows: 1. If the enterprise is owned by a natural person, the following information must be reported:

    1°.   his name, address and the country where located, if other than The Netherlands;
    2°.   his date and place of birth, as well as country of birth, if other than The Netherlands;
    3°.   his nationality;
    4°.   the trade name under which he operates the enterprise;
    5°.   a short description of the business or businesses carried on by the enterprise;
    6°.   the place of establishment of the enterprise;
    7°.   the signature and initial he uses to sign documents concerning the enterprise.

[6] Asser/Maeyer, 1989, p. 32. Note that the entitlement not to file annual accounts will in certain circumstances be lost as a result of the adoption of Directive 90/605 EEC, in essence where all the members of the partnership are companies already subject to the Fourth and Seventh Company Law Directives, see footnote 14 above.

[7] Article 1679 D Civil C reads as follows: The partners are not each liable for the entirety of the debts of the partnership; and each of the partners cannot bind the others if they have not given him the authority to do so.
and Asser/Maeyer, 1989, 153–6.

[8] Article 1680 D Civil C reads as follows: The partners can be held liable by a creditor with whom they have concluded a transaction for equal sums and equal shares, even if the share in the partnership of one is less than that of the others; unless it was expressly agreed when the debt was incurred that each would be responsible for a share proportionate to his contribution to the partnership.

[9] Asser/Maeyer, 1989, 155. Pro rata his capital contribution.

[10] District Court Utrecht, December 10, 1924, Netherlands Jurisprudence ('NJ') 29, 815. District Court Rotterdam, November 29, 1932, NJ 37, 324. District Court Roermond, October 4, 1951, NJ 52, 771.

Internally he might be able to recover some part of the costs from his other partners.

(ii) *Each partner can bind the partnership (externally)*: Each partner is presumed to be the representative of the other partners, unless it has been agreed otherwise (article 1676 D Civil C).[11] It is not even necessary that a partner clearly states that he represents the partnership for the presumption to arise.[12] The absence of a statutory defined management arrangement, in contrast, for example, to jvcs, makes it possible for each partner to bind the others without their consent. It can, on the other hand, be agreed that only one partner, the 'managing partner' can represent the other partners (article 1673 D Civil C).[13]

(iii) *External finance*: Although the partners may jointly grant charges over their joint assets, in practice, banks prefer to obtain personal guarantees from the individual partners. The difficulty of raising external finance is a clear disadvantage of the Dutch partnership.

Floating charges or other types of security interest on assets do not have to be registered publicly in The Netherlands. A partnership can grant a floating charge, but banks are generally reluctant to accept them.

(iv) *Automatic dissolution in certain events*: If there is no continuation clause (voortzettingsbeding), (*see* 3.2 iii above) the partnership agreement will be dissolved if one of the partners dies or goes bankrupt or terminates voluntarily. Therefore, it is important to include a continuation clause in the agreement so that the other partners who remain may continue in partnership.

(v) *Limited ability to transfer a partnership interest*: It is impossible to transfer an interest in a partnership without the consent of all other partners. If such

---

[11] Article 1676 D Civil C reads as follows: In the absence of special stipulations concerning management, the following rules must be observed:

    1°. The partners are deemed to have granted each other the power to conduct the management on the other partners' behalf. Acts performed by each of them are binding on the share of the other partners, without it being necessary to obtain their consent, without prejudice to the right of the other partners or one of them to object to a transaction before it is concluded.

    2°. Each of the partners may use the property owned by the partnership provided that he does so in accordance with its ordinary intended purpose, and provided that he does not use it against the interest of the partnership or in such a way that the other partners are thereby prevented from exercising their concurrent right to use such property;

    3°. Each partner has the authority to require the other partners to share in the costs which must be incurred for the preservation of property belonging to the partnership.

    4°. None of the partners can without the consent of the remaining partners bring about any changes in real estate owned by the partnership, even if he asserts that such changes were advantageous to the partnership.

[12] Asser Maeyer, 1989, p. 138. Dutch Supreme Court, April 10, 1942, NJ 42, 501.

[13] Article 1673, D Civil C reads as follows:

1. A partner who is charged with the management of the partnership by a special provision to that effect in the partnership agreement can, even against the will of the other partners, perform all acts relating to the management of the partnership provided that he does so in good faith.

2. This authority cannot be revoked other than for lawful reasons for as long as the partnership continues, but if this authority is granted not by the partnership agreement but by a later deed, it is, like a simple mandate, revocable.

a clause has been included, the new 'buying' partner takes the position of the old 'selling' partner as co-owner of the partnership assets. Generally, the mechanics of transfer are more complicated than the transfer of shares in a jvc.

3.4   When to select

The partnership has the clear disadvantage of unlimited liability for its partners. As a result, the structure of a company (jvc) is more frequently chosen. Tax reasons, in particular the possibility of tax transparency, generally motivate the selection of the partnership or limited partnership structure.

3.5   Formation documentation/key aspects

In practice, a partnership is usually formed by a written agreement. However, there is no statutory requirement to file the terms of a partnership agreement. Partnerships can also be formed orally.[14] Typical provisions include the following.

(i) *Name*: Ordinary partnerships may not have a separate name, but will simply list all or some of the names of the partners. If a commercial partnership operates under a separate name, the rules of the VOF become applicable, thus conferring full liability for all of the firm's obligations upon each partner.

(ii) *Purpose clause*: The aim of the joint business to be conducted through the partnership is usually described in a short statement.

(iii) *The contribution*: The contribution of the partners may take the form of capital, goods or even intangible assets such as intellectual property rights. The most common contribution is the 'work capacity' of the partners themselves.

(iv) *Management*: It is important to lay down each partner's responsibility in terms of the conduct of the partnership business. Externally it prescribes the extent to which a particular partner may contract in the name of the partnership. Specific managing partners can be appointed. Of course, third parties may not know who the managing partner is and, as a matter of law, an individual partner will bind his other partners if his actions fall within the usual and/or expected sphere of his authority. Voting procedures and the creation of committees are also commonly provided for. Usually, the partners do not receive remuneration apart from their portion of the partnership's profits.

(v) *Allocation of profits and losses*: Unless the agreement provides otherwise, profits and losses will be divided in proportion to the contribution of each of the partners to the capital of the partnership (article 1670 D Civil C) (*see* note 19, *supra*).

(vi) *Accounts*: The agreement should provide for the keeping of books of

---

[14]   *See* note 6, *supra*.

account. All businesses in The Netherlands are required to keep proper books of account (article 14 of book 2 D Civil C and article 6 D Commercial C).

(vii) *Duration, termination, dissolution*: A partnership can be designated to expire upon the occurrence of a specific event (e.g. the completion of a project) or after the lapse of a given period of time. If there is no such stipulation, the partnership will continue indefinitely, although it can always be terminated by one of the partners upon reasonable notice (provided such party acts in good faith, for specific reasons and takes the interests of the other partners into account – see articles 1683, 1686 and 1687 D Civil C).

(viii) *Continuation clause (voortzettingsbeding)*: Where a partner ceases to be a partner as a result, for example, of death, bankruptcy, liquidation, the transfer of his partnership interest or termination (for cause by the remaining partners) the partnership will dissolve automatically unless the agreement contains a mechanism by which the outgoing partner's portion of the capital and profits of the partnership can be evaluated and distributed and an express provision that the other partner(s) can continue in partnership. A dissolution could have serious tax consequences if there is substantial goodwill in the partnership (*see* further 3.2 (iii) and 3.6.3 (2)).

(ix) *Non-competition clause*: It is possible to agree that a partner will not compete with the business of the partnership or attempt to entice away any of its employees during or for a limited number of years after his membership of the partnership.

3.6 Tax

3.6.1 Income Tax

The ordinary partnership and the VOF are treated similarly for income tax purposes. Both vehicles are not taxed as entities as such, instead the partners are taxed directly for their portion of partnership profits and losses. (This approach, as in other EC jurisdictions, is commonly referred to as 'tax transparency'.)

For income tax purposes the partnership is not considered to be a separate legal entity. The partnership will consist of a collection of separate undertakings (in a commercial context, typically limited companies). In the case of a foreign corporate partner, membership of a Dutch partnership will require either the establishment of a Dutch registered subsidiary or a Dutch branch. With respect to resident partners, the partnership income will form part of their total taxable income. With regard to non-resident partners, the transfer of profits from a branch to a partner's head office will not qualify as a dividend or other distribution since it will be treated as a payment within the same legal entity (or group).

The distinction as to residency made under 2.6 in respect of contractual joint ventures applies equally to partnerships:

1. Resident partners will have to account for their partnership income

(whether positive or negative). Such income will be subject to tax in The Netherlands.

2. Non-resident partners in a treaty country will be taxable in The Netherlands when their share in the partnership income is attibutable to a Dutch situate permanent establishment. The same applies to non-resident partners in a non-treaty country. In addition, non-resident partners in a non-treaty country can still be within the Dutch tax net where they receive payments from a profit sharing scheme (see 2.6.3 above).

Generally a partnership will result in the setting-up of an office or factory in The Netherlands and in the appointment of personnel as third party distributors or agents. As a result it will typically be pointless to attempt to deny the existence of a permanent establishment.

3.6.2 Taxable profit

Initially, the taxable profit of the partnership is calculated as if it were an individual taxpayer in The Netherlands. After this calculation the total taxable profits (or losses) will be apportioned to the partners in proportion to their profit shares.

Normally capital gains realised in a partnership will be taxable at the ordinary corporate income tax rate. In the case of capital gains realised as a result of the sale of fixed assets it is possible to postpone the payment of the tax.[15] If the asset is replaced (within four years) by a similar asset the amount of the capital gain realised with the sale of the former asset can be deducted from the purchase price of the new asset.

It is a generally accepted principle that no deduction of interest and royalty payments is possible when a branch pays such amounts to its foreign head office.[16] The logic behind this approach is that there cannot be payments within one and the same legal entity. This approach is likely to change as a result of the Dutch Supreme Court decision of 8th November 1989 BNB 1990/36 which recognised the existence of a loan between a head-office and a permanent establishment. The decision of the court was based on the principle that the branch should be treated as if it was an independent enterprise.

Where a partnership receives a loan from a third party in order to finance the acquisition of an asset for its own business activities the interest payments in respect of the loan will be fully deductible.

The provisions under Dutch law with respect to compensation for losses in a partnership are similar to those applying to companies[17] (see further paragraph 5.6).

---

[15] Partly based on article 14 ITA and partly based on some court decisions such as: Supreme Court: 4th April 1951 B 8970; 5th June 1968 BNB 1968/196.
[16] *See*: commentary on paragraph 7 of the OECD-model treaty 1977.
[17] Article 51 ITA, article 20 CITA.

As regards the issue of pricing services supplied by partners to the partnership, the revenue have published some guidelines[18] (which also apply to companies). The guidelines provide that the basic principle as to such services is that they should be priced upon an arm's length basis. The guidelines also deal specifically with 'preparatory and auxiliary activities'. These are, in essence, services provided by the partnership to its partners which are peripheral or auxiliary to such partners' activities – i.e. services that do not form an essential element of the main activities of the partners. The provision of management services by a partnership to its partners would not fall within the definition since such services would be seen as forming an essential element of the respective partners' businesses. The rule as to pricing set out in the guidelines is that where preparatory and auxiliary activities bear no significant business risk a basis of cost plus 5% will be considered to be at arm's length.

3.6.3 Access of new partners/termination of partnership

(1) *Access of new partners*: Where a new partner joins the partnership his capital contribution may give the rise to a taxable profit in the hands of the other partners. This profit is calculated as the difference between the contribution by the new partner and the net bookvalue of the partnership's assets prior to such contribution. The profit is allocated to each partner according to his profit share. The creation of a taxable profit can be avoided by providing that the new partner will not be entitled to already existing reserves and goodwill. The taxable profit can also be avoided when, prior to the new partner joining, the partnership is transferred at bookvalue to a resident company in exchange for shares.[19] Although the partners in such company cannot sell the shares (without tax consequences) within three years, the new company can issue new shares to the new partner. The new partner will also generally contribute an amount by way of share premium to which the other shareholders (former partners) will also become entitled.

(2) *Winding up of partnership*: When the partnership is dissolved, or when a partner retires, there is likely to be a taxable profit calculated as the difference between the amount which the partner receives for his partnership interest either from the other partners or from a purchase (third party) and the bookvalue ascribed to such partner's share.[20]

3.6.4 Distribution of profits

The transfer of profits by a branch to its non-resident 'parent' will not be subject to tax, *see further* 3.6.1 above.

---

[18] Resolutioin of 25th April 1985 No. 084–2737 BNB 1986/196.
[19] Individuals: Article 18 ITA. Companies: Article 14 CITA.
[20] Article 16 ITA.

3.6.5 VAT

The partnership itself will be a taxpayer for VAT purposes. This means that the partnership must submit VAT invoices to its customers and that VAT paid can be deducted by the partnership itself from VAT owed as a result of the provision of goods or services.

3.6.6 Real Estate Transfer Tax (RETT)

When real estate, which has been used during a period of at least two years, is transferred by one of the partners to the partnership, a 6% RETT will be due unless it amounts to the transferring partner's contribution to the partnership *and* the real estate forms part of a contribution of an entire enterprise.[1] The latter is generally not the case with a joint venture partnership, therefore real estate is typically made available under a lease in order to avoid paying the RETT.

3.7   Foreign involvement

There are no restrictions upon foreign nationals or companies participating in a Dutch partnership, including the VOF. As a result of tax transparency the foreign partner will be treated as if maintaining an enterprise in The Netherlands unless he can successfully contend that he does not have a permanent establishment in The Netherlands.

3.8   Acquisition/use of intellectual property and other assets

One must be very careful to distinguish between 'partnership property' (in the strict sense of the term) and property belonging to an individual partner which is made available for the partnership's business under a licence agreement. It is important to specify which property has been contributed and by whom. The following 'rules' apply to 'partnership property':

(a)   an increase in the value of partnership property belongs to all of the partners;

(b)   partnership creditors are entitled to recover first against partnership assets; creditors can act against property belonging to individual partners only after the partnership assets have been exhausted;

(c)   real estate owned by a partnership is regarded as the joint property of the partners and can be registered in the name of all the partners;

[1] Article 15.1.e. Real Estate Transfer Tax Act.

(d) intellectual property can also be registered as joint (partnership) property. Usually, intellectual property rights are not transferred to the partnership. Instead, individual partners grant licences to the partnership for the use of their individually owned intellectual property.

The partnership may, of course, develop its own intellectual property. In such case, the resulting rights can be registered in the name of the partnership. If a partner, or an employee of the partnership, invents a patent or a copyright, it will be owned by the partnership, unless agreed otherwise (article 10 Patent Act and article 7 Copyright Act 1912).

3.9 Competition law

No specific Dutch competition law applies to partnerships. However, partnerships are subject to the Economic Competition Act, considered below.

The Economic Competition Act ('Wet Economische Mededinging'). This Act is an instrument for implementing the economic policy of the government and generally seeks to protect free competition within The Netherlands. The Act does not prohibit outright all types of arrangement that restrict competition but only certain categories of agreement. Chief amongst these are price maintenance agreements for specified consumer durables and penalty clauses; articles 9e, 9f and 9g ECA. Almost all types of restrictive agreement must be notified to the Minister of Economic Affairs, who has the power to intervene in cases where an arrangement restricting competition is considered detrimental to the public interest ('algemeen belang'). Upon the basis of the public interest, the Minister can declare an arrangement partly or wholly void and unenforceable (article 19 paragraph 1 sub b ECA) or suspend the validity of the arrangement if an immediate intervention is necessary (article 23 paragraph 1 ECA). Furthermore, the Minister can declare arrangements or provisions of arrangements generally void and unenforceable ('generieke onverbindendverklaring', article 10 ECA). This means that that particular type of arrangement will always be void and unenforceable.

With respect to the applicability of the ECA to joint ventures, it is necessary to make a distinction between joint ventures which amount to a concentration and joint ventures which are merely cooperative in character. A 'concentrative' joint venture will give rise to an independent economic entity ('zelfstandige economische eenheid') with its own assets and personnel, that operates independently. Such a joint venture will not result in the founding undertakings coordinating their competitive market behaviour. All other forms of cooperation between undertakings by way of a joint venture are considered to be cooperative joint ventures.

Because the ECA can not be used to control concentrations, it will not apply to concentrative joint ventures. Cooperative joint ventures will need to be considered in the light of the ECA. However, the Minister of Economic

Affairs has never to date taken the view that a particular joint venture was contrary to the public interest.

3.10   New Civil Code: public and silent partnership

The New Civil Code (NCC), of which the section on partnerships will come into effect a few years after 1992 (the exact date is still uncertain), will provide for just two types of partnership: 'public partnerships' and 'silent partnerships'.

A partnership will be deemed public if it acts under a common name like the present VOF. Public partnerships will have legal personality. The assets of a public partnership will not constitute jointly owned assets of the partners, but rather assets belonging to the public partnership *per se*. Despite its legal personality, the partners will remain jointly and severally liable and their mutual relationship will continue to be regulated by the partnership agreement. The NCC will mark a radical departure in partnership law since, *inter alia*, under the present law partnerships are not considered independent legal entities. Silent partnerships will be governed by the rules currently pertaining to ordinary partnerships (see 3.1 *et seq* above). Perhaps the most notable aspect of this type of partnership is the fact that the liability of parties is limited to their capital contribution.

3.11   Conclusion

Although easy to form and flexible in terms of operation, the lack of limited liability in the partnership structure has meant that it is not often used for joint ventures. Where tax transparency is required, it is more common for parties to select the limited partnership structure (considered below). This last combines the advantages of tax transparency with limited liability.

4.   LIMITED PARTNERSHIPS

4.1.1 Introduction

The limited partnership ('commanditaire vennootschap') is, like the VOF, a type of statutory partnership; it is described in articles 19 to 35 'D Commercial C'. In the text that follows the term 'limited patnership' will be used to describe this form.

4.1.2 Liability

The limited partnership consists of two types of partner: 'general partners' (also known as 'managing partners') who like partners in a VOF have unlimited liability and 'limited partners' (or 'commanditaire vennoten') who do not participate in the management of the partnership business and whose liability is limited to the amount of their capital contribution to the partnership.

The advantage of limited liability for the limited partners can be lost in a number of ways:

   (i)   where the partnership is not properly registered (article 29 D Commercial C);

  (ii) where the partnership has the same name as the limited partner (article 20 section 1 D Commercial C); or

 (iii) where the limited partner takes part in the management of the partnership's business (article 20 section 2 D Commercial C).

It is important to be able to ascertain whether the property of the limited partnership will be viewed as separate from the property of the managing partners. First, this can be important in determining the transfer tax on real estate when real estate is transferred to and/or from the managing partner(s). Secondly, this property classification is important in determining whether it is possible to separate the creditors of the limited partnership, on the one hand, from the creditors of the managing partners on the other. The Supreme Court of The Netherlands has ruled that if there is only one managing partner, there can be no separate property of the partner in question: Supreme Court decision January 4, 1937 Netherlands Jurisprudence, 1937, 586 (Erik Schaaper Radio) and Supreme Court decision February 3, 1956 Netherlands Jurisprudence, 1960, 120 (Hardy). Both specialist literature and lower case law support a contrary view. In practice, it is safest to establish a limited partnership with at least two managing partners, since this ensures that the property of the managing partners will be viewed separately from that of the limited partnership.

Frequently, in The Netherlands, at least one managing partner (and usually both managing partners) are companies. This way the managing partners can enjoy the advantages of limited liability and the organised struture of the corporate form. In fact, such an arrangement is often the ideal combination of the partnership and jvc structures.

4.2   Advantages

Article 15 D Commercial C provides that, in general, the limited partnership is subject to the same rules as an ordinary partnership (described in the D Civil C). The advantage of this form is that financing can be obtained from the limited partners without subjecting them to unlimited liability. As mentioned above, there are specific tax advantages to this form, since the limited partners can, under certain circumstances, be regarded as taking part in the business as general partners for tax purposes. As a result, they will be able to take advantage of tax transparency and the ability to deduct partnership losses from their own profits.

4.3   Disadvantages

The same disadvantages apply here as with the ordinary partnership form (*see* 3.3 above), except that the liability of the limited partners can be limited.

4.4   When to select

The limited partnership structure is used quite often in The Netherlands as a result of its specific tax advantages. It is used in venture capital investments, in real estate development projects, in shipbuilding, ship operating projects and in many other situations where investors (typically foreigners) provide the financing but not the management skills necessary for a particular venture.

4.5   Formation documentation

Article 22 Dutch Commercial Code states that a limited partnership should be founded by a notarial deed or by a written agreement. However, this is not in fact a strict formation requirement. The absence of such a document cannot be used as a defence to a claim that an individual was acting as a partner. Such documentation is, of course, evidence of the existence of the limited partnership, but it is theoretically possible (although virtually unheard of in practice), to form a limited partnership by oral agreement.

4.6   Taxation

Most of the remarks made under 3 above in respect of ordinary partnerships, are applicable to limited partnerships. However, a number of additional points need to be made.

4.6.1 Corporate income tax

A distinction that needs to be made is between an 'open' and a 'closed' limited partnership. A limited partnership will be considered 'closed'[2] when the transfer of partnership shares (save in the case of inheritance) may not be effected without the prior consent of all the other partners. A limited partnership which is not 'closed' will be considered 'open'.

4.6.1.1 Open limited partnerships. An open limited partnership will be treated as a taxable entity for corporate income tax purposes (there is accordingly

[2]   Article 2 paragraph 3 section C AWR.

no tax transparency). Distributions of profits will be subject to dividend withholding tax. (This is generally at a rate of 25% although subject to moderation by tax treaties.) For further tax consequences *see* generally 5.6 below in respect of the tax treatment of JVCs.

4.6.1.2 Closed limited partnerships. In a closed limited partnership a distinction needs to be made between limited partners who are carrying on a business and those who are merely making a passive investment.

The distinction is of prime importance for individuals.

The general partner will always be considered to be carrying on a business and accordingly the rules set out in 3.6 above will apply.

Whether or not a closed limited partnership carries on a business depends on the amount of the combination of capital and labour involved in the partnership. However when the partnership is considered to carry on a business this does not necessarily mean that the limited partners receive their income out of the partnership as business income, as opposed to the general partners who do receive their partnership income as business income. In principle the limited partners will be considered to receive business income out of the partnership when they are entitled (for their share) to the hidden reserves at the occasion of the dissolution of the partnership.

4.6.1.2.a Limited partners carrying on a business. When a limited partnership is considered to be a business *and* the limited partners are considered to receive business income out of this activity, the limited partners will be treated in the same was as general partners although their tax deductible losses will be limited to the amount of their capital contribution.

The distinction between business income or not of the partnership *as a whole* appears to be especially relevant in the case of investments.

So the questions to be answered are, is the partnership considered to be a business and if so will the respective partners be considered to receive business income.

A limited partner will be considered to receive business income himself when he is entitled to the hidden reserves in the partnerships at the moment of dissolution of the partnership.[3]

4.6.1.2.b Limited partners not carrying on a business. The main differences between individuals receiving business income and those who do not are that the latter:

1   will not be subject to tax on capital gains (and correspondingly capital losses will not be deductible); and

---

[3] Due to a much criticised press release (6–11–1986) the Revenue created some confusion on this subject. However the courts do not seem to follow the point of view of the Revenue.

2   will be charged to income tax on a cash basis and not on an accrual basis.

Where the partner in question is not an individual but is a company or other legal person, that partner may, exceptionally, be considered not to be carrying on a business. This would be a rare case and would never apply to a resident company. However, if it were to apply to a non-resident company the rules would be the same as for an individual limited partner. Thus, for a non-resident partner situate in a treaty state, there would be no taxable event in The Netherlands assuming that the partner has no permanent establishment in The Netherlands and the partnership has made no investments in Dutch real estate. For a non-resident partner situate in a non-treaty state there may be a taxable event in the Netherlands even in the absence of a permanent establishment in the Netherlands and any Dutch real estate investments by the partnership.

4.6.2 Real Estate Transfer Tax

See 3.6.6 above.

4.7   Foreign involvement

A foreign corporate partner which participates in a Dutch partnership, will normally pay Dutch corporation tax on the partnership's trading profits. This is almost always true as to managing partners, but limited partners may escape this tax liability. There is a substantial body of law on the question of whether a limited partner is deemed to be subject to Dutch tax (whether corporation or personal income tax).

4.8   Acquisition/use of intellectual property rights and other assets

As with a general partnership (*see* 3.2. (iii) and 3.7 above) it is essential that the partnership agreement contains a continuation clause (voortzettingsbeding) specifically describing what happens to the limited partnership in the event that one of the partners leaves the venture or transfers his interest in it.

With respect to intellectual property rights, the rules are the same as for general partnerships (*see* 3.8 above). Partners typically retain ownership of their own intellectual property and grant licences to the limited partnership. If intellectual property rights are developed by the partnership, they can be jointly registered in the name of all the partners.

Real estate can be registered in the name of the joint partners. It is the general view of Dutch law that partnership property is separate from the property of the partners. Therefore, if real estate has to be transferred from the partnership to a partner, transfer taxes must be paid.

4.9 Competition

See 3.9 above.

4.10 Conclusion

The limited partnership is used in The Netherlands quite frequently for partnerships involving substantial economic risk and requiring external financing. It is often used in venture capital transactions, in real estate development projects and in ship-building and ship operating projects. The structure offers the advantage of limited liability for limited partner(s). The managing partners are wholly liable, but this liability can be limited if the managing partners are limited liability companies. In that case, corporate law also provides a structured management and monitoring system for the managing partner companies.

From a tax viewpoint, the structure offers the advantage of tax transparency for closed limited partnerships.

5. JOINT VENTURE COMPANIES

5.1 Introduction

A joint venture company (jvc) is typically used where the parties contemplate the creation and continuing operation of a jointly owned business. The cooperation results in the establishment of an independent legal entity (the jvc). Although its constitution, its operation and the rights and obligations of jvc shareholders are, to a large extent, prescribed and described by the Ducth Civil Code in book 2,[4] it is customary, in addition to the company statutes to negotiate and draft a separate joint venture agreement.

5.2 Advantages

(i) *Limited liability*: The maximum liability of the shareholders is limited to the amount they have paid in respect of their shares or, in the case of partly paid-up shares, the amount owing in respect of their shares.[5] This limited liability can be contrasted with an ordinary partnership where each partner is personally liable for the liabilities of the partnership *pro rata* to his contribution to the partnership's capital and to the VOF where each partner is fully liable for all partnership debts (and other obligations).

---

[4] The two Dutch Companies NV (comparable with PLC, AG or SA) and BV (comparable with Ltd, GmbH or SARL) are dealt with in Book 2 D Civil C, respectively articles 64–174 and 175–284.
[5] W. J. Slagter, Compendium van het Ondernemingsrecht, 1990, p. 173. *See also* article 64 Book 2 D Civil C and article 175 Book 2 D Civil C.

Although the limited liability of a jvc seems a clear advantage, there are in practice a number of legal and commercial constraints upon its availability. Examples of these constraints include:

(a)   the frequent requirement of banks and other lenders to the jvc for security in the form of personal guarantees from the joint venturers;

(b)   the fact that the protection of limited liability will not apply in certain situations, for example joint venturers will be personally liable:

   –   for debts incurred in the period before the jvc was founded (sometimes referred to as the 'pre-incorporation period') (articles 93 and 203 Book 2 D Civil C);

   –   where a company brings about a reduction of capital as a result of the payment of a dividend, *see* articles 93a and 203a D Civil C, 98a and 207a Book 2 D Civil C and 98c and 207c Book 2 D Civil C;

   –   in certain very specific cases where the courts will look beyond the corporate veil; such cases are rare.[6]

(ii) *Liability of directors*: In The Netherlands, there is specific legislation on the liability of Directors of a jvc. This legislation can be found primarily in the Second and Third Mismanagement Acts (Misbruikwetten). Under the Second Mismanagement Act,[7] in the event of the insolvency of the jvc, the jvc's directors will be held personally liable for unpaid taxes and social security premiums. Under the Third Mismanagement Act,[8] the directors will be held personally liable for clear mismanagement if a jvc is declared insolvent. In addition, jvc directors can be held personally liable for the preparation and filing of misleading accounts.

(iii) *Separate legal entity*: A jvc has a distinct legal personality whose interests are separate from those of its shareholders. This is in contrast to the position of partners in a partnership. A jvc is able to sue (or be sued) in its own name and to enter into contracts with third parties. A jvc may own property in its own right and register its title thereto. The separateness of the corporate identity from that of its shareholders avoids many of the potential difficulties involved in the use of a partnership structure, for example:

   –   the potential confusion between a partner's and the partnership's property;

   –   the implied right of all partners to participate in the day-to-day management of the business; and

   –   the ability of all partners to bind the partnership.

---

[6] Dutch Supreme Court September 29, 1981 Netherlands Jurisprudence 1982, 443 (Osby) and Dutch Supreme Court February 2, 1988 Netherlands Jurisprudence 1988, 37 (Albada Jelgersma).
   In cases where the shareholders have given the impression of creditworthiness and have made the jvc enter into transactions while they knew the jvc could not fulfil the obligations.
[7] This Second Mismanagement Act is laid down in many tax and social security Acts. *See* W. J. Slagter, Compendium van het Ondernemingsrecht 1990, p. 126.
[8] This Third Management Act is laid down in articles 138 and 248 Book 2, D Civil C.

(iv) *Commercial understanding/familiarity*: The jvc structure is more familiar to most businessmen than the partnership form. This is not only an attraction to those organising the joint venture, but also to those subsequently doing business with the jvc. The jvc form simply works better in commerce because it is more widely known and raises less questions internally and externally.

(v) *Ability to transfer interests*: In theory, it is easy to assign interests in a jvc – a party need simply sell his shares. In practice, however, the joint venturers will often wish to limit the extent to which joint venture partners can transfer their shares. This reflects the fact that the choice of joint venture partner is a personal matter and that joint venturers generally wish to avoid being confronted with new persons or companies as their partners. The mechanics for the transfer of shares are straightforward – use must be made of a Deed of Transfer. No transfer tax is levied on the transfer.

(vi) *Permanence of the structure*: If one of the partners dies, or if he wishes to transfer his interests, the jvc will continue to exist. There is no requirement, for example, for a continuation clause, as would be the case with a partnership (*see* 3.5 (viii) above).

(vii) *External finance*: The jvc will be a much better vehicle than a partnership when it comes to obtaining external financing. A jvc, unlike a partnership, can grant a floating charge. Such a charge is not attached to specific items, but rather floats over all of the company's assets. Until the charge is called in by the lender, the floating charge permits the company to buy, sell and otherwise deal in its assets. In addition, a company can issue loan stock or loan notes, usually called 'obligaties'.

(viii) *Basis for further expansion*: The jvc, through its ability to form subsidiaries and undertake corporate reorganisations offers a very effective base from which to expand the joint venture's operations. Different activities can be undertaken by separate companies within the jvc's corporate group and holding companies can be established. Also, a jvc is able to apply for a listing of its shares on the Amsterdam Stock Exchange. None of the above are available to other joint venture structures.

(ix) *Tax*: The jvc offers an important advantage with regard to the deferment of taxes, *see* 5.6 below.

5.3 Disadvantages

(i) *The formation of the company*: There are two basic types of corporation under Dutch law: the NV which is comparable with a PLC, an AG or a SA; and the BV which is similar to a Ltd, a GmbH or a SARL. Both NVs and BVs must have Articles of Association drafted and submitted to the Ministry of Justice in order to obtain a declaration of non-objection or 'nil obstat' which is required before operations can begin. It takes six to ten weeks to obtain this declaration. After that, the company can be founded with a minimum capital of fls 100,000 for an NV and fls 40,000 for a BV.

Usually, the parties will agree to a text of the jvc's Articles of Association (in Dutch 'Statuten') and a Shareholders or Joint Venture Agreement. The negotiation and preparation of all of these agreements, along with the preparation of and the submission of the request for the Ministry of Justice's approval for the Articles of Association can be quite expensive.[9]

(ii) *Lack of flexibility*: In comparison with a partnership or a limited partnership, there is slightly less flexibility with regard to the interal organisation of the jvc because of the mandatory laws concerning the structure and capital of companies. On the other hand, many variations in structure are possible in terms of establishing subsidiaries and holding companies.

(iii) *Dissolution more difficult*: The dissolution of a company involves the parties in a complex series of procedures.[10] The requirements of dissolution include the public announcement of the liquidation of the jvc, setting up a plan to pay creditors, announcing the creditor payment plan publicly, and waiting a period of at least two months before the actual liquidation can take place. Note that this final act of dissolution must be publicly announced again.

(iv) *Lack of secrecy*: As a result of the implementation of the 4th EEC Company Directive in Dutch law, each Dutch company must file its annual audited accounts in Dutch, French, German or English,[11] particulars of the directors and a copy of its Articles of Association with the Trade Register.[12] The ownership of the share capital does not have to be (and in fact, never is) registered in The Netherlands.[13] In practice, the Articles of Association will be registered, but the Joint Venture (or the Shareholders) Agreement will not be registered. This will remain a confidential document.

(v) *Tax*: *See* 5.6 below.

(vi) *Foreign participation*: From the perspective of a foreign participant, the lack of tax transparency may make the jvc structure less attractive than other business forms, especially when there is a loss situation and these losses can not be offset against profits in the State of residence of the joint venturers.

5.4   When to select

The jvc is very often the preferred structure for a joint venture contemplating the establishment and operation of an independent business involving substantial profits and/or losses and contractual relations with third parties. In some cases, however, either for tax reasons or because the scope of the project is too small, it may be uneconomical to use the jvc structure.

[9] The cost of formation of a BV is about Dfls. 4,500.
[10] Articles 167 *et seq*. and 277 *et seq*. Book 2 D Civil D.
[11] 4th EEC Council Directive July 25, 1978 (78/660/EEC) OJ L222 August 14, 1978.
[12] Section 69 and 180 Book 2 D Civil C and section 8 paragraph 2 and section 9a Trade Register Act.
[13] In the near future an Act will be adopted that a shareholder who owns 100% of the shares in a company must be registered. Clearly, this will not be relevant to joint ventures.

5.5 Formation documentation

The jvc will require two principal documents: a Shareholders Agreement (or a Joint Venture Agreement) and Articles of Association. The NV and BV are ruled by their Articles of Association, which is a notarial deed. The deed serves as the deed of foundation of the company and, at the same time, provides the text for the Articles of Association ('Statuten'). Before foundation, it is necessary to obtain Ministry of Justice approval for the text of this deed. For this reason these deeds are usually drafted in conformity with standard models; it is difficult to have tailor made Articles of Association. In the event of a change in the Statuten, a declaration of non-objection is required from the Ministry of Justice. No company can be founded without a declaration of no objection or 'nil obstat'.[14] No change in the Articles of Association can be made without such a declaration.[15] It takes ten weeks to get the declaration for a foundation and about five for a change to the Articles of Association. The aim of the control of the Ministry is to avoid the misuse of companies.

The Articles of Association (Statuten) usually include:

Article
1 Definitions
2 Name and Location of Registered Office
3 Objects
4 Capital and Shares
5 Register of Shareholders
6 Notices, Announcements, Communications and Statements
7 Issue of Shares
8 Ownership of Shares
9 Decrease in Capital
10 Transfer of Shares, Usufructary, Right of Pledge
11 'Blokkeringsregeling': provisions governing the Transfer of or other Change in the Ownership of Shares.
    The two general forms are:
    – the obligations to offer first to other shareholders (right of first refusal); and
    – the obligation to obtain shareholder consent (*see* further 5.5 (xiii)
12 Management; by whom appointed and for what decisions shareholder or supervisory board consent is needed
13 Board of Supervisory Directors (not obligatory)
14 Financial Year, Annual Accounts, Annual Report and Publication
15 Profit Distribution
16 General Meeting
18 Resolutions without a Meeting

[14] Article 68 and 179 Book 2 D Civil C.
[15] Articles 123 and 223 Book 2 D Civil C.

19   Alteration of the Statutes/Dissolution
20   Winding-up

Usually, these topics are covered in this standard order. It is in the Share-holders (or Joint Venture) Agreement that the parties can introduce special agreements. The following major headings are likely to be addressed.

(i) *The Joint Venturers (the parties)*: There should be no misunderstanding concerning the identity of the parties to the agreement. Especially where a joint venturer is a member of a group of companies, there should be clarity concerning the relationship between the joint venturer and that group of companies. This can be important for matters such as whether the joint venturer's group will guarantee its obligations under the agreement and whether its group will be subject to any non-compete clauses, *see* further (xix) below.

(ii) *Preamble*: It is important to lay down in a preamble the intentions of the parties concerning the foundation and purpose of the joint venture. The intent of the parties may be used to interpret the agreement.

(iii) *Finance*: As in any joint venture, it is important to define the contribution of the individual joint venturers (e.g. cash, assets, know-how, capital, loans or personal guarantees). The agreement will typically record the manner in which the share capital is to be subscribed. Subscription can be paid-up in cash or by providing valuable assets, such as machines, real estate or even know-how. In the case of non-cash contributions, an accountant must confirm the value of the assets contributed.[16]

It is customary to allocate a different class of share to each party (e.g., A and B ordinary shares). The two shareholders might be entitled to a different dividend policy and may reserve profits in their own A and B accounts. Also, since A shareholders can appoint A directors and B shareholders can appoint B directors, this method can be used to determine which shareholders have the power to appoint directors, e.g. A shareholders owning 60% could make binding nominations for three A directors, while B shareholders owing 40% could make binding nominations for two B directors. It is usually the case that complex share structures with preferred shares and other types of shares are used by venture capital funds where the proportion of an individual investor's equity in the company can be adjusted by reference to its solvency. In the normal case of a joint venture, there will be separate classes of ordinary shares (A and B shares). In all cases, even if there are preferred shares, all shares will have the same voting rights. In The Netherlands, it is *not* possible to have non-voting shares or to limit a shareholder to a certain amount of votes.

The capital duty in The Netherlands is a one-time payment of one per cent of the total contribution. This must be paid by the company itself. However exemptions of capital contribution may under certain circumstances be obtained when more than 75% of the shares in an EC company are contributed.

It is normal to include clauses providing that each of the parties will provide

[16]   Articls 94a and 204a Book 2 D Civil C.

loans to the jvc or personal guarantees in support of its obligations (usually in proportion of their shareholding; sometimes jointly and severally) if the Board of the jvc and/or the shareholders deem such action necessary. These 'extra' agreements in respect of financing, of course, expand the shareholders' liability.

(iv) *Obligation to vote according to the agreement*: It has been argued that it is void for a shareholder to restrict his freedom to vote as he wishes. However, the Dutch Supreme Court (Hoge Raad) has in a number of judgments ruled that it is possible to include such 'restrictions' in Shareholders Agreements see – June 30, 1944 (NV Wennex),[17] November 13, 1959 (Distilleerderij)[18] and February 19, 1960 (Aurora)[19] – that agreements binding shareholders to vote a certain way are valid, e.g. two 50% shareholders agree that they will always vote the way one of the parties wishes.

It is possible to make provisions in the Shareholders Agreements to break a deadlock (or tie vote) situation, e.g. if parties can not agree, they ask a third party to decide the issue – his view of the matter being binding upon the parties.

One can also draft the Shareholders Agreement so as to avoid the situation where a minority shareholder or minority shareholders together (owning say 30% of the shares) are powerless in certain voting situations (such as the appointment of directors). Dutch Company Code law states that if two-thirds of the shareholders vote at a meeting to appoint or dismiss a director(s) (articles 133 and 243 Book 2 D Civil C), no Shareholders Agreement can overcome this vote. It is, however, possible to construct a valid Shareholders Agreement such that a minority shareholder in this situation may appoint one member of the board of directors. It is then agreed that the minority shareholder may propose one director and that the other shareholders will then vote for that proposal. Such an agreement can be given extra enforceability by adding a penalty clause for cases of default.[20]

(v) *Appointment of board of directors*: The right of the joint venturers to appoint supervisory directors and managing directors will typically be expressed as a class right. The A shareholder, the B shareholder, etc. will each be entitled to appoint (and dismiss) a specified number of directors to the board of managing directors and the board of supervisory directors of the jvc.

It is even possible to agree that the A shareholders will appoint specific specialised directors while the B shareholders will appoint other specialised directors. Provisions relating to the constitution of the board will typically be addressed both in the Shareholders Agreement and the Articles of Association.

In The Netherlands these agreements sometimes will, but usually do not, provide for the voting division within the board(s) (boards are normally allowed

[17] Dutch Supreme Court June 30, 1944, Netherlands Jurisprudence 1944/45, 465.
[18] Dutch Supreme Court November 13, 1959, Netherlands Jurisprudence 1960, 472.
[19] Dutch Supreme Court February 19, 1960, Netherlands Jurisprudence 1960, 473.
[20] Slagter, Compendium p. 251; Hendriks-Jansen, NV, 60 p. 7.

to make their own voting arrangements). Sometimes, the parties agree that certain board decisions must be unanimous.

(vi) *Supervisory directors and managing directors*: The Netherlands has a two-tier system which povides for managing directors, who do all the day-to-day managing as well as represent the company (in effect executive directors) and a separate board of supervisory directors who simply supervise the managing directors. One person cannot simultaneously be both a supervisory director and a managing director as it is impossible to adequately supervise oneself.

(vii) *Possibility to instruct directors*: The managing directors direct the company. This means guiding the company, making decisions, buying and selling the assets of the company and determining the day-to-day activities of the company. Dutch Company law assumes that the members of the board of managing directors are autonomous and have their own responsibility to the company. However, it is possible for the shareholders to have influence on the managing directors:

1. The Articles of Association may determine that the shareholders may give general directions in the areas of financial, social, economic and personnel policy.[1]
2. The Articles of Association may give powers of instruction to shareholders, i.e. the power of the shareholders to instruct the directors to act according to shareholder's instructions, however such powers may not be used to an extent where the directors no longer retain the initiative to act independently.
3. The Articles of Association may provide that the Board requires shareholder consent for certain decisions.
4. Ultimately, the shareholders meeting retains the all important power to appoint and dismiss the managing directors.

(viii) *Information to shareholders*: The joint venturers will require full information regarding the jvc. Normally, shareholders receive only such information that the managing directors (and supervisory directors), judge to be in the company's interest to disclose. It is possible that the interests of the company (or the separate interests of the nominated directors) would prevent the giving of information to joint venturers, in particular minority shareholders. Therefore, it should be expressly agreed that the individual joint venturers may receive all the information about the company they desire, including the right to inspect the company's books.

(ix) *Minority protection*: This is a very important part of the Shareholders Agreement; it lays down a requirement for common accord among the shareholders on certain material issues. Minority shareholders are not well protected under Dutch law. It is advisable to provide that certain decisions of the jvc require the unanimous vote of all the parties to give the minority shareholder some protection. Such decisions may include: alterations to the Statutes; the

---

[1] Slagter, Compendium, p. 258; Ministerial Directives 1986, paragraph 9.

issue and/or allotment of share or loan capital; the granting of charges; mortgages and other security; the provision of guarantees; the entering into of contracts outside the usual course of business; the entering into of agreements with one of the joint venture partners; the employment of key personnel; variations to the terms of employment of key personnel. It can be specified in the Shareholders Agreement and/or the Articles of Association that the board of directors can make none of these decisions without the permission of the shareholders in general meeting. In addition, a unanimous vote of the shareholders may be required for such decisions as well as a unanimous vote among directors on the board.

The Shareholders Agreement should contain provisions addressing a 50/50 tie vote. Such a 'deadlock' clause might call for the appointment of an arbitrator to make a final binding decision. If there are more than two shareholders, each of them must be protected against a possible combination of the others. A typical solution is to give each party veto rights, e.g. if they each have more than 20% of the voting rights, by requiring a minimum vote of 80% for certain decisions.

(x) *Disharmony and termination*: If the Shareholders Agreement provides that certain key actions can only be taken by common accord, the question remains: what happens if the parties fail to reach such common accord? It is possible to make a number of (alternative) arrangements to cover a failure to agree:

(a) Refer the dispute to the chairmen of the respective joint venture parties;
(b) Refer the dispute to arbitration;
(c) Refer the dispute to the district court;
(d) Terminate the joint ownership of the jvc by forcing a buy-out or a sale of the shares. (The defaulting shareholder would be forced either to sell his shares at a low price or to buy the shares of the other party at a high price, a low price would be the net asset value and a high pice would be a price with goodwill.) If one party is insolvent, the other should be able to buy the shares at a low price.
(e) If all else fails, the jvc can be liquidated.

(xi) *Statutory provisions for disputes between shareholders*: Articles 335 to 343 Book 2 D Civil C provide for the regulation of disputes. One or more shareholders who, solely or jointly, owns at least one-third of the issued capital may institute proceedings against any shareholder who, by his conduct, prejudices the interests of the company in such a way that the continuation of that shareholding cannot reasonably be tolerated by the other shareholders. The complaining shareholder(s) may demand the transfer of the offending shareholder's shares. The Court shall appoint either one or three experts to prepare a report to establish the value of that party's shares. Examples of prejudicing the interests of the company would be: refusing to cooperate in its financing, hindering the board, refusing to give consent to important decisions and competing with the jvc in an aggressive way or in other words in a manner exceeding normal competition.[2]

(xii) *Termination of the joint ownership of the joint venture company*: Common methods include:

(a) An agreement that one of the parties must give notice (or will be deemed to have given notice) under certain circumstances and that he must offer to buy the shares owned by the other party or offer to sell his shares. If one wishes to add a penalty element, the terminating party could be obliged to sell his shares at a low (net asset value) price, or to buy the other's shares at a high (with goodwill) price.

(b) It is also possible to use the 'pre-emption right' system. If such a system is employed, it will be set forth in the Articles of Association. Under this system, if a party wishes to sell his shares, that party must first offer to sell his shares to all the other shareholders in proportion to their holdings.

(xiii) *Transferability of shares*: The Articles of Association will prescribe one of two possible mechanisms:

(a) the 'consent procedure', under which shareholders present or in the shareholders meeting must consent to any transfer of shares; or

(b) the 'offering system', whereby a shareholder wishing to transer his shares must always offer his shares first to the existing shareholders in proportion to their holdings. This is like the pre-emption right described above under xii(b).

These two systems are in general collectively referred to as 'blockade clauses'.

In joint venture agreements the following specific provisions are generally included:

(a) a shareholder may not transfer his shares within a specified period;

(b) if a joint venture partner wishes to sell, he must offer his shares first to the other joint venturers;

(c) a joint venturer may elect to transfer its shares within the group to which it belongs provided the transferee assumes its obligations under the Shareholders Agreement and the former joint venturer guarantees the performances of its obligations by the transferee;

(d) if one of the joint venturers suffers a change of control, it will be forced to offer its shares to the other parties;

(e) special formulas for determining share values in the different situations described above.

(xiv) *Termination*: The Shareholders Agreement will specify a number of circumstances that will bring about the termination of the jvc:

(a) immediate termination for cause in the event of a serious default of

[2] Slagter, Compendium, p. 428.

the Shareholders Agreement (which is not remedied within a reasonable time); the insolvency of one of the parties; or a change of control of one of the parties;

(b) termination without 'cause' upon giving reasonable notice (e.g. 6, 12 or 24 months). In such case, it may be agreed that the terminating party will be forced to sell his shares or, in the alternative, buy the shares of the other party(s) (*see* (xii) above for the penalty element).

(xv) *Mutual confidentiality*: Each joint venture agreement should, and typically does, include a confidentiality clause.

(xvi) *Manufacturing and production*: There are often specific clauses which describe the way in which the parties will work together, coordinate the work of the joint venture, develop products and acquire equipment to be used in manufacturing. Frequently, the jvc buys raw materials and components from one or more of the joint venturers. Such agreements should be fair, negotiated at arm's length, and well drafted to ensure that all the joint venturers are treated fairly.

(xvii) *Distribution*: Sometimes the distribution of profits is determined by the joint venturers. In such cases certain general rules are typically agreed upon, e.g. not more than 50% of profits to be distributed. It is also possible to have different distribution policies for different joint venturers by creating different classes of shares with separate reserve accounts. It is important commerically to provide for a distribution policy so that all joint venturers will be treated fairly and there are no disagreements upon the manner or extent to which profits are extracted.

(xviii) *Non-competition clause*: In most cases a joint venture agreement will include specific agreements that the joint venturers shall not compete with the jvc. Also, typically, a clause is included that the jvc will not compete with the joint venturers. These clauses, as is the whole arrangement, are subject to article 85 of the EEC Treaty. For Dutch competition law *see* 3.9 above.

(xix) *Licence agreements concerning the intellectual property of the joint venture*: It is important to have specific licensing agreements between the joint venturers and the jvc for any relevant intellectual property rights. These agreements should be fair and negotiated in detail. It is possible that the joint venture company will develop its own intellectual property rights. One should determine at the outset which party is to own such rights (normally it will be the jvc) and the extent to which the joint venturers will be entitled to have access to rights generated by the jvc.

(xx) *Regulation of dispute*: A clause specifying whether disputes should be resolved by arbitration or civil court proceedings are frequently used. It is also possible to agree that disputes should be initially addressed to the chairman of the joint venture parties.

(xxi) *Choice of law*: It is normal to agree that the law governing the operation of the jvc will be the law applicable to the agreement.

In the creation and operation of a jvc, there are likely to be a number of important additional agreements such as agreements regarding the purchase of raw materials, distribution agreements and licensing agreements. There are also service agreements with the key employees as well as property documentation or lease agreements when real estate is involved.

5.6   Tax

Corporate taxes will apply to a jvc:

(i) *Corporate income tax*: Corporate income tax is levied on the profits of resident and non-resident legal entities as well as certain other associations.

A legal entity (hereinafter 'corporation') is resident if it is managed and controlled in The Netherlands.[3]

Also, a corporation will be deemed to be resident if it is incorporated under Dutch law.[4] Taxwise there is no difference between NV and a BV.

Resident corporations are taxed on their total worldwide income, i.e. all profits from all activities.

Non-resident corporations are taxed only on their Netherlands source of income, i.e. profits derived from a permanent establishment, dividends received from a Dutch corporation (and capital gains and losses realised on the alienation of a substantial (33⅓%), interest in a Dutch corporation only in the theoretical situation that the non-resident corporation does not carry on a business) and income out of real estate situated in The Netherlands.[5]

As of October 1, 1988, the corporate income tax rate is 40% on profits up to fls 250,000 and 35% on all profits exceeding fls 250,000.

(ii) *Computation*: Taxable corporate income is equal to the jvc's corporate net income minus loss compensation. Corporate net income is all income generated by the corporation minus allowable deductions.[6]

Generally, all business-related costs are deductible, e.g. interest, wages, etc. Some costs having both a business and personal character (e.g. canteen provisions, entertainment costs, etc.) are deductible up to 75%.

Distributions of profit (either in the form of dividends or disguised, or hidden profits distributions) are not deductible.

(iii) *Loss compensation*: Both the off-setting of tax losses and the carrying back of negative income against profits earned in other years is favourably treated in The Netherlands. A loss, or negative income, can be carried back for three years. In addition, if the loss exceeds the profits of the previous three years, the balance can be carried forward for up to eight years.

Losses incurred during the first six years of incorporation (starter losses) may be carried forward indefinitely. The general rule is that the oldest losses

---

[3] Article 4 AWR.
[4] Article 2 paragraph 4 CITA.
[5] Article 49 ITA.
[6] *See also* the principles of computation of taxable profits of partnerships.

must be set-off first. Non-starter losses will have to be off-set before starter losses.[7]

(iv) *Interest and royalties*: No withholding tax is due on interest and royalties paid by a Dutch company. However, when the interest is received by the holder of a substantial interest in the company, the interest will sometimes be taxable under the normal corporate income tax rate (40–35%). When a treaty applies these rates will be lowered to the treaty rates on interest, even though this cannot be considered a withholding tax.[8]

(v) *Dividends*: Dividend tax is withheld on distributed dividends. The rate is 25%, although this rate is often reduced under tax treaties.

The dividend tax can be credited against both personal and corporate income tax as far as residents are concerned. If a dividend is distributed by a company to its shareholders, the company must withhold 25% of the dividend as tax. Consequently, the company only really distributes 75% of the gross dividend to its shareholders. The shareholders, in turn, are allowed to credit the dividend tax against their personal or corporate income tax.

(vi) *Participation exemption*:

A. The Netherlands' participation exemption or affiliation privilege (deelnemingsvrijstelling) ranks as one of the most well known international tax planning schemes.[9] In its present form, companies are exempt from corporate income tax on all benefits (including dividends and capital gains realised upon disposition of shares) deriving from qualifying shareholdings. The basic philosophy underlying the participation exemption is to avoid double taxation of profits, i.e. once a profit is distributed by one company to another company acting as shareholder that income should not be retaxed. Lacking such a privilege, corporate income tax would be imposed twice in The Netherlands, i.e. once at the level of the distributing company and once at the level of the recipient corporate shareholder.

One of the basic principles of Dutch fiscal legislation is that a legal entity is deemed a separate entity and therefore (in principle), is subject to tax on its total worldwide income. The ultimate owner of such an entity cannot take the corporate income tax due by the entity into account when determining its own (corporate or individual) tax liability.[10] However, there are two important exceptions to these fundamental principles, i.e. the affiliation privilege and the concept of the 'fiscal unity' (fiscale eenheid).[11]

Under the aegis of the affiliation privilege, profits which have been subject to corporate income tax once will not be retaxed. The profits received (e.g.

---

[7] Article 20 CITA.

[8] Article 49.1.b ITA and Supreme Court 11–101978 BNB 1978/300.

[9] Combined with the extensive network of tax treaties concluded by The Netherlands, the beneficial tax arrangement with The Netherlands Antilles and the absence of withholding taxes on interest and royalties the country offers an extremely favourable investment climate.

[10] *See* Betten, R., 'The Fiscal Unity: International Aspects and Recent Developments', 27 European Taxation 3 (1987) at 78.

[11] *See* Article 2 CITA. Certain other companies, however, are not eligible for the benefits of the participation exemption (*see* Article 28 CITA 1969) and text below.

dividends) are, in fact, profits of the shareholder but they have already been subject to tax at the level of the shareholders participation in the relevant company.

The affiliation privilege is set forth in Article 13 of the Corporate Income Act (CITA). In general, all corporate taxpayers may avail themselves of the privilege. The affiliation privilege applies to participations in both resident and non-resident companies, although additional requirements must be satisfied for non-resident participations.

1. *Resident companies*: In order for a corporate taxpayer to benefit from a participation in a resident company several conditions must be fulfilled:

(a)   *Participation of at least 5%*:[12] The participation must be at least 5% of the shares of the nominal paid-in capital of the company invested in.[13]

(b)   *Capital divided into shares*:[14] The second requirement is that the company invested in must be a company whose capital is divided into shares.[15]

2. *Non-resident companies*: Participations in companies incorporated under foreign law also qualify regardless of whether the company is resident in The Netherlands but, as mentioned above, several additional requirements must be met.

(a)   *Subject to a profits tax*: Article 13 CITA provides that the participation exemption is only available for participations in non-resident companies if the non-resident company is subject to a profits tax, i.e. the company invested in must be subject to income tax on its profits.

(b)   *Passive investment* (belegging):[16] Passive or portfolio investments do not qualify for the participation privilege.[17] A passive investment exists, for instance, when shares are held in a foreign portfolio investment company for the mere purpose of receiving a return on an investment. A participation exists when a nexus between the business activities of the two companies can be established.[18]

B. *Expenses*

Expenses in this context include interest costs on loans which the parent company has made to finance the purchase price of the participation, capital tax

---

[12] A shareholder within the meaning of Article 13 is any corporate taxpayer which has legal ownership of the shares. Certain exemptions, however, have been granted to economic owners.
[13] Certain exceptions apply to this rule as well.
[14] Article 13 paragraph 1.
[15] A foundation is not considered to have a capital divided into shares. However, a participation in a cooperative society or in a resident 'fund for joint account' may qualify, but these participations are not discussed here.
[16] For a discussion of the passive investment issue, *see* the Spenke, Gerrit, Taxation in The Netherlands, Kluwer Law and Taxation Publishers, Deventer, The Netherlands (1985) at 64.
[17] *See* Article 28 CITA.
[18] *See also* the Official Explanation to the Bill introducing CITA 1969.

with respect to an increase in share capital in order to finance the purchase price and management and accountancy expenses.[19]

Expenses related to a participation are only deductible from the shareholder's taxable profit if these costs can be considered to contribute to profits which are taxable in The Netherlands.[20] Profits distributed by a Dutch subsidiary company are considered to have contributed to such taxable profits so that expenses connected to a qualifying participation in a Dutch company are deductible. However, expenses incurred in connection with a qualifying non-resident participation are not deductible for Dutch income tax purposes because they do not generate profits taxable in The Netherlands since the profits distributed will be exempt; under the affiliation privilege.[1]

C. *Miscellaneous*

If the participation exemption applies, no dividend tax will have to be withheld. Thus, if Dutch company A distributes dividend to Dutch company B, who benefits from the participation exemption, A is not obliged to withhold dividend tax.

(vii) *Fiscal unity*: Fiscal unity[2] is only possible between parent companies and wholly owned subsidiaries which are both NV or BV and both resident, for Dutch corporate income tax purposes, in The Netherlands. A NV/BV which is a non-resident for tax treaty-purposes can also form part of a fiscal unity.[3]

The effect of fiscal unity is the immediate intragroup compensation of losses of one group company with profits of the other group company. Moreover transactions within the group do not trigger much attention as far as inter-company-pricing issues are concerned.

Consequently, interest paid by the parent company (e.g. if it borrows money to purchase the subsidiary) can be off-set against profits generated by the subsidiary. A fiscal unity is, subject to certain conditions, granted upon request by the Dutch tax authorities. Standard conditions for approval have been issued by the Ministry of Finance.

(viii) *Transfer of assets*:[4] In the event of a transfer of assets (when a whole enterprise is transferred) this transfer may take place against bookvalue provided that the transferor receives shares in the company to which the enterprise was transferred and the transferor does not sell these shares within three years. The receiving company has to continue with the bookvalues as they appeared in the balance sheet of the contributing company at the moment of the transfer.

This facility is open in the following situations:

(1)   BV transfers enterprise to another BV or other resident company.

---

[19] Article 13 paragraph 1 does not include losses of the participation. These are taken into account upon formal liquidation of the participation.
[20] *See* Article 13 paragraph 1.
[1] Article 20 CITA.
[2] Article 15 CITA.
[3] Supreme Court 29 June 1988 BNB 1988/331.
[4] Article 14 CITA.

(2)   permanent establishment transfers an enterprise to a BV or other resident company.

When the joint venture company itself carries on the business of the joint venturers, this company will be subject to corporate income tax.

(ix) *Investment deduction*: As of January 1, 1990, an investment deduction is granted for a percentage of the investment on a sliding scale: 18% for investment of fls 3,000 decreasing to 2% for investment of fls 441,000.

5.7   Foreign involvement

There are no general restrictions on foreign involvement in a Dutch jvc. However, restrictions do apply in certain regulated businesses such as banking and air transport.

Banking: Any joint venture involving a Dutch Bank will require the consent of the Central Bank under the terms of the banking licence held or to be held by the Dutch Bank concerned. Where a person is to hold shares in excess of 5% of the capital of a Dutch Bank, the ability to exercise voting rights in excess of 5% will be conditional on the issue of a statement of non-objection by the Central Bank. Such a statement will be forthcoming unless the Central Bank or the Ministry of Finance is of the opinion that the acquisition of such voting rights might adversely affect the Dutch Bank in question or the banking sector in general. The requirement to obtain a statement of non-objection also extends to any holding of shares of any holding company of a Dutch Bank.

Insurance: Equivalent restrictions apply in relation to mergers or joint ventures involving Dutch insurance companies. Under the licence required to be held by companies carrying on insurance business in The Netherlands, a statement of non-objection must be obtained from the Insurance Chamber before any person who is to hold shares in excess of 5% of the capital of an insurance company or its holding company may exercise more than 5% of the voting rights in that company. A statement of non-objection will be forthcoming unless the Insurance Chamber considers that the holding of voting rights might adversely affect the insurance company in question or the insurance sector in general.

As these regulations are currently applied, banks may hold up to 15% of the capital in a Dutch Insurance Company and Insurance Companies may hold up to 15% of the capital of a Dutch Bank. However, in neither case may the shareholder exercise more than 5% of the voting rights in the bank or insurance company concerned.

Air transport: Under the Aviation Act, the operation of an airline from The Netherlands may only be carried out with the benefit of a licence from the Ministry of Transport. Such a licence will only be granted to enterprises which demonstrate that the majority of their capital in their effective management are in Dutch hands. This requirement effectively precludes a jvc of which more than 49% is in foreign hands.

The Netherlands has an open attitude to foreign investment. Many jvcs are in place. The Netherlands uses itself as a 'transit' country.

Directors of BVs or NVs can be of any nationality or residence.

5.8 Acquisition and use of business assets and intellectual property rights

Business assets are often transferred to the jvc. They can be sold to the jvc by the shareholders, or they can be contributed to the capital of the jvc. Book 2 of the D Civil C comprises several articles, which require shareholders of the jvc to be very exact in the valuation of the assets that they sell or contribute to the jvc. These rules are there to protect the creditors of the jvc, as well as the other shareholders of the jvc. The rules are there to avoid that shareholders would sell or contribute assets to the jvc and receive a too high value for those assets. Articles 94A/204A and 94C/204C Book 2 D Civil C determine that founders or shareholders who sell or contribute assets to the jvc must provide an accountants' report confirming that the value of the assets is at least equal to the amount they receive in return either selling price (if it is a sale) or in shares (if it is a contribution).

The joint venturers may of course also consider leasing assets to the jvc. This not only to avoid disclosure requirements but may also be advantageous from a tax perspective.

Intellectual property rights are often licensed rather than transferred to the jvc. If intellectual property rights are transferred outright, the jvc may need to enter into licence agreements with the joint venturers in order to allow them to continue to make use of their rights.

5.9 Competition law considerations

See 3.9 above.

5.10 Conclusion

Most joint ventures in The Netherlands are organised in the form of a jvc. Although subject to higher formation and running costs, the structure is familiar to businessmen, is governed by an established body of corporate and tax law and is generally the most appropriate choice for a commerical collaboration of reasonable substance and duration.

CHAPTER 6

Joint ventures in Spain

1.   GENERAL INTRODUCTION

There is no good translation into Spanish for the words 'joint venture' and it is for this reason that these English words are widely used in Spanish legal and commercial practice, lacking however any legal support since Spanish law provides for no specific regulation of joint ventures.

In Spanish legal parlance, the English words 'joint venture' in a strict sense are used to refer to two particular types of agreement called respectively the 'cuentas en participación' and the 'Unión Temporal de Empresas'. In both cases, the underlying principle is the undertaking of a specific project over a short period of time.

However, sometimes the terms 'joint venture' are also interpreted in a much broader sense, meaning any kind of gathering of various entities or individuals with common objectives or a common project.

Joint ventures in Spain can be studied under two basic categories: contractual joint ventures which do not create a separate legal entity and which are mostly used for short term collaborations ('Cuentas en Participación' and 'Unión Temporal de Empresas') and incorporated joint ventures which create a new legal entity and which are mostly employed for long-term collaborations. The two most common forms of jointly controlled legal entities are limited liability and stock companies. Other types of incorporated entities could also be used, such as partnerships, limited partnerships and collective companies. However, we prefer not to discuss these alternatives since they are seldom used in Spain, save in very specific situations which are not relevant to the present study.

2.   CONTRACTUAL JOINT VENTURES: 'CUENTAS EN PARTICIPACIÓN'

2.1   Introduction to Structure

The 'cuentas en participación' is a type of agreement regulated under Title II of Book 1 of the Commercial Code (hereinafter, the 'CommC.').[1] Pursuant

---

[1] The legal definition of 'cuentas en participación' is contained in article 239 of the CommC., which states the following:
> Art. 239. Prodrán los comerciantes interesarse los unos en las operaciones de los otros, con-tribuyendo para ellas con la parte del capital que convinieren, y haciéndose participes de sus resultados prósperos o adversos en la proporción que determinen.

A free translation of this article is as follows:
> Art. 239. Merchants may take an interest in the transactions of other merchants by contributing a pre-establshed amount of capital and becoming participants in the results whether positive or negative in a predetermined proportion.

to an agreement of 'Cuentas en participación', a person (whether an individual or a corporation) (hereinafter, the 'investor') contributes funds to a business carried out by another person (which similarly might be an individual or a corporate entity) (hereinafter, the 'entrepreneur'). The entrepreneur remains the sole manager of the business, the only obligation of the investor being the contribution of the funds. The business is carried out by the entrepreneur in its own name and responsibility, without disclosing to third parties the existence of the association with the investor. It is for this reason that it has been said that the 'cuentas en participación' is in a way a hidden corporate entity or a company whose existence is kept secret by the parties.[2] The parties can freely determine the rules that are to govern their mutual relationship. The use of a commercial name is however specifically prohibited by Article 241 of the CommC. This structure purports to obtain: (i), for the entrepreneur, sufficient funds to carry on his business activities without the burden of obligations that arise from a loan (for example the mandatory payment of interest and the obligation to reimburse the principal thereof after a fixed period of time) and, (ii) for the investor, participation in the profits of a business activity without risking more capital than he actually contributes, i.e. with liability limited to the amount of the capital contribution.

2.2 Advantages

(i) *Ease of formation.* No formalities are required by law to enter into this agreement. They can even be created by oral understanding between the parties involved.[3] All terms of the association can be freely established by the parties thereto.

(ii) *Flexibility in operation.* Since this structure is barely regulated, the parties can freely determine how they will operate it. The 'cuentas en participación' will at all times act in the name of the entrepreneur and may not use a different name. The entrepreneur is solely liable to undertake all obligations imposed on the business by law.

(iii) *Liability.* Even though the results of the business are shared between the parties in the manner agreed upon by them, as to third parties the only party liable is the entrepreneur, those third parties having no possibility of

---

[2] Joaquin Garrigues, Curso de Derecho Mercantil, Volume II, 6th Edition, Imprenta Aguirre, 1,974, p. 60.
[3] Article 240 of the CommC. states as follows:

Articulo 240. Las cuentas en participación no estarán sujetas en su formación a ninguna solemnidad, pudiendo contraerse privadamente de palabra o por escrito, y probándose su existencia por cualquiera de los medios reconocidos en Derecho, conforme a lo dispuesto en el articulo 51

which can be translated as follows:

Article 240. The formation of 'cuentas en participación' shall not be subject to any formalities whatsoever, and could be created privately orally or in writing; its existence being proved by any manner within those recognised by law, pursuant to article 51.

redress against the investor.[4] The investor has in this way limited his liability to the amount of his contribution to the 'cuentas en participación'. The entrepreneur always acts in his own name and no disclosure of the 'hidden partner' is made. Third parties have thus no possibility of holding the investor liable for whatever acts or omissions arise from the business activities carried out within the scope of the 'cuentas en participación'.

(iv) *Ease of termination*. There are no formal requirements. The agreement can be terminated in any manner determined by the parties at the time of its execution. Common examples of grounds for termination might be the expiry of a defined initial term or the fulfilment of the task entrusted to the 'cuentas en participación'. According to article 243 of the CommC., upon termination the entrepreneur must give a proven report of the results of the association to the investor.

(v) *Confidentiality*. The terms of the agreement are not disclosed to third parties but rather are kept in secret. This is particularly advantageous to the investor since his responsibility is limited to his contribution to the 'cuentas en participación'.

(vi) *Minimal costs*. No registration or other formal costs are involved in the creation of the 'cuentas en participación'. However, if the investor instead of contributing money contributes goods, the transfer of title to such goods will trigger the payment of transfer taxes at rates varying from 1% (in the case of certain personal property) to 6% (in the case of real estate property) applicable to the value of the goods transferred (*see* further 2.5.1 below).

2.3   Disadvantages

(i) *Liability*. *Vis-à-vis* third parties, liability for the activities of the Cuentas en participación is borne solely by the entrepreneur. This means that the association with the investor adds nothing to the creditworthiness of the entrepreneur, except for the specific goods contributed by the investor. All the property of the entrepreneur, whether or not used in the business activities the subject matter of the 'cuentas en participación', is at risk to claims from creditors. By the same token all property used in the business subject of the 'cuentas en participación' (including that of the investor transferred to the entrepreneur by reason of the creation of the 'cuentas en participación') is potentially at risk to claims resulting from other business activities of the entrepreneur it

---

[4] Article 242 of the CommC. states as follows:

> Articulo 242. Los que contraten con el comerciante que lleve el nombre de la negociación sólo tendrán acción contra él, y no contra los demás interesados, quienes tampoco la tendrán contra el tercero que contrató con el gestor, a no ser que éste les haga cesión formal de sus dereohos chos.

which can be translated as follows:

> Article 242. Those contracting with the merchant carrying the name of the association will have action only against him and not against the other interested parties, who shall equally not have any action against the third party contracting with the entrepreneur, unless a formal assignment of its rights is made.

follows that the investment of the investor is not protected from claims from the general creditors of the entrepreneur.

(ii) *Limited field of use.* Theoretically, the structure has a wide range of application. In practice, it is for a number of reasons, unsuited to large scale ventures requiring material financial backing: (a) lack of limitation of the liability of the entrepreneur, (b) the charge triggered on assets transferred by the investor to the entrepreneur for the purposes of the 'cuentas en participación', (c) the inability of the arrangement to increase the entrepreneur's credit capacity and (d) the disadvantageous tax treatment accorded to a cuentas en participación.

(iii) *External relationships – funding.* The contributions made by the investor for the funding of the 'cuentas en participación' are potentially subject to taxation and a general lack of protection. In the case of outright transfers of goods and land, the transfer of title will give rise to a tax change (see further 2.5.1 below). In addition, as discussed in (i) above, the investor's contribution will fall subject to claims from the general creditors of the entrepreneur.

(iv) *Lack of permanent structure.* Since no entity is created by the 'cuentas en participación', the interest of the investor is not well protected should the entrepreneur decide to change the purpose or object of the relevant enterprise. Only a contractual responsibility is placed upon the entrepreneur to continue to carry out the business activities for which the investor has joined the 'cuentas en participación'.

(v) *Limited ability to transfer contractual interest*: Since this is an agreement between two (or more) parties, any transfer of interest will require the agreement of the other party(s). The interest of the investor would be easier to transfer, since he has contributed only funds to the 'cuentas en participación'. On the contrary the interest of the entrepreneur will require the substitution of another capable entrepreneur since his position is that of a manager.

2.4   When to select

It is very difficult to determine when to select this structure. We would not recommend it in the case of large scale business activities or activities which are to be carried out over a lengthy period of time. In all other respects this vehicle can be used in a wide variety of activities. It might better (or perhaps more accurately) be viewed as a way by which the entrepreneur obtains funding for his business rather than a real joint venture to promote joint commercial objectives.

2.5   Formation documentation, key aspects

2.5.1 Funding

If the investor's contribution is in kind rather than liquid funds, then the investor will (typically) transfer to the entrepreneur title to the property the subject of his contribution. This will trigger the charge of a transfer tax. This tax is applicable on all transfers of title to property. The rates levied are 1% in the case of the assignment of a debt, 2% in the case of other tangible and intangible property (such as machinery, tools, vehicles, patents and trademarks) and 6% in the case of real estate property (i.e., land and buildings). When the 'cuentas en participación' is terminated, the same tax will apply to the transfer back to the investor of property the subject of his contribution in kind. Contributions by the investor can also be made by way of licences to use intellectual property rights, leases of properties, and the secondment of personnel to the entrepreneur.

2.5.2 Liability to third parties

As stated previously, liability to third parties remains with the entrepreneur since the existence of the investor is kept hidden.

2.5.3 Liability between members

Between members, liability is governed by the agreement. As a rule, liability resulting from the activities carried out under the umbrella of the 'cuentas en participación' will be shared jointly and severaly by the parties.

2.5.4 Management

Management is entrusted solely to the entrepreneur. He alone is liable for mismanagement.

2.5.5 Allocation of profits and losses

The profit and losses resulting from the activities of the 'cuentas en participación' will be allocated between the parties in the manner set forth in the agreement between them.

2.5.6 Resolution or disputes

This matter can be freely determined by the parties

2.5.7 Leaving the joint venture

Termination of the joint venture might occur either as a result of the express terms of the agreement (for example its expiry) or at the initiative of the investor for example, in the event of the gross negligence of the entrepreneur in carrying out his obligations as manager of the 'cuentas en participación'. According to Article 243 of the CommC., upon termination the entrepreneur is under obligation to give a proven account of the results of the 'cuentas en participación' to the investor.

2.6 Taxation

The 'cuentas en participación' does not create a new tax centre, because, as stated above, (a) the 'cuentas en participación' does not create a new corporate entity and the business activities are carried on in the name of the 'entrepreneur' and (b) no disclosure is made of the existence of the investor, not even to the tax authorities. Therefore, the total profits of the 'cuentas en participación' are taxed in the hands of the entrepreneur. The investor's share of the profits of the 'cuentas en participación' are not tax deductible for the entrepreneur and are taxable again as income of the investor. Hence the share of profits allocated to the investor is taxed twice: once as part of the income of the entrepreneur and then as part of the income of the investor. The share of the entrepreneur is taxed only once.

2.7 Foreign involvement

There is no legal limitation upon an investor in a 'cuentas en participación' being a foreign individual or entity. Equally, a 'cuentas en participación' may participate in investments abroad provided that the regulations governing foreign investments are compiled with. (In this respect it should be noted that Spain is still a foreign exchange regulated country, even though the Spanish government is slowly lifting restrictions for foreign investments into and from Spain.)

The Spanish Foreign Exchange Authorities are aware of the fact that joint ventures are widely used in other countries and that lack of sufficient regulation and inappropriate tax treatment runs counter to the governmental policy of opening Spanish markets to foreign investors. This might lead to changes in the treatment and regulation of the 'cuentas en participación' or a recommendation to use the structure known as the 'Unión Temporal de Empresas' (see further 3 below).

2.8 Acquisition and use of business assets and intellectual property rights

Business assets acquired or intellectual property rights generated during the course of the joint venture will be the property of the entrepreneur. If upon termination this property is to remain with the entrepreneur then no further action would be required. However, if such property is to be allocated to the investor, this is likely to trigger transfer taxes. This is a clear disadvantage for the investor.

2.9   Competition

For the Spanish rules on competition which might be applicable to this vehicle *see* 5.9 below.

2.10   Summary

The 'cuentas en participación' is not very widely used in Spain. Even though it can be attractive for an investor not wishing to be involved in the management of the relevant business it has the disadvantage of exposing the investor to mismanagement by the entrepreneur, for which his only remedy will be a claim in contract. However, the most critical disadvantage is the fact that profits accruing to the investor are taxed twice, once in the hands of the entrepreneur and once more in the hands of the investor.

3.   CONTRACTUAL JOINT VENTURES: 'UNIÓN TEMPORAL DE EMPRESAS'

3.1   Introduction to structure

The Unión Temporal de Empresas (hereinafter, the 'UTE') is a vehicle created by a tax law and presently governed by Law 18/1982 of 26th May 1982 as amended by Law 48/1985 of 27th December 1985 (hereinafter, the 'UTE Law'). The UTE Law was enacted under the provisions of the Fourth Transitory Provision of the Corporate Income Tax Law 61/1978 dated 27th December 1978. This law makes a distinction between an 'agrupación de empresas' (a grouping or association of enterprises) and a 'unión temporal de empresas' (a temporary union of enterprises). The difference is that in the first case, two or more enterprises agree to collaborate to develop a common commercial activity for their own benefit, while in the latter one or more enterprises combine to implement a project, provide a service or supply goods to third parties.[5] We will not address the former alternative since its purpose is limited to serving the needs of the joint venturer, in particular it is not able to deal with third parties. The latter structure is a clear case of a joint venture and the only one which is regulated in Spanish law. As stated, the UTE Law is a tax law and as such its purpose is to regulate the tax consequences of the vehicle rather than to develop a comprehensive set of rules and regulations governing the formation and operation of the structure. It is, as a result, that the UTE Law has a number of material loopholes. The UTE can be created by individuals or corporate entities, whether resident in Spain or not. (Being a tax law, residency should be taken as tax residency rather than corporate residency, concepts that usually but not necessarily coincide.) The existence of a UTE is limited

---

[5]   Resolution of the Economic-Administrative Tribunal dated 24th May, 1988.

to the time needed to carry out its objective subject to a maximum of ten years.[6] No corporate entity is created.

3.2 Advantages

(i) *Ease of formation*. According to paragraph (e) of Article 8 of the UTE Law, the UTE must be created by public deed executed before a Notary Public. Once created, UTEs may request registration in the special Registry opened in the Ministry of Economy. It should be noted that some of the advantages of the UTE Law will not be available to non-registered UTEs. In the discussion that follows it is assumed that the UTE has been registered.

(ii) *Flexibility in operation*. The manner in which a UTE operates is a matter for agreement between the parties. One must remember that since this vehicle has been created by a tax law, its operational aspects are subtantially unregulated.

(iii) *Liability*. According to the provisions of Article 7 of the UTE Law no new legal entity is created when a UTE is formed. This being the case, liability remains in the hands of the participants who, according to article 8.8 of the UTE Law, are jointly and severally liable to third parties. This unlimited liability to third parties is without prejudice to any internal regulation of liability between the parties inter se.

(iv) *Ease of termination*. Termination of the UTE is typically provided for in the founding deed; there are no set procedures to be followed.

(v) *Tax transparency*. According to Article 10.2 of the UTE Law, a registered UTE is tax transparent. Tax transparency means that no tax centre exists and therefore that profits are not taxed at the level of the UTE, but in the hands of the members. A registered UTE is not subject to corporate income tax. In contrast, a non-registered UTE is subject to corporate income tax, and thereafter the net profit allocated to its members is again subject to corporate income tax (in the case of an incorporated member) or to personal income tax (in the case of an individual member).

(vi) *Confidentiality*. In the case of registered UTEs, the founding deed is registered in a special Registry of the Ministry of Economy, and therefore the terms of the deed are disclosed to the tax authorities. Aside from this disclosure, secrecy is permitted. In the case of non-registered UTEs, its terms are not disclosed at all.

(vii) *Minimal costs*. The creation of the UTE is subject to transfer tax at a rate of 1% of the stated capital. The transfer of property to the UTE is subject to transfer tax at the rate of 1% in the case of the assignment of debts, 2% in the case of tangible and intangible goods and 6% in the case of land

---

[6] As an exception UTEs can request a one year extension of their existence. Under article 8 of the UTE Law the Ministry of Economy is authorised to grant or refuse this extension at its discretion.

and buildings. Under the UTE Law a 99% rebate of transfer taxes is available. This reduces the actual rate applicable (for example in the case of the assignment of a debt from 1% to 0.01%). Besides this tax, one should take into account the notarial fees which can be estimated at around 0.5% of the capital of the UTE.

3.3   Disadvantages

(i) *Liability*. The unlimited liability of the members *vis-a-vis* third parties is a considerable disadvantage.

(ii) *Limited field of use*. The UTE can only be used in those cases where the implementation of a project, the rendering of a specific service or the supply of goods requires the temporary collaboration of two or more enterprises (corporate or individual).

(iii) *External relationships, funding*. The transfer of property to the UTE is subject to transfer tax, *see* 3.2 (vii) above.

(iv) *Lack of permanent structure*. Since the UTE's purpose is a specific project, service or supply of goods it has a limited life and after the performance of such purpose it must be dissolved.

(v) *Limited ability to transfer contractual interest*. There is no clear rule upon the transfer of an interest to a new member, however, we understand that this is only possible by the creation of a new UTE. As explained above, the UTE is created by a public deed; therefore the amendment of this contract would require the agreement of all the parties and would imply the creation of a new UTE. Moreover, in the case of a registered UTE the new public deed must be recorded in the special Registry of the Ministry of Economy and thus the members thereof would automatically change, and accordingly give rise to a new UTE.

3.4   When to select

According to Article 7 of the UTE Law, the UTE is a vehicle whereby its members undertake to cooperate between themselves for a certain period of time for the development or execution of a *specific* work, service or supply of goods. The distinction between a UTE and a grouping of enterprises ('agrupación de empresas') which is also regulated by the UTE Law is that the purpose of the former is the development of a work in favour of third parties while the purpose of the latter is to carry out a project in favour of the members themselves.[7]

---

[7] Written answer from the General Tax Directorate dated 8th of July 1988 to a question raised by an undisclosed taxpayer.

3.5 Formation documentation, key aspects

3.5.1 Funding

The UTE need not necessarily have a paid up capital at the time of its creation. The contract creating the UTE can, on the contrary, state that the parties shall transfer funds as they are needed for the project to be developed by the UTE.

3.5.2 Liability to third parties

Since no corporate entity is created, the liability of the members to third parties is joint and several.

3.5.3 Liability between members

This is a matter that can (and should) be freely determined by the members in the contract creating the UTE.

3.5.4 Management

The UTE is managed by a manager duly appointed by the members. This manager can be either one of the members, a manager of one of the members or a third party.[8]

3.5.5 Allocation of profits and losses

This subject is also a matter for agreement between the parties at the time of creation of the UTE and should be spelt out in the contract.

3.5.6 Resolution of disputes

No regulation is made by the UTE Law on this subject and therefore the parties can freely regulate the point. Usually this is done by means of a reliance upon arbitration by the Chamber of Commerce of the city where the UTE has its domicile or by arbitrators appointed by the relevant Chamber of Commerce.

3.5.7 Leaving the joint venture

Again this point is also left to the agreement of the parties at the time of creation of the UTE.

---

[8] The Resolution of the Central Economic-Administrative Tribunal of 24th May, 1988 clearly states that one of the alternatives for the appointment of a manager is the manager or managing entity of one of the members.

3.5.8 Termination of the joint venture

The contract creating the UTE can freely regulate this subject. In principle the UTE should be terminated when the purpose of the UTE has been fulfilled. In this regard, the parties should determine at the outset how the remaining proceeds of the UTE will be distributed between them.

3.6 Taxation

Profits of a registered UTE are not subject to corporate income tax; they are allocated directly to its members who are then subject either to corporate income tax at the general rate of 35% or to personal income tax whose rates go up to 56%, depending on whether the member is a corporate entity or an individual. Provided that the UTE so elects in writing, losses can be treated in the same way: they can be allocated to each member and thus offset against profits obtained by the relevant member during the same year or during the following five years.[9] Each member is severally liable for its own income tax. However, the UTE and all the members are jointly and severally liable for:

  (i)   taxes to be withheld at the time of distribution of the UTE profits to its members (25% of such amounts so distributed);
  (ii) all indirect taxes applicable to the activities of the UTE (VAT and other sales taxes); and
  (iii) all other taxes applicable to an ongoing concern (licence tax, municipal taxes, etc.).

3.7 Foreign involvement

The UTE can develop activities abroad. In this case the members are entitled to a tax credit for the foreign taxes paid. Another important point is that foreign enterprises or individuals can be members of a UTE, in which case it will be considered that the foreign entity or individual has a permanent establishment in Spain and therefore will be taxed as a resident on profits allocated by the UTE. Finally, it is possible for Spanish entities or individuals to create (together with foreign entities or not) a UTE that operates abroad. In this case the UTE itself cannot be registered in the special Registry of the Ministry of Economy but its Spanish members (entities or individuals which according to Spanish tax law are considered resident in Spain) should be registered therein in order to obtain the special tax treatment discussed above.

As stated above, it should be noted that Spain is a foreign exchange regulated country and therefore the participation of foreign entities in a UTE should

[9] Article 10.2 of the UTE Law, article 19.3 of the Corporate Income Tax Law 48/1985 of 27th December 1985 and answer dated 16th March 1988 from the General Directorate of Taxation to a query filed by an undisclosed taxpayer.

be previously approved by the Spanish exchange authorities. Likewise, if the UTE wishes to undertake business outside Spain, special authorisation should also be obtained. Spain is presently in the process of lifting a variety of restrictions on both incoming and outgoing investments, so it should be expected that in the near future all such investments will be capable of being effected freely.

3.8 Acquisition and use of business assets and intellectual property rights

Business assets acquired by the UTE or intellectual property rights generated by the UTE will become the property of the UTE unless otherwise agreed by the parties in the contract creating the UTE. The contract should state how assets, including intellectual property rights, are to be distributed to its members upon termination. Even though the UTE does not create a legal entity separate from its members, in practice it can act as such and therefore can lease and/or licence all kinds of property, including land and intellectual property rights.

3.9 Competition

The creation of a UTE will be subject to the Spanish Law on Competition which is discussed at 5.9 below.

3.10 Summary

The purpose of the UTE is to undertake the performance of a specific work, service or supply of goods; its existence is thus limited to the period of time required to perform such work, service or supply of goods. Individuals and corporate entities, whether resident in Spain or abroad, can become members of a UTE. The UTE can operate in Spain or abroad. UTEs may be registered in a special registry of the Ministry of Economy and should do so in order to obtain the special tax treatment provided for by the UTE Law. UTEs can only be created to undertake a specific work, service or supply of goods. The UTE does not create a legal entity that is separate and distinct from its members.

4. INCORPORATED JOINT VENTURES: LIMITED LIABILITY COMPANIES

4.1 Introduction to structure

Under prior legislation in Spain the limited liability company could not have a capital of more than Ptas 50,000,000. This was in practice a reason not to use it as a vehicle for medium to large scale commercial ventures. As a consequence of the limitation upon capital the limited liability company was viewed as a 'small' company and in practice was used mainly for family or closely-held businesses.

The situation has changed as a result of the enactment of Law 19/1989 of 25th July, 1989. This amended the regulations that applied to limited liability companies, one of the principal changes being that there is now a minimum capital requirement (which is lower than that of a stock company) but no limitation as to the maximum capital.

Since as aforesaid this type of company has been seldom used, there is little practical experience of their use for joint ventures. However we believe that this structure will be used more often in the future as a result, inter alia, of the removal of the restriction on maximum capital.

In general terms, both the stock company and the limited liability company are very similar in legal nature and structure.

To avoid unnecessary repetition we will only discuss those aspects where the limited liability company differs from the stock company. The main differences are the following:

(1) *Limited number of partners.* The law provides that the limited liability company can not have more than fifty partners at any time.

(2) *Minimum capital.* A limited liability company can be incorporated with a minimum capital of Ptas. 500,000, while a stock company requires a minimum capital of Ptas. 10,000,000.

(3) *Totally paid-up capital.* The limited liability company must have all its capital fully paid-up. In the case of the stock company, only 25% of the capital need be paid-up provided that the entire capital has been subscribed for.

(4) *Transfer of interests.* The law protects the closeness of the limited liability company by regulating the manner in which the interests can be transferred to third parties. In essence, the other partners will have a right of first refusal. All transfers must be made by public deed. Upon the death of a partner his heirs will acquire his interest in the company. In addition, the Bye-laws may provide that the remaining partners may acquire the interest of a former partner from his heirs at an agreed price.

(5) *Lack of secrecy of shareholders.* The incorporation of the limited liability company is made by a public deed which is registered in the Mercantile Registry. Transfers of interests must also be made by means of a public deed. Therefore the partners are always identifiable. Moreover, there is a special book where the partners should be registered. This book exists only for registered shares in the case of the stock company. Therefore in this latter company the name of the shareholders can be kept secret if all shares are bearer shares. This secrecy is not available in the limited liability company.

(6) *Formalities for resolutions of partners.* The law of limited liability companies states that if the number of partners is less than 15, resolutions do not require a special meeting of all the partners and can be adopted in writing or by mail or in any other informal way, provided that there is evidence that

a majority of shareholders have agreed to the resolution. This alternative is not available in the case of the stock company.

(7) *Non-competition*. Officers are prohibited from directly or indirectly competing with the business activities of a limited liability company.

5.   INCORPORATED JOINT VENTURES: STOCK COMPANIES

5.1   Introduction to structure

The most common vehicle in Spain for the establishment of a joint venture has been the stock company (sociedad anónima). The stock company has been widely used because of its well-known structure and because, even though extensively regulated, the former statute governing the creation and life of stock companies stated only minimum requirements which, in the absence of specific regulations in the Bye-laws of the company, were to rule the company. These minimum regulations helped to create a basic structure but at the same time left parties substantial freedom to tailor the constitution and structure of the company to suit their requirements.

To comply with EEC legislation, a new law of stock companies has been recently passed by Parliament. The governing statute was approved by Royal Legislative Decree 1564/1989 on 22nd December, 1989 (the 'LSC'). Following the enactment of the LSC, the government approved new regulations governing the Mercantile Registry by means of Royal Decree 1597/1989 of 29th December, 1989 (the 'RRM').

The stock company is an entity which is created by an agreement between the incorporators which must be in the form of a public deed and which obtains its legal status upon its registration in the Mercantile Registry. There is a complete separation of interest between the shareholders or owners of the stock company and the company itself. In practice this distinction becomes somewhat blurred when the person who owns most of the shares of the company is at the same time the manager of the company's business. This is the case of stock companies owned by a few shareholders. In most cases these closely-held companies are owned by members of the same family and are therefore known as 'family companies'.

The basic characteristics of a stock company are:

(1)   *Separate entity*. A new legal entity is created which has separate and distinct interests from those of its shareholders;

(2)   *Continuity of life*. The death or retirement of a shareholder, or the sale of its shares will not affect the life of the company;

(3)   *Limited liability of shareholders*. Shareholders are not personally liable for the liabilities and obligations of the company but only for the amount paid-up or owing in respect of their shares;

(4) *Centralised management.* The management of the company is centralised in a limited number of people;

(5) *Transferability of interest.* Shareholders may transfer their shares in the company without affecting its existence.

5.2   Advantages

(i) *Ease of formation.* Even though the formation of a Spanish company is regulated by the LSC, this does not mean that it is a complicated task. Normally standard Bye-laws are used and, as stated, points not specifically covered by the Bye-laws will be governed by Spanish company law. The incorporation can be effected within a week. Registration in the Mercantile Registry formerly took three to four weeks, but since the enactment of the new Corporate law it now takes around two months. As stated previously, incorporation does not take effect until registration in the Mercantile Registry.

(ii) *Separate entity.* Once the public deed has been signed and registered in the Mercantile Registry a new entity is created and starts to have an existence and interests that are independent from its shareholders. A stock company is capable of owning assets and may enter into contracts and sue in its own name. This separateness of identity will have many consequences, such as the limitation of shareholder liability for corporate activities, the continuity of the company despite changes in shareholder and a greater facility for transfering interests (i.e. shares) in the company.

(iii) *Commercial understanding, familiarity.* The stock company is by some margin the most frequently used incorporated structure in Spain. Even though the CommC provides for alternative incorporated entities, such as partnerships, collective companies, limited liability partnerships and limited liability companies, only the stock company has been widely used. This has contributed to the fact that the laws relating to the structure and operation of a stock company are generally well known. This is a clear advantage in the use of this structure. Familiarity with the structure is also advantageous from the point of view of external financing, since banks and other lending institutions are used to dealing with stock companies and therefore parties using this vehicle will be in a better position when seeking external finance.

The new LSC has created restrictions in respect of: the formation of stock companies (i.e., minimum capital of Ptas 10,000,000); their operation (i.e., rules governing Directors' liability: *see* 5.2, (vi)); accounting (very strict rules on this point). These restrictions have created a tendency for parties to avoid using the stock company structure for family or closely-held stock companies. As an alternative, the use of commercial limited companies (sociedad de responsabilidad limitada) is more and more being used in these cases. These companies have an important draw-back in that no shares can be issued and therefore a transfer of an interest in the company is more difficult than the transfer of shares in stock companies. This reason coupled with the fact that stock companies were not at the time very strictly regulated (in constrast to the position under the new LSC) are the main reasons why stock companies have traditionally been used even in small businesses and in family enterprises instead of commercial limited companies which would have been a more suitable vehicle for these closely held enterprises.

(iv) *Limited liability*. An important aspect to be taken into consideration when selecting a vehicle for creating a business concern is the limitation of the risks involved. Often businessmen are unaware of many of the liabilities facing their business.

In the case of stock companies, liabilities arising out of the transactions carried out by them are limited to their own assets; in other words, only the assets of the company underwrite its transactions with third parties. The shareholders are not normally liable for the obligations or liabilities of the company (save to the extent that amounts are owing in respect of their shares), unless they have failed to comply with legal formalities in the formation or operation of the company.

However, limited liability can sometimes be more theoretical than real in family or closely-held companies. On the one hand, banks normally request that loans given to these type of companies be personally guaranteed by the shareholders or at least by those entrusted with the management of the company. On the other hand, in many cases a large proportion of the personal assets of the shareholders are owned by the company.

The requirement for personal guarantees is likely to occur in the case of a company formed to carry out a joint venture if the assets transferred to the new company are not large enough to secure its external financing requirements or if the stock company is newly formed.

(v) *Continuity*. As a consequence of having a separate entity from its shareholders, the death or retirement of a shareholder will not affect the life of the stock company. Similarly, the transfer of a shareholders' interest in the company will not alter the existence of the company.

(vi) *Centralisation of management*. The business of the company is managed only by the directors or managers. They and not the shareholders manage the day-to-day operation of the business. This centralisation is derived from the legal distinction between ownership and the right to manage. Where there is a large number of shareholders, the management of the company will be centralised in a limited number of people. Where there is a small number of shareholders who also manage the business, they do so in a different capacity: as directors or administrative officers and not as shareholders. It is in their capacity as officers of the company that directors and managers can be liable to the company, its shareholders and creditors for mismanagement, illegal acts, breaches of the Bye-laws and the improper fulfilment of their duties and obligations.

(vii) *Transferability of interest*. Shareholders may transfer their interest in the company without affecting its existence. The company's existence does not depend upon the identity of the persons who are its shareholders.

Normally transfers of shares can be freely made. Sometimes transfers of registered shares are made subject to special formalities which should be stated in the Bye-laws of the company.

Bearer shares should be transferred before a public attesting officer: a Notary Public or a Spanish Stockbroker (Agente de Cambio y Bolsa or Corredor Colegiado de Comercio). The transaction is therefore subject to the payment of notarial or stockbroker fees (in both cases the fee is assessed by reference to the price paid).

(viii) *External finance*. The stock company, being a separate entity can request financing from banks and other institutions subject to the provision of its own security. (However, this advantage may not apply in closely-held or family companies, since as stated in 5.2 (iv) above, financial institutions are likle to require personal guarantees from some of the shareholders or at least from the managing shareholder.)

5.3   Disadvantages

(i) *Administrative complexity*. Day-to-day activities will be undertaken by the management; more strategic decisions will be taken by the directors; the appointment of all directors and managers must be registered in the Mercantile Registry. The above are examples of the complexity of managing a stock company.

(ii) *Lack of flexibility*. Resolutions of shareholders and directors require the observance of certain formalities in order to be valid and enforceable, for example, proper notice of meetings, minimum quorum for the holding of the meetings, and minimum number of votes to take decisions. The net result is that the structure lacks flexibility when compared to essentially contractural arrangements such as the cuentas en participación or the partnership.

(iii) *Lack of secrecy*. As discussed earlier, the formation of the company requires registration in the Mercantile Registry. All important acts and resolutions of the company (such as the appointment of directors and administrative officers, changes to the Bye-laws, reductions or increases of capital) also require registration in the Mercantile Registry, as do the annual accounts and accounting documents (the balance sheet, the report to shareholders and the profit and loss account). It follows that neither the existance of the company nor its important data are kept secret from third parties.

(iv) *Difficulty of termination*. Termination of the joint venture vehicle is not a simple process. For such purpose a shareholders meeting must take place and majority approval obtained for the dissolution and liquidation of the company. The resolution will start a long process that includes publications in newspapers, the preparation of a final balance sheet, the appointment of liquidators, the actual liquidation of assets and the payment of liabilities.

(v) *Costs of incorporation*. The formation of the stock company is subject to the payment of transfer tax by reference to its stated capital. Further increases of capital are also subject to this tax. Notarial and registry fees will also be incurred. These costs will be discussed further in 5.6 below.

5.4   When to select

The stock company is the right choice for any important project or business objective of medium to longterm duration. In the case of smaller short-term projects it might not be advisable to choose this type of company but rather the commercial limited company which, from an administrative point of view, is less complicated to manage.

5.5   Formation documentation, key aspects

The stock company can be formed in two ways: by agreement between the founding shareholders or by public subscription. The latter method is not widely used and in any case would not be appropriate for joint ventures. Therefore we will only discuss the former method. The founding shareholders should be at least three and the founding agreement should be a public deed, which means that it should be signed before and attested to by a Public Notary. The agreement should thereafter be registered in the Mercantile Registry. Registration is a precondition to the legal existence of the company.

The public deed of formation of a stock company should contain: details of the founding shareholders, the amount and description of the property transferred to the company by way of capital (depending on whether the capital is paid in in assets or in cash), the Bye-laws that are to govern its existence and details of the persons appointed as its directors and auditors. The general rule contained in article 10 of the LSC is that the Bye-laws can contain any terms and conditions provided that they are not against the law or against the basic principles of the stock company.[10]

The Bye-laws should at least contain:

(a)   *The name of the company.* Shareholders can choose any name provided it is not already used by another company. To determine this fact prior to its formation, the founders should request a certificate stating that the chosen name is not registered and can be used. This certificate

---

[10]   Article 10 of the LSC literally states the following:
   Articulo 10. En la escritura se podrán incluir, además, todos los pactos y condiciones que los socios fundadores juzguen conveniente establecer, siempre que no se opongan a las leyes ni contradigan los principios configuradores de la sociedad anónima
   which can be translated as follows:
   Article 10. Besides (those points set forth in the preceding article) the founding shareholders may include in the public deed whatever agreements and conditions that they see convenient, provided that they do not go against the law or contradict the basic principles of the stock company.

should be given to the Public Notary at the time of signing the founding deed.

(b) *The objects of the company*. The founders can state a wide or a restricted object. The object stated in the Bye-laws will define and limit the scope of company's activities. The objects of the company can be changed at a later stage.

(c) *The duration of the company*. The Bye-laws should state the duration of the company in terms of years elapsing after its foundation or the reaching of a certain date.

(d) *The date when the company starts its operations*. The founders can select the date on which the company will start its operation (this must be after the date of the deed of foundation). It should be noted that all acts performed or contracts executed after such date, but prior to the registration of the company in the Mercantile Registry, will be the responsibility of the persons who have performed such acts and executed such contracts. This responsibility ceases if the company ratifies them within three months of its registration in the Mercantile Registry.

(e) *The domicile*. The domicile should be stated. The domicile and the headquarters can be different.

(f) *The capital, stating the amount already paidin*. The capital should be stated in Spanish pesetas even if the shareholders are foreign and have made a foreign investment in foreign currency. The minimum capital is Ptas 10,000,000. At least 25% must be paid-in at the time of the company's foundation. The same 25% rule applies in case of increases of capital. Shareholders have a pre-emptive right to acquire new shares in the same proportion as their shares bear to the existing capital.

(g) *The number of shares, their par value and other information relating to them*. The par value should be a division of the stated capital by the number of shares issued and it should be fixed in Spanish pesetas. Different kinds of shares are permitted (such as shares with special voting or without voting rights; privileged shares) provided that each form part of the same series or class of shares.

(h) *The structure of the body which is to govern the company*. This can comprise a sole director, a board of directors or a committee of directors to whom particular powers have been delegated, see further 5.5.4 below.

(i) *The manner in which corporate decisions will be taken*. The following will, inter alia, be specified: quorums to hold meetings, quorums to take decisions, persons to chair meetings and minutes of meetings.

(j) *The date when each accounting year will end*. This may or may not coincide with the calendar year.

(k) *The limitations, if any, upon the transfer of shares*. The transfer of registered shares may be subject to a wide variety of limitations, provided that after compliance with said limitations the seller can actually transfer his shares. Absolute prohibition upon the transfer of shares is not permitted.

(l) *Any further payment or services to be carried out by the shareholders, if any.*

(m) *Any special rights that the founders of the company may have.* This is more common where the company is founded by public subscription. Here the founders on occasion obtain special rights, for example, the right to receive a special priority share of the profits of the company.

In certain circumstances stock companies must appoint auditors to verify their accounts. Shareholders should elect the auditors of the company prior to the end of the relevant year. Auditors can be elected for a period of no less than three nor more than nine years. They can be re-elected only after another term of three years has elapsed.

It is not common practice for shareholders to sign a special shareholders agreement. In principle the Bye-laws should contain all the provisions necessary for the management and operation of the company. Shareholders Agreements are, however, not prohibited and are sometimes used. The problem is that these agreements are not enforceable against third parties since they are generally not registered in the Mercantile Registry.

In cases of 50–50 shareholders, it might be advisable to have a Shareholders Agreement to agree on how resolutions should be taken in the event of deadlock. No legal provision exists on this matter since the LSC generally approaches the stock company from the perspective of an 'open' company (i.e. one not closely-held).

Similarly, when a stock company is created by two or more joint venturers, it is advisable that a Shareholders Agreement be signed to solve some important aspects not usually covered by the Bye-laws. Among these are the following:

(a) *Termination.* Joint venturers typically like to agree that in certain instances the joint venture should be terminated. This will trigger the dissolution and liquidation of the company, which will have to be resolved in a shareholders meeting.

(b) *Confidentiality.* Secrecy during and after the joint venture's activities is essential in some cases.

(c) *Dividend policy.* To safeguard proper and continuing funding of the company it is often advisable to establish a dividend policy, to avoid distribution of funds needed to continue the business activities, or alternatively to ensure that profits are extracted.

(d) *Special quorum for specific decisions.* Certain actions, such as the appointment of management, the salaries of key management, the disposal of important assets, contracts not in the ordinary course of business, increases in capital, loans to or from the company exceeding a certain limit, might be made subject to special voting, quorum and other requirements.

(e) *Jurisdiction in case of conflicts.* Parties often prefer to resort to arbitration in place of court proceedings as a means of settling disputes.

5.5.1 Funding

Contributions to the company can either be in money or in kind. If in money they should necessarily be in Spanish pesetas; hence in case of foreign investments, the foreign currency should be exchanged for pesetas and the investment will thus be registered in pesetas. Under the LSC, contributions in kind should be valued by specially appointed appraisers and can comprise all kinds of assets, intellectual property rights, know how or even a whole business.

5.5.2 Liability to third parties

This matter has been discussed in point 5.2 (vi) above.

5.5.3 Liability between members

The liability of shareholders is limited to their contribution to the company, i.e., their share of the capital. No special liability exists from one shareholder to another save where a shareholder is also an officer of the company. Directors and managers are liable to the company, the shareholders and creditors of the company for damages caused by their alleged act or omission, their breach of the Bye-laws or their failure to exercise diligence in the exercise of their duties and obligations.

5.5.4 Management

There are three levels at which decisions are taken in a stock company: the shareholders, the director or directors and the managers. Managers are appointed by the directors who in turn are elected by the shareholders.

The shareholders meeting is the body that adopts resolutions approved by the shareholders and is therefore the highest level of decision-making body in the company. There are two kinds of shareholders meeting: ordinary and extraordinary. Ordinary meetings must be held annually within the first six months of each year to approve the management of the company, its annual accounts and the proposed allocation of profits. All other shareholders meetings are extraordinary meetings and can adopt resolutions on any matter which is within the competence of the meeting. Meetings must necessarily take place within the territory of the domicile of the company unless all shareholders are present and decide to hold the meeting elsewhere.

Management of the day-to-day operations of the stock company is entrusted to one or more directors.

5.5.5 Transactions with shares

No shares of the company may be transferred prior to its registration in the Mercantile Registry. In principle shares are freely transferable between shareholders or to third parties. However, limitations can be imposed provided that the shares are registered shares, that the limitations imposed do not make transfers impossible and provided that such limitations are contained in the Bye-laws of the company.

Companies can only acquire their own shares or shares of their parent company in specific cases and subject to very strict rules, non-compliance with which [will] render the transaction null and void or bring about a reduction in capital of the company. The same principle applies to the acceptance by the company of shares (its own shares and/or those of its parent company) as guarantee for the performance of obligations of the shareholders or third parties.

A very important new rule of the LSC is that contained in Article 81 which limits the ability of a company to give financial assistance for the acquisition of its own shares by a third party.[11] No such restriction had existed prior to the enactment of the new LSC and many acquisitions by third parties of shares in stock companies had been carried out by using the assets of the company whose shares were being acquired as security for the financing of the acquisition. This is, in principle, no longer permitted by the new LSC. As a result, a common method of financing acquisitions has been outlawed.

5.5.6 Allocation of profits and losses

Profits and losses must be allocated equally to shares of a given class. However, different kinds of shares or shares having special rights can be issued. An example of a share with special rights would be one with a preferential right to receive up to a certain percentage of the profits prior to other classes of share.

[11] This article literally states as follows:

Articulo 81. Asistencia financiera para las adquisiciones de acciones propias. – 1. La sociedad no podrá anticipar fondos, conceder préstamos, prestar garantias ni facilitar ningún tipo de asistencia financiera para las adquisiciones de sus acciones o de acciones de su sociedad dominante por un tercero.

2. Lo dispuesto en el apartado primero no se aplicará a los negocios dirigidos a facilitar al personal de la empresas la adquisiciones de sus acciones o de acciones de una sociedad del grupo.

3. La prohibición del apartado primero no se aplicará a las operaciones efectuadas por bancos u otras entidades de crédito en el ámbito de las operaciones ordinarias propias de su objeto social que se sufraguen con cargo a bienes libres de la sociedad. Esta deberà establecer en el pasivo del balance una reserva equivalente al importe de los créditos anotados en el activo.

which can be translated as follows:

Article 81. Financial assistance for the acquisition of its own shares. – 1. The company may not advance funds, grant loans, give guarantees or any type of financial assistance for the acquisition of its shares or of shares of its dominant company by a third party.

2. The provisions of the first paragraph shall not apply to transactions addressed to help acquisitions by its employees of its own shares or shares of a company belonging to the group.

3. The prohibition of the first paragraph shall not apply to transactions made by banks and other credit institutions within the scope of the ordinary transactions of their corporate object which are paid out with free resources of the company. It shall establish a reserve among its liabilities equivalent to the amount of the credits which are reflected in its assets.

5.5.7 Resolution of disputes

Disputes are in principle solved by the shareholders meetings where all resolutions taken in compliance with the Bye-laws bind the remaining shareholders. Shareholder Agreements should take care of this matter in the case of joint venture companies.

5.6   Taxation

The taxation of stock companies focusses upon three aspects.

(1) *Taxes applicable on formation.* The funding of a stock company is subject to a 1% transfer tax applicable on the capital of the company. At the time of formation other expenses (not taxes) may be incurred: (a) notarial fees, applied on the basis of a specific schedule (but which can be estimated at approximately Ptas. 250,000 or 0.5% of the capital, whichever is the lesser) (b) registry fees, applied also according to a specific schedule and which are roughly equivalent to notarial fees and (c) legal costs which in the absence of special circumstances can be estimated at around Ptas. 500,000. All figures are given on the assumption that the company created will have a large capital. Foundation costs are therefore likely to be around 1.5% to 2% of the stated capital of the company.

(2) *Taxation of profits.* Profits of stock companies are taxed at the corporate income tax rate of 35% which is applicable on the net profits, i.e., revenues of all sources minus expenses incurred in connection with such revenues. Losses can be carried forward during a period of five fiscal years. The company will have to submit its tax return within 25 days after the date on which the Shareholders approved the accounts of the company, which must take place within the first six months of each year.

(3) *Taxation of dividends.* Dividends are subject to a withholding tax of 25%. This withholding tax is, in the case of resident shareholders, an advance payment on account of the personal income tax of the individual shareholder or of the corporate income tax of the corporate shareholder, as the case may be. The amount withheld may be refunded to the shareholder (whether individual or corporate) if at the time of filing his personal or corporate tax return, he or it is not subject to actual taxation on his or its income or profits. In the case of non-resident shareholders this withholding is the only Spanish tax to be paid. Spain has treaties with the USA, almost all the European countries and some other countries to avoid double taxation on income from Spanish sources.

(4) *Group relief.* Group relief will be available only if the dominant entity (the parent company) is resident in Spain and its participation in the joint venture company amounts to over 90% of its capital. Although group relief will rarely be available in a jvc context, Spanish law does provide a range of provisions allowing for a tax credit in respect of the payment of dividends.

5.7 Foreign involvement

Stock companies can receive foreign investments and be involved in investments abroad.

Foreign investments in Spanish stock companies up to or over 50% of their capital require (as a general rule) the filing of a special form with the Exchange Authorities. Once this form has been cleared by said Authorities, the foreign currency can be sent to Spain. The bank receiving the foreign currency will then issue a document certifying the currency received which will be included among the notarial documents of foundation of the company.

Spanish companies should also request special authorisation from the Exchange Authorities to make investments abroad. In certain investments this authorisation is not required provided some conditions called for by law are met.

5.8 Acquisition and use of business assets and intellectual property rights

All assets contributed by the shareholders to the company become the property of the company. Likewise, assets bought or in any way acquired by the company also become the property of the company. The company can thus use freely such property.

It is recommended that in the case of intellectual property rights, these are made available to the company under licence rather than by outright transfer. This will avoid, inter alia, difficulties upon termination.

Upon liquidation, the assets of the company will either be sold or allocated to the shareholders. This means a new transfer of title to such properties, and the payment of transfer taxes.

5.9 Competition

The New Spanish Competition Law (hereinafter the 'Competition Law') was passed on 17th July, 1989. It is based both upon the Competition Law and Law 110/1963, of 20th July, 1963 on the Repression of Practices Restrictive of Competition (now superseded by the Competition Law.[12]

The Competition Law regulates joint ventures in four main chapters: (1) Prohibited anti-competitive practices; (2) Abuse of dominant position; (3) Unfair acts; and (4) Economic concentrations.

5.9.1 Prohibited anti-competitive practices

Article 1 of the Competition Law prohibits and declares void 'all agreements, decisions, collective recommendations or concerted or consciously parallel prac-

---

[12] Third paragraph of the preamble of the Competition Law.

tices which have as their purpose to produce or which may produce the effect of impeding restricting or falsifying competition in all or part of the national market'. Examples of such prohibited practices indicated in Article 1 paragraphs a to e include: price fixing, agreements on market shares or production quotas and tie-in clauses.[13]

As under EEC competition law, the Competition Law is applicable to all kinds of practices, without taking into consideration whether they are conducted by a party which does not have legal personality. Therefore, conduct resulting from a contractual joint venture, (i.e. a joint venture without legal personality), will also be caught by the Competition Law. The prohibition, as in Article 85 EEC Treaty, applies both to so-called horizontal agreements (agreements between undertakings at the same level of commercial activity, i.e., between competitors) and to vertical agreements, (agreements between undertakings at different levels of trade, for example, manufacturers and distributors.)

Although the Competition Law is not very clear on the point, it is thought that arrangements falling subject to article 1 will nevertheless be authorised where they are not capable of significantly affecting competition, provided that they are justified by the general economic situation or public interest.[14]

Article 2 of the Competition Law states that the prohibitions set out in Article 1 will not apply to agreements, decisions, recommendations and practices that result from the application of law or regulation.

Under the Competition Law, as under Article 85, EEC Treaty arrangements prima facie caught by the prohibition set out in Article 1 can be authorised (or "exempted") by the appropriate bodies when the practices involved contribute to the improvement of production or marketing of goods and services or promote technical or economic progress, provided that: (1) they allow consumers or users a sufficient share of such benefits; (2) they do not impose restrictions on the parties that are not indispensable to the achievement of their objectives; and (3) they do not afford the parties the possibility of eliminating competition in the whole or a substantial part of the market affected by the arrangements.[15] As under EEC competition law, the aforementioned conditions must be satisfied in order to get an individual exemption.

In addition, it will be possible to obtain an exemption for practices caught by Article 1 where they are justified by the general economic situation or the public interest so long as: (1) the purpose is to maintain or promote exports (to the extent that they are compatible with obligations that result from international treaties ratified by Spain); or (2) the purpose thereof is to align supply and demand; or (3) they would produce a sufficiently material rise in the social or economic level of depressed zones or sectors; or (4) due to their slight importance, they would not be capable of significantly affecting competition.[16]

---

[13] The article is almost identical to the first part of Article 85 of the EEC Treaty.
[14] *See* Article 3, paragraph (2), (d) of the Competition Law.
[15] *See* Article 3.1 of the Competition Law.
[16] *See* Article 3.2 of the Competition Law.

If the criteria for exemption from article 1 are met, the Court for the Defence of Competition (hereinafter the 'Court'), may grant an individual exemption for a defined period of time and subject, where appropriate, to terms and conditions. Exemption may only be obtained if the arrangements have been notified. An exemption will be deemed to have been granted if the Court fails to reach a decision within three months of receipt of a notification.

The Spanish Government is empowered to adopt certain bloc exemption regulations for the categories of agreement mentioned in Articles 3.1 and 3.2, with the collaboration of the Court. The bloc exemptions will resemble those existing under EC Law.

The Court may require those who perform practices mentioned in Article 1 to cease such acts and, if applicable, to eliminate the effects of such practices. The Court may impose fines of up to Ptas. 150,000,000 upon companies, associations, unions or groups who deliberately or negligently infringe the provisions of Article 1. This amount may be increased by up to 10% of the total volume of sales for the fiscal year preceding the Court's decision. The Competition Law in addition provides that when the infringement is committed by a legal entity, a fine of up to Ptas. 5,000,000 will be imposed on its legal representatives or the persons forming the administrative bodies that participated in the agreement or decision that restricted competition.

5.9.2 Abuse of dominant position

The Competition Law states that the abusive exploitation by one or more companies of their dominant position in all or part of the national market is prohibited. This prohibition will also apply to those cases in which the dominant position of one or various companies in the market has been established by law.

5.9.3 Unfair acts

Article 7 of the Competition Law states that the Court is competent to determine, on the terms established by the Competition Law regarding prohibited conduct, those acts of unfair competition which affect the public interest by falsifying, in an appreciable manner, free competition in all or part of the national market.

5.9.4 Economic concentrations

All transactions involving the concentration of companies or the assumption of control of one or various companies by one or more other persons, company(s) or groups of companies, that affects or could affect the Spanish market, especially through the creation or reinforcement of a dominant position, may be referred to the Court by the Ministry of Economy and Finance for its report:

(1) when as a result of the concentration the target's market share in the relevant goods or services becomes equal to or exceeds 25% of the national market or a substantial part thereof; or (2) when the volume of the target's sales in Spain surpasses, in the preceding fiscal year, Ptas. 20,000,000,000.

Concentrations may be voluntarily notified to the Ministry by any of the parties, prior to or within three months of its implementation. Prior notification does not either require the suspension of the performance of the concentration before its express or tacit authorisation. However, the concentration will remain, in any case, subject to the power of the Government which could decide that the concentration is contrary to the law and order appropriate measures to ensure that effective competition is established, including divestment, the cessation of control and the imposition of fines of up to 10% of the parties' volume of sales in Spain.[17]

5.10 Summary

The best vehicle for a joint venture established to carry out a large business undertaking is a stock company ('sociedad anómnima'). A general familiarity with the structure exists not only in Spain but also abroad.

---

[17] *See* Articles 15.1, 17. c.2. and 18 of the Competition Law.

CHAPTER 7

Swiss joint ventures

1. GENERAL INTRODUCTION

The term 'joint venture'[1] covers a variety of cooperation arrangements between two or more parties[2] for a common project or enterprise. There is no body of law that specifically covers the formation or operation of joint ventures; accordingly, there is no statutory definition of the term 'joint venture'.[3] Most rules on the formation and operation of a joint venture are found in the Swiss Code of Obligations ('CO') which covers the contractual as well as company law aspects of joint ventures. Tax law, intellectual property law and certain governmental regulations[4] often have a major impact on the choice of the legal structure of a joint venture. Restrictions of Swiss competition law may also apply; but these rules are of minor importance compared to other jurisdictions.

Swiss law allows basically two forms for a joint venture: the contractual joint venture and the joint venture company.[5] Formation of a partnership or a limited partnership is generally excluded because Swiss law requires that the general partners (not, however, the limited partners) be natural persons.[6]

A Swiss joint venture which attracted considerable attention in recent years was the 'merger' between Sweden's ASEA and Switzerland's BBC. The two (listed) companies contributed all their electrotechnical operations (mostly subsidiaries) to a joint venture company (ABB Asea-Brown Boveri) in exchange for a 50% participation in the joint venture. ASEA and BBC thus became holding companies, their major asset being the shareholding in ABB.

[1] Swiss legal doctrine as well as the economic literature generally use the English term 'joint venture'; sometimes, authors use the German term 'Gemeinschaftsunternehmen' for corporate joint ventures.
[2] Partners are usually corporations but it is conceivable that one of the parties to a joint venture might be e.g. a contractual joint venture, i.e. not a legal entity.
[3] *See* Claude Reymond, Le contrat de 'Joint Venture', Innominatverträge, Festgabe zum 60. Geburtstag von Walter R. Schluep (Zurich 1988), p. 383 *et seq*; Matthias Oertle, Das Gemeinschaftsunternehmen (Joint Venture) im schweizerischen Recht (Zurich 1990) p. 2 *et seq*.
[4] E.g. in certain regulated businesses (such as banking and insurance) or with respect to working permits for foreign employees.
[5] Some authors restrict the term joint venture to corporate joint ventures.
[6] Article 552 and 594.2 CO.

2.   CONTRACTUAL JOINT VENTURES

2.1   Introduction

Contractual joint ventures are subject to Articles 539 to 551 CO,[7] but the parties may contract out of most of these rules.

Contractual joint ventures are chosen in cases where no permanent structure is required or where flexibility is a key element for the success of the joint venture. Tax considerations may influence the decision as to the legal form as well.

A common example of a contractual joint venture is a consortium, formed for a construction project.[8]

2.2   Advantages

(i) *Ease of formation.* No formal procedure needs to be observed for the constitution of a contractual joint venture. The contract can be concluded orally although parties will usually enter into a written agreement. No capital has to be put up for the joint venture and no formal management structure is required.

(ii) *Flexibility in operation.* Joint venturers can simply change their contractual agreement in order to adapt to new circumstances. By contrast, a joint venture company will be less flexible in operation, in particular with respect to the provision of funding by means of additional subscriptions for equity.[9]

(iii) *Ease of termination.* There is – again contrary to the corporate joint venture – no formal procedure which has to be observed for the termination of a contractual joint venture.

(iv) *Tax transparency.* The contractual joint venture is not subject to any taxation and offers total tax transparency. Profits and losses accrue directly to the partners.

(v) *Confidentiality.* The contractual joint venture offers complete secrecy to the joint venturers if such secrecy is desired. Parties could even choose a form under which only one party to the contractual joint venture deals with third parties, the other parties being undisclosed partners.

---

[7] So-called 'einfache Gesellschaft' or 'société simple', often translated as 'ordinary partnership' as opposed to the general partnership of art. 552 to 593 CO. As seen above the latter form is generally not suitable for a joint venture in Switzerland, *see* § 1 at footnote 6.

[8] Reymond, op. cit., p. 385, points out that the majority of the cases cited under the heading 'joint ventures' in the Yearbook for Commercial Arbitration concern contractual joint ventures. Of course, one could argue that this is no indication as to the number of contractual joint ventures versus corporate joint ventures, but is rather due to the fact that contractual joint ventures do not offer a secure structure for the parties.

[9] Under Swiss law it is not possible to have (as for example in the UK) an 'authorised' share capital which would permit the issue of additional equity up to the authorised maximum. Instead, every increase in equity will require an amendment to the jvc's by-laws.

(vi) *Costs.* The absence of a formal structure and certain tax advantages generally lead to lower costs in a contractual joint venture as opposed to a joint venture company.

2.3 Disadvantages

(i) *Liability.* There is no limited liability for the parties (or 'partners') of a contractual joint venture; they may even become liable for debts[10] incurred by other partners of the joint venture.[11]

(ii) *External relationships, funding.* Third parties will often find it difficult to deal with a contractual joint venture as they will prefer to deal with one specific contractual party, preferably a legal entity. This is even more so if parties to a joint venture are based abroad. Funding will generally only be available for the joint venturers and not to the joint venture itself.

(iii) *Lack of permanent structure.* While parties may prefer the flexibility that a contractual joint venture offers, third parties are likely to point out that only a corporate joint venture guarantees the permanent structure necessary for a long-term business relationship. The lack of a permanent structure will, in addition, make it difficult for the joint venturers to define the rights and obligations between them.

(iv) *Limited ability to transfer contractual interest.* Swiss law does not allow the transfer of a stake in an ordinary partnership (which typically will include a contractual joint venture) without the consent of the other partners.[12] Even where there is such consent, the withdrawing partner will remain liable for debts of the joint venture for two years following the date of transfer of his share.[13]

2.4 When to select

A contractual joint venture should be chosen for short-term projects or projects which do not require a permanent structure. Common examples would be the formation of a consortium for a given project or joint research and development in a specified field.

Cost considerations may be a further reason to prefer a contractual joint venture to a corporate structure.[14]

---

[10] There is only liability for debts which have been incurred on behalf of the joint venture.
[11] *See* Article 544 CO. A contractual joint venture generally qualifies as a so-called ordinary partnership (defined as combination of two or more persons with a view to the attainment of a common goal through joint endeavours and resources).
[12] Article 542 CO.
[13] Article 181 CO.
[14] A partnership is generally excluded under Swiss law, *see* § 1 above at footnotes 5–7.

2.5   Formation documents, key aspects

As indicated above, there is no legal requirement for any formal documentation. Rules of the CO will fill gaps not covered by the agreement between the parties. Generally, the following issues are likely to be addressed by parties entering into a contractual joint venture.

(i) *Name*. Under Swiss law, a contractual joint venture cannot carry a registered corporate name.[15] On the other hand, the joint venture can appear under a name or label freely chosen by the parties.

A contractual joint venture cannot be registered in the commercial register.

(ii) *Purpose and scope*. The purpose and scope of the joint venture will define the parameters within which the partners may act on behalf of the joint venture. Consequently, the partners may have an interest in agreeing on a rather narrow definition.

(iii) *Funding, contributions*. Article 531 CO states that – unless agreed otherwise – each partner must make a contribution, either in cash, assets or in the form of services in order to achieve the agreed purpose of the business. If the partners transfer assets to the business, these will be jointly owned by the partners, because the joint venture is not a legal entity (*see also* § 2.8 infra).

Article 537 CO states that each partner has the right to be reimbursed for all expenditure incurred by him on behalf of the joint venture. However (unless agreed otherwise), a partner will have no claim for compensation for work performed. Despite the lack of an automatic entitlement to compensation, each partner is responsible to all other partners for losses resulting from his acts or omissions.

(iv) *Management, decision-making and power to deal with third parties*. The contractual arrangement will generally define which partner will be in charge of the management of the contractual joint venture. If there is no express agreement on the point, Article 535 CO applies, which states that each partner may act on behalf of the business but that the other partners have a right to veto any act prior to its completion.

If the contract confers the right to manage the joint venture on one (or more) partners, the others may (according to the mandatory rule of Article 539.2 CO) revoke such power for 'important reasons'.[16]

A partner not entrusted with the management has certain statutory rights to inspect the books and correspondence of the business.[17]

Decisions by the partners must generally be taken unanimously; however,

---

[15] Protection for the name of the joint venture may however be available under the Unfair Competition Act of December 19, 1986. This statute offers a remedy that is broadly similar to the UK law of 'passing off' – i.e. the joint venturers may be able to prevent a third party from trading under a name that as a result of its similarity (to that employed by the joint venture) is likely to cause confusion in the minds of the public.

[16] Article 539.3 CO defines important reasons as a major breach of the duties of the managing partner or a loss of the partner's ability to manage the business.

[17] Article 541 CO.

the contract may provide for the possibility of a majority vote on certain issues. Parties are likely to agree that – as a means of minority protection – certain transactions require the consent of all partners involved (*see* § 3.5.viii infra).

When dealing with third parties, each managing partner may conclude contracts which are binding upon the other partners of the joint venture, according to the rules of agency.[18] All partners will be jointly and severally liable in respect of such third party dealings.

(v) *Profit and loss allocation.* Article 532 CO provides that each partner must share any benefit that 'by its nature belongs to the joint venture'. Article 533 CO provides that – unless otherwise stipulated in the contract – each partner will share equally all profits and losses without regard to their respective contributions. The law furthermore states that if the parties only allocate profits, losses are to be borne in the same proportions.

(vi) *Non-competition.* Article 536 CO states that no partner shall do business for his own account which would prejudice the purpose of the joint venture. It is therefore not necessary to include an express non-competition clause in the contract.[19] This is an aspect of a Swiss contractual joint venture that is often appreciated by foreign partners who are reluctant to include express clauses restricting competition due to restraints imposed by their domestic competition law.

(vi) *Confidentiality.* Partners will often agree to treat certain information received with regard to the business and affairs of other partners as confidential.

(viii) *Transfer of interest.* Swiss law does not provide for the transfer of a stake in a contractual joint venture from one party to another. A transfer would require a liquidation of the old joint venture, followed by the creation of a new joint venture with different partners.

(ix) *Duration and termination.* Parties often agree on a certain duration for the agreement because Article 546 CO provides that the contract may be cancelled at 6 months notice if the agreement has been entered into for an indefinite duration.

The law provides for a termination of the agreement: (i) if the purpose of the joint venture has been attained or has become unattainable; (ii) in the event of the death or bankruptcy of a partner; (iii) by mutual consent; (iv) by decision of a court if there are valid reasons to dissolve the joint venture.

If the joint venture is dissolved, partners have no entitlement to receive back the assets originally contributed by them; there is, however, a right to claim the value of the contributions; unless the parties agree otherwise (possibly already in the joint venture agreement), assets will therefore be sold upon dissolution.

The dissolution of the joint venture does not affect the liability of the partners towards third parties.[20]

---

[18] *See* Article 543 and 544 CO for details.
[19] A breach of this implied non-competition covenant would lead to a claim for damages (but not necessarily to an account of profits made by the partner wrongfully 'competing').
[20] Article 551 CO.

2.6 Taxation

A contractual joint venture is not taxed as such and is fully tax transparent unless the joint venture qualifies as a permanent establishment.[1] Losses of the joint venture may therefore be offset against the income of the partners.

2.7 Foreign involvement

There are generally no limitations on foreign involvement in a Swiss contractual joint venture. Rules restricting foreign ownership of Swiss real estate and regulations on employment by foreign nationals may, however, have an impact upon a contractual joint venture in Switzerland (*see* § 3.7 for details).

2.8 Acquisition and use of business assets and intellectual property rights

Article 531.3 CO specifically mentions the possibility of transferring assets to the business (respectively into joint ownership, *see* § 2.5 (iii) supra) or the leasing of assets to the joint venture.

Intellectual property rights are hardly ever transferred to a contractual joint venture because of the complicated formalities to be observed. Parties may, however, agree upon a licence between a partner and the contractual joint venture.

If the joint venture is likely to create intellectual property rights, parties should choose the form of a corporate joint venture (*see* § 3). The contractual joint venture, lacking an independent legal identity, is an inappropriate structure for the creation and holding of intellectual property rights. If parties do choose a corporate joint venture form, however, they must be aware that intellectual property rights (with the exception of copyrights) created by employees of the joint venture will belong to their employer and not the joint venture company.[2] Parties must therefore agree that the other partner in the joint venture either obtains joint ownership or a licence to use the rights.

2.9 Competition

Contractual joint venture agreements may limit competition in certain areas. Swiss competition law does not, however, outlaw such agreements unless third parties are either excluded from competition or considerably hindered from

---

[1] In such a case the parties will become liable to cantonal and federal taxes in the domicile of the permanent establishment (the definition of permanent establishment used in Switzerland – even in domestic cases – is substantially equivalent to the definition in the OECD model double taxation convention). If taxes are lower in the place of the permanent establishment than in the domicile of the partners, the parties may prefer to have the income of the joint venture taxed separately in such place.

[2] *See* Article 332 CO.

competing. Joint venturers may even then claim that there are overriding interests justifying the agreement (*see* § 3.9 infra for details).

2.10 Summary

The contractual joint venture allows great flexibility and is mostly used for short-term projects. The statutory non-competition provision applying to contractual joint ventures is very often appreciated by foreign parties to a joint venture who might be reluctant to include non-competition clauses due to restraints imposed by their domestic competition law. Tax transparency may be a further reason to choose a contractual joint venture.

Because Swiss law does not allow corporate entities to form partnerships,[3] the contractual structure is always chosen when a corporate joint venture is excluded for cost reasons.

3. CORPORATE JOINT VENTURES

3.1 Introduction

Swiss joint venture companies are generally organised as corporations limited by shares,[4] regulated by Articles 620 to 763 CO. The company with limited liability[5] is hardly ever chosen,[6] mostly because of the lack of confidentiality[7] and the formalities to be observed in the event of a transfer of shares.[8]

In contrast to the contractual joint venture, the joint venture company (hereinafter 'jvc') is an independent legal entity with distinct and separate interests from those of its members and shareholders (the 'joint venturers'). The relationship between the joint venturers is generally governed by a shareholders' agreement. The provisions of the shareholders' agreement could also be incorporated in the articles of association of the jvc, but parties are usually reluctant to do so, mainly because the articles of association: (i) can only be changed by means of a formal procedure;[9] and (ii) may be inspected by anyone at the commercial register.

---

[3] *See* § 1 at footnote 6; corporate entities may be limited partners in a partnership, but at least one *natural* person must act as a general partner.

[4] In German 'Aktiengesellschaft' (abbreviated 'AG'), in French 'Société Anonyme' (abbreviated 'SA').

[5] 'Gesellschaft mit beschränkter Haftung' ('GmbH'), 'Société à responsabilité limitée' ('Sarl'), Articles 772 to 827 CO.

[6] The equity of a company with limited liability may furthermore not exceed Sfr. 2,000,000 (Article 773 CO).

[7] Article 790 CO. A list of the shareholders must be deposited with the commercial register and is publicly available for inspection. The transfer of the shares must be published in the commercial gazette.

[8] The shares (respectively the 'parts' or 'quotas' as the law calls them) can only be transferred by means of a notorised deed of assignment to be made in a public deed.

[9] A shareholders' meeting must pass the respective resolutions, a notarised deed must be drawn up and changes must be notified to the commercial register.

The shareholders' agreement may be signed prior or subsequently to the formation of the jvc; in the former case, the agreement may also address the formation of the jvc. Joint ventures can also be formed by means of a subscription for new shares or transfer of shares in an existing company. The special aspects of such a jvc (and its contractual basis) are not specifically dealt with in the text that follows. The documentation for such structures is rather similar to that where a new jvc is formed. The principal difference lies in the fact that the 'old' partner will typically be required to give warranties and representations with respect to the company to his new partner(s) upon the subscription for or transfer of the shares.

3.2   Advantages

(i) *Ease of formation*: A Swiss jvc is relatively easy to incorporate, the process taking no more than two to three weeks. Counsel will often advise the use of standard articles of association (since, *inter alia*, parties generally place all commercially sensitive provisions in the shareholders' agreement)[10] which adds to the ease of formation.

(ii) *Separate entity*. The fact that the jvc is a distinct legal entity enhances the stability of the joint venture structure; this has advantages for the joint venturers for their relationships *inter se* as well as in the jvc's dealings with third parties. The ability to enter into contracts and to own property (including intellectual property rights) is a clear advantage over the contractual joint venture.

(iii) *Limited liability*. The liability of each joint venturer is limited to the amount subscribed in the share capital of the jvc.[11] However, a joint venturer will often not be able to take advantage of this limited liability, because: (a) the insolvency of the jvc will damage the standing of the joint venturer in the capital market, possibly also triggering cross default clauses in loans to the joint venturer; and (b) one or more joint venturers may have personally guaranteed the debts of the jvc.

(iv) *Transferability of interest*. Shares of the joint venturers can easily be transferred either to other joint venturers or to a third party.

(v) *Commercial understanding/familiarity*. Parties dealing with a corporate joint venture will undoubtedly find a structure that is more familiar than that of a contractual joint venture. Furthermore, a jvc will often appear as a 'domestic' company, even if it is controlled by foreign joint venturers. This may be especially helpful where the jvc bids for public works.

---

[10]   *See* § 3.1 supra and § 3.5 infra.

[11]   More precisely, if shares are not fully paid up, the shareholders remain liable for the balance owing on their shares. Because joint venturers will often make a contribution in kind, there may also be a liability if the contribution is overvalued, Article 753 CO.

   On the other hand, if the contribution is undervalued, or if the shareholders contribute more than the nominal share capital (a so-called 'agio' or surplus), this amount is not recoverable by the shareholders in the event of an insolvency.

(vi) *External finance.* A jvc is generally much better placed to deal with banks and other lenders than a contractual joint venture, where finance is usually provided by the joint venturers themselves.

3.3 Disadvantages

(i) *Formation and running costs.* A jvc has higher formation and running costs than a contractual joint venture. Attorney's fees, notarisation costs and registration fees usually amount to approximately Sfr. 5,000 – 10,000. There is furthermore a capital duty (referred to as 'stamp tax') of 3% payable on the issue of share capital.[12] The requirement for a board of directors, the costs of book-keeping and auditors must all be taken into consideration when comparing the running costs of a jvc to those of a contractual joint venture. Costs associated with the shareholders' agreement may be comparable to the costs of drafting and negotiating the agreement for a contractual joint venture.

(ii) *Termination.* The termination of a jvc is a formal procedure that involves – *inter alia* – the threefold publication of such intention to potential creditors in the *Swiss Commercial Gazette*. Assets of the company may only be distributed after the expiry of one year after the third publication.[13]

(iii) *Taxation.* The jvc is taxed as an independent entity; there is consequently no tax transparency. Dividends paid to the joint venturers[14] are subject to a 35% withholding tax which may be fully reclaimed by Swiss joint venturers, and partially – i.e. by virtue of double taxation treaties – by foreign joint venturers. Because Swiss tax law does not tax groups on a consolidated basis – but treats each corporation as an independent entity[15] – a joint venturer will be unable to set off a loss from the jvc againt other income.

(iv) *Lack of flexibility.* A jvc has to comply with certain minimum legal requirements, namely with respect to its share capital (at least Sfr. 50,000),[16] the payment of dividends,[17] and the internal organisation (book-keeping requirements, auditors, board of directors with a majority of Swiss citizens residing in Switzerland). A change in the capital structure or in the articles of association of the jvc will require a formal procedure.[18]

(v) *Lack of secrecy.* The disclosure requirements of Swiss companies are not stringent in comparison to other jurisdictions. However, certain requirements apply if the joint venturers contribute a business, know-how or certain assets to the jvc in exchange for shares.[19]

---

[12] Respectively on the fair market value of the consideration received if the joint venturers contribute their business.

[13] Certain exemptions may apply, Article 745.3 CO.

[14] Including constructive dividends, i.e. other distributions of assets that are treated as if they were a dividend.

[15] There is, however, a relief on dividends received by a parent company; see § 3.6 for details.

[16] Article 621 CO.

[17] Article 671 CO: The jvc must build up certain reserves.

[18] A shareholders' meeting in the presence of a notary public and the changes must be notified to the company registrar. *See* § 3.5 post.

[19] Article 628, 630, 636 CO. In essence the nature and value of the assets must be identified.

3.4   When to select

The jvc is almost always selected for a joint venture in Switzerland unless
the type of activity contemplated: (i) is of a short-term nature; or (ii) requires
little or no contact with third parties. Tax considerations may, however, lead
to a selection of a contractual joint venture.[20]

3.5   Formation documentation, key aspects

If the jvc is established for the purpose of cooperation between two (or more)
joint venturers, the latter will usually enter into a shareholders' agreement[1]
for the formation and the running of the jvc. Certain provisions of this agreement may be entered in the articles of association of the jvc (e.g. clauses regarding the transferability of the shares or the powers of the shareholders' meeting);
such incorporation in the articles of association has certain advantages over
a purely contractual arrangement (with standard articles of association), namely
with respect to third party rights;[2] third parties are deemed to have knowledge
of the contents of the articles of association; the principal disadvantage of
placing commercial terms in the articles of association lies in the fact that
clauses in the articles of association are open to public inspection; they can
furthermore only be changed by means of a formal procedure.[3] Standard
articles of association must include (Article 626 CO): (i) the corporate name
and the registered office of the company; (ii) an objects clause; (iii) the nominal
amount of the share capital and the number, type and nominal value of the
shares; (iv) the notice period for shareholders' meetings; (v) the manner in
which directors can enter into legal documents on behalf of the company;
(vi) the manner in which notices are communicated; and (vii) the number of
shares the directors must deposit with the company when in office (it is a
requirement of Swiss company law that directors be shareholders).

The following key aspects are likely to be addressed in the shareholders'
agreement (or in the articles of association).

(i) *Name and registered office of the jvc.* Certain rules apply under Swiss
law with respect to the names of companies: they must not be designed solely
for publicity purposes and must not deceive third parties. Parties sometimes
use a combination of their own names for the jvc;[4] often, the name will be

---

[20] *See* § 2.6 and § 3.6 for details.
[1] The term 'shareholders' agreement' is actually too narrow: when entering into the agreement,
the parties are not yet shareholders but plan to become shareholders of the jvc. It is maybe
for this reason that some authors prefer to refer to the contractual arrangement as the 'basic
contract' ('contrat de base'). The contents of shareholders' agreements vary widely in practice.
If the agreement is concluded prior to the formation of the jvc (which is generally the case)
a draft of the contemplated articles of association should be annexed to the agreement.
[2] Third parties are deemed to have knowledge of the articles of association since they are placed
on the commercial register and third parties have unrestricted access to their terms.
[3] A shareholders' meeting must be convened. Generally a simple voting majority is required
although the bye-laws may specify otherwise: Art 698 CO.
[4] E.g. ABB Asea-Brown Boveri AG.

registered in German, French, Italian and English (X AG/SA/Ltd). The registered office does not have to coincide with the location of the company's headquarters and is often chosen as a result of tax considerations. However, if the business is conducted in a location other than that of the registered office, the business will generally qualify as a permanent establishment in such location and will therefore be subject to taxation there and not (or only to a certain extent) at the company's headquarters.

(ii) *Objects clause of the jvc.* The purpose clause limits the scope of activity that the jvc may engage in. Sometimes the clause is drafted as widely as possible (and thus rendered practically meaningless) in order to allow an expansion into other areas of business. Sometimes the clause is very narrowly drafted in order to ensure that the jvc limits itself to clearly defined activities. After the formation of the company the purpose clause can only be changed if the holders of two-thirds of the share capital agree.[5]

(iii) *Share capital, number and type of shares.* The articles of association must contain a provision regarding the amount of the share capital. The minimum share capital is Sfr. 50,000 – 20,000 of which must be fully paid-up. The share capital is usually divided into shares of Sfr. 1,000 each.[6] The joint venturers usually agree to issue registered shares, although the law also allows bearer shares.[7] The articles of association may limit the transferability of registered shares, e.g. by granting the board of directors or the shareholders' meeting the right to refuse to enter the acquirer into the shareholders' register.[8]

Swiss law also allows the use of different classes of shares, e.g. 'A' shares and 'B' shares, entitling the holders of each type of share to propose a number of directors for election at the shareholders' meeting.[9] The shareholders' meeting may then only refuse to elect the proposed director for 'valid reasons'.[10]

Parties may furthermore agree to create shares with super voting or dividend rights,[11] or shares without voting rights, so-called participation certificates. These differing share structures can be used to reflect and reward differing contributions made to the jvc by the joint venturers.

A subsequent change in the share capital necessitates approval by the shareholders. Shareholders have a statutory option to purchase newly issued share capital *pro rata* to their existing shareholding at the issue price fixed by the

---

[5] Article 648 CO. This rule is mandatory, i.e. the articles of association may not lower this threshold.

[6] The minimal nominal value is Sfr. 100.

[7] Note that the transfer of 'bearer' shares cannot be controlled. Like a £1 note, possession alone confers title. There will be no register of holders of bearer shares – the identity of holders will be unknown.

[8] Article 686 CO.

[9] Article 708.5 CO.

[10] Such valid reasons would, for example, exist if the proposed director did not have the necessary professional experience or background. *See also* § 3.5. (vii) *infra.*

[11] Shares with super voting rights can only be issued by creating shares with a different nominal value (e.g. shares with a nominal value of Sfr. 100 and Sfr. 500) and giving each share one vote. In other words, super voting rights can only be achieved by increasing the number of shares and therefore available votes. Shares with super dividend rights are regulated by Articles 654 to 656 CO.

board of directors. This option may be waived (for all shareholders) by a majority vote.

(iv) *Subscription of the joint venturers to share capital.* This clause will address the amount of equity each joint venturer takes in the jvc. Often, the joint venturers will contribute a business, intellectual property rights, know-how or other assets to the jvc. In such cases, the parties will need to agree upon a valuation of these contributions. Parties may agree to give warranties and representations as to title, value and condition of the contributions either to their fellow joint venturers and/or to the jvc.

If there is to be a contribution in kind (or if the shares are subscribed for cash, but there is an understanding that the jvc will purchase certain assets from a shareholder) there are disclosure requirements in the articles of association that must be complied with; the board of directors must, in addition, draw up a report on the nature, condition and adequacy of the contribution.[12]

(v) *Transferability of shares.* The transferability of shares in a jvc is often restricted. Swiss law specifically allows such restrictions to be incorporated in the articles of association. If the acquirer and seller do not abide by these rules, the acquirer will not be entered into the shareholders' register and will not be able to vote his shares in a shareholders' meeting.[13] Often, the articles of association of a jvc will demand that a majority – of say 80% – of the shareholders agree to any given transfer. Such a clause can in practice confer a power of veto upon each joint venturer with respect to a proposed transfer. A right of first refusal is also often used in joint venture agreements.[14] Sometimes, these agreements will even provide that the remaining partners may purchase the shares at book value if one party intends to sell its shares to a third party. There are various means by which a right of first refusal can be secured *vis-à-vis* third parties. Such measures are necessary where the right is placed in a shareholders' agreement but not the bye-laws since in such circumstances third parties will not have notice of the restriction and will not be bound by a transfer of shares in breach of the contractual agreement between the joint venturers. Perhaps the most common solution to this dilemma is to place the shares of all joint venturers in escrow with a trusted third party. The terms of the escrow arrangements will provide, *inter alia*, that no shares can be transferred unless they have first been offered to existing shareholders.

The agreement sometimes contains also a 'take-me-along' clause that requires a joint venturer willing to sell his stake to seek a purchaser for the shares of all other joint venturers.

(vi) *Future funding.* Swiss tax law generally requires that the debt-equity ratio does not exceed 6:1.[15] If loans are granted by shareholders, tax authorities furthermore define a maximum interest rate. Tax considerations will often force

---

[12] Article 630 CO. The disclosure covers a list of all assets contributed, the method and appropriateness of valuation, the number of shares, the contributing shareholder received.

[13] Articles 685/6 CO.

[14] In the sense that a shareholder wishing to transfer his shares must first offer them to the club of existing joint venture shareholders. Such rights may also be found in the articles of association.

[15] If the ratio is exceeded, the tax authorities will not recognise the deduction of interest payments.

the joint venturers to consider further equity funding for the jvc, even though such funding is subject to a 3% capital duty. Generally, the joint venturers will agree in the shareholders' agreement to subscribe for newly issued share capital under certain conditions, for example, to make up losses incurred by the jvc.[16]

Financing by third parties (namely banks) is often only possible if the joint venturers guarantee repayment of the loan. Such a guarantee clearly increases the personal exposure of the joint venturers and alters fundamentally the limited liability aspect of the jvc.

The parties may also raise finance through the issue by the jvc of non-voting shares (so-called 'participation certificates') to third parties. Such shares carry dividend rights and an entitlement to future liquidation proceeds.

(vii) *Constitution of the board of directors.* The number of board members is usually defined in the articles of association. Swiss law requires that a majority of the directors be Swiss citizens residing in Switzerland.[17] Sometimes the articles of association provide for two classes of shares (e.g. 'A' shares and 'B' shares) giving the holders of each class the right to propose a number of directors.[18] Swiss law does require that the shareholders' meeting formally elects these board members; the shareholders' meeting may refuse to elect a proposed board member only, though, if there are valid reasons for doing so.[19] The law provides further that the right of the shareholders' meeting to remove directors from office at any time cannot be waived by contractual arrangements.[20]

The joint venture agreement often contains detailed rules as to the election of the president and the vice-president of the board. Contrary to the practice in other companies,[1] the articles of association of a jvc often provide for an election of the president by the shareholders. The articles of association (or the shareholders' agreement) may also define the minimum number of directors necessary to form a quorum and may furthermore address the question of whether or not the president will have a casting vote. The articles of association or the shareholders' agreement are finally likely to limit the types of transaction that the board can enter into without shareholders' approval (see below).[2] If the board issues regulations as to the frequency, quorum and other administrative aspects of its meetings and with respect to the rights of its members to enter into legal documents on behalf of the jvc, such regulations are usually made conditional upon approval by the shareholders meeting.

---

[16] There is a statutory option under Swiss law to subscribe for newly issued shares, Article 652 CO. This option can be waived by a majority vote in a shareholders' meeting.
[17] Article 711 CO. An exception applies to holding companies.
[18] *See also* § 3.5 (iii) for the possibility of shares with super voting rights.
[19] *See* supra.
[20] *See* Article 705 CO.
[1] Where the board constitutes itself.
[2] Such restrictions will usually not be binding upon third parties.

The parties may also agree on the manner in which directors and officers may execute agreements that bind the jvc.[3]

It should be noted in this context that directors are personally liable for damages caused by their unlawful conduct (including a breach of their fiduciary duty towards the jvc). Directors may find themselves in a conflict between the interests of 'their' joint venturer and the interests of the jvc; if their decision is solely made in favour of the joint venturer, they may become personally liable.[4]

(viii) *Minority protection.* Minority protection in a typical joint venture agreement is achieved by requiring approval by: (i) either both (or all) parties; or (ii) by all board members for a range of transactions specified in the shareholders' agreement. Such transactions typically include:

- The hiring of senior management;
- Loan agreements exeeding a certain threshold;
- Contracts outside the ordinary course of business;
- Contracts with a joint venturer or a party associated with a joint venturer;
- Capital expenditure exceeding a certain amount;
- The sale of important business assets.

A change in the articles of association will often require a special quorum (e.g. 80%).

(ix) *Deadlock devices.* Especially in 50:50 joint ventures, the parties may agree on certain deadlock devices for cases where the articles of association or the shareholders' agreement require approval by both parties and they fail to reach agreement. Parties sometimes agree to a form of arbitration procedure, in which each party may elect an additional board member who will in turn propose a third member. The newly composed board of directors will then decide the issue. Alternatively, some agreements provide that one party will prevail on certain questions in one year, while the other will in the next. Some agreements state also that if the parties fail to agree, the jvc must be wound up, or that so-called 'Russian Roulette' clauses will apply. Under Russian Roulette clauses, one party will need to specify the price at which it is willing to purchase or sell the shares to the other party. The other party may then choose to acquire or dispose of the shares at that price. This mechanism is destined to ensure that the shares change hands at a fair price.

(x) *Auditors.* A Swiss jvc must have auditors. Parties will generally choose a well-known, possibly international, accounting firm for this task.

(xi) *Termination.* The shareholders' agreement (or the articles of association)

---

[3] It is common that the articles of association provide that not less than two signatures of directors are required.
[4] Of course, in such circumstances the joint venturer would have to indemnify a director who was ordered to act in a certain manner.

may provide for a number of instances where the jvc must be dissolved.[5] Generally, shareholders must decide on the liquidation of the company in a shareholders' meeting. The meeting will also elect liquidators, who will – among other duties – have to publish three notices to creditors in which creditors are asked to file any claims they might have. Generally, the proceeds of the liquidation may only be distributed to the shareholders one year after publication of the last of the three notices to creditors.[6]

(xii) *Non-competition*. Parties will usually undertake not to compete with the business of the jvc. Under Swiss competition law it will generally be possible to give such an undertaking.[7]

(xiii) *Confidentiality*. Parties often undertake to keep confidential all information relating to the business of the jvc and relating to the business and affairs of other joint venturers.

(xiv) *Contractual arrangements with joint venturers*. Parties will often require that all joint venturers consent to agreements between the jvc and one of the joint venturers. According to the specific circumstances, the parties may also undertake to provide certain services to the jvc.

(xv) *Use of intellectual property rights created*[8] *by the jvc*. Parties will generally agree that the jvc will grant free of charge licences to the joint venturer unless there are competition considerations to be taken into account.

(xvi) *Dividend policy*. The dividend policy of a jvc is typically interrelated with the question of future funding and the abstraction of profits. Swiss companies generally have a policy of paying out only a small portion of their net income in order to finance 'internally' expansion into new areas. Tax considerations (in particular, withholding tax) may also lead to a low pay-out ratio.

(xvii) *Costs*. Formation costs of the jvc will generally be borne by the jvc; the respective costs are often capitalised and written off over a period of 5 years.[9]

(xviii) *Applicable law, jurisdiction*. In an international context, it is necessary to specify the law applicable to the shareholders' agreement. Generally, the parties select the law of the country where the jvc is domiciled. But other solutions are conceivable, e.g. if two German companies form a jvc in Switzerland: in such a case, parties are likely to specify that German law covers their

---

[5] Article 736 CO states four reasons for dissolving a company: (i) reasons enumerated in the articles of association (ii) bankruptcy (iii) judgement if shareholders representing 20% of the share capital demand liquidation in the event of the oppression of a minority (such cases are very rare) and (iv) in certain special cases, such as if the company fails to elect a board of directors.

[6] A judge may allow an earlier distribution, Article 745.3 CO.

[7] *See* § 3.9 infra on competition law aspects.

[8] Technically, employees will create such intellectual property rights which may – by operation of law or by contract – be passed to the jvc.

[9] Article 664 CO.

relationship.[10] Parties furthermore often agree on the jurisdiction of an arbitral tribunal in case of a dispute.

3.6 Taxation

A jvc is taxed just like any other Swiss company. In particular, the following taxes will be levied:

(i) *Stamp duty* (Securities Issuance Tax). There is a stamp duty of 3% on the nominal value of newly issued share capital. If there is a contribution in kind, the 3% is levied on the fair market value of such contribution. Under special circumstances, namely if the joint venturers both contribute parts of their business, the creation of a jvc qualifies as a reorganisation which lowers the tax rate to 1%. The debt – equity ratio must in such a case not exceed 1:1.[11]

(ii) *Corporate income tax*. Corporate income is taxed by the Federal Government and by the Cantons (States). The tax rate at the federal level is progressive and ranges from 3.63% to 9.8% of the income (after cantonal taxes). No exemptions or deductions are granted for foreign source income except if derived from a permanent establishment or real estate located abroad. Cantons each have their own tax laws which vary with respect to tax base, tax period and tax rates. Whereas the maximum income tax rate in the Canton of Zug amounts to approximately 12% of net income, other Cantons may charge income taxes of more than 30%. In contrast to the federal government, many Cantons grant a privileged tax treatment to foreign-controlled companies which mainly generate foreign source income (*see also* (iv) below for holding companies and dividends received from subsidiaries).

(iii) *Capital tax*. The federal capital tax is annually levied at a rate of 0.0825% of shareholders' equity. Capital tax levied by the Cantons varies (generally 0.3 to 0.6% per year).

(iv) *Special rules for holding companies*. Income received from subsidiaries of a jvc is generally tax free due to an intercompany dividend received exemption; there are also reduced capital taxes on such companies at the Cantonal level.

(v) *Group relief*. There is no group relief under Swiss law; losses of a jvc may therefore not be offset agaist other income of a joint venturer. However, as stated above, there is an exemption on dividends received by holding companies.

---

[10] However, the parties will need to seek advice from a Swiss lawyer whether their agreement is in conformity with mandatory provisions under Swiss law.
[11] As opposed to 6:1 under 'normal' circumstances.

3.7 Foreign involvement

There are no rules prohibiting foreign involvement in a Swiss jvc; however, certain rules and regulations apply.

(i) *Regulated businesses.* Certain regulated businesses – namely banks – need a special permit or licence if they are controlled by foreigners.

(ii) *Exchange control.* There are as a general rule no restrictions on capital transactions between Switzerland and other countries. The Swiss National Bank may, however, regulate the country's money supply and implement credit and currency policies. While foreign entities who want to raise capital in the Swiss market must seek approval by the Swiss National Bank,[12] a Swiss jvc would generally not require such permission. The sale of any type of securities issued by Swiss companies may be prohibited by the Swiss Government under certain circumstances. Such prohibition was in force in 1978 in order to maintain a certain exchange rate level of the Swiss franc.[13] No such rules are currently in force.

(iii) *Other restrictions on foreign investment.* Non-residents may acquire all types of domestic assets or shares in domestic companies without obtaining special approval with the exception of (i) companies engaged in certain regulated businesses (such as banking or insurance) and (ii) real property or companies that hold real property (see below for details). The contribution of a business to a jvc that needs a licence (or a concession) to operate (i.e. a business involved in transportation, the health sector or the import of certain agricultural goods) may be subject to approval by the competent authorities.

(iv) *Rules regarding the acquisition of real property by foreigners.* The Federal Law on the Acquisition of Real Property by Foreigners of December 16, 1983 (usually referred to as the Lex Friedrich) limits not only the acquisition of real property but also the purchase of shares or the participation in companies which own real property.[14] The Lex Friedrich applies to a purchase or subscription of shares in a jvc that owns real property only if (i) the purchaser is a foreigner, a foreign corporation or a Swiss corporation which is controlled by foreigners, (ii) such purchaser obtains or re-enforces a controlling position (the test for such control is met – *inter alia* – if foreign ownership exceeds one third of all shares), and (iii) the market value of the real property is more than one-third of the market value of the total assets of the jvc. Unless the value is clearly below this threshold, the purchaser must seek a decision of the competent authorities that the Lex Friedrich is not applicable to the purchase of the shares. If the value of the real property exceeds one third of the total assets, the foreign joint venturer must seek the approval of the competent authorities to purchase a controlling interest. Such authorisation is granted if the real property is necessary for the corporation to conduct its business (e.g. for manufacturing purposes or to meet office space requirements). The

---

[12] This permission is generally granted.
[13] Article 16i I.3 of the Federal Law on the National Bank.
[14] As further defined in Article 4 Lex Friedrich and Article 1 of the implementing ordinance.

authorisation will often only be granted under certain conditions such as a prohibition resale or a requirement that the shares be deposited with the competent Cantonal authorities or agencies. No authorisation will be granted if the real property is near a military installation or if the acquisition is considered contrary to the public interest. A purchase of shares in a company holding Swiss real estate without the necessary approval is considered null and void under the Lex Friedrich.

(v) *Rules on the employment of foreign nationals.* Switzerland imposes very strict limitations upon the grant of work permits to foreign employees. Each Canton has (according to the size of its economy) a yearly quota of working permits it may grant. If a foreign group enters into a Swiss joint venture, the jvc cannot expect to be staffed entirely with management from the home country of the joint venturer. However, working permits for top executives, skilled technicians and specialists essential to the establishment and the smooth operation of a business will usually be granted, subject however to the availability of such permits in that Canton.

3.8   Acquisition and use of business assets and intellectual property rights

Business assets are often transferred to the jvc. There are certain disclosure requirements[15] and tax consequences[16] if such a transfer is made in return for shares.[17] Parties may of course also consider leasing assets to the jvc; this not only avoids disclosure requirements but may also be advantageous from a tax perspective.

Intellectual property rights are often licensed rather than transferred to the jvc. If intellectual property rights are transferred outright, the jvc may need to enter into licence agreements with the joint venturers in order to allow them to continue to make use of their rights. However, competition considerations may render necessary an exclusive use of the intellectual property rights by the jvc. Intellectual property rights (with the exception of copyright) created by employees of the jvc belong – by operation of law – to the jvc.[18] In some instances the jvc will licence such rights to the shareholders.[19]

3.9   Competition law considerations

The Federal Law on Cartels[20] ('FLC') was revised on December 20, 1985 and came into force on July 1, 1986. In contrast to the national laws of most

---

[15] *See* § 3.5 (iv) supra.
[16] *See* § 3.6 (i) supra.
[17] Or against cash shortly after a capital increase against cash.
[18] Article 332 CO.
[19] *See* § 3.5 (xv).
[20] Cartels are, inter alia, defined as agreements, resolutions, or non-binding agreements which influence or are liable to influence the market for specific goods or services by means of a joint restriction of competition, especially by regulating the manufacturing, the sale and resale of goods or the prices or terms upon which they are offered.

European jurisdictions – and in particular Articles 85/86 of the EEC treaty – Swiss law in principle allows companies to enter into agreements that may restrict or distort competiton,[1] unless such agreements or measures exclude third parties from competition[2] or considerably hinder them from competing (Article 6 FLC), or have socially or economically detrimental consequences (Articles 29, 32 FLC). So-called quasi-cartel organisations – defined *inter alia* as undertakings with a dominant market position – are subject to the same regulations (Article 4 FLC). The shareholders' agreement or the jvc itself may therefore be subject to the FLC.

The Federal Cartel Commission ('the Commission'), the administrative agency responsible for the enforcement of the FLC, must investigate a merger or any other combination of enterprises (such as a joint venture)[3] if the combination leads to or enforces a dominant market position (i.e. qualifies as a quasi-cartel organisation) and (cumulatively) if there is an indication of economically or socially detrimental consequences as a result of such merger.[4] The Commission has so far only investigated one merger.[5]

The Commission can make preliminary inquiries (Article 28 FLC) which may lead to an informal settlement; it can also start formal investigations (Articles 29, 30 FLC). The Commission may then issue recommendations, (Article 32 FLC). If the parties concerned do not accept these recommendations (which are in essence non-binding) the Federal Economic Department ('FED') may issue orders.[6] The FED is responsible for monitoring whether parties comply with such orders or recommendations.

It is important to note in the present context that neither the Commission nor the FED have the power to order the divestiture or break-up of a jvc. There are no criminal penalties provided for in the FLC for hindering third parties from competing.[7]

Third parties who are excluded from competition (or considerably hindered from competing) may claim damages or other appropriate relief.

Article 137 of the new Federal Statute on Private International Law of December 18, 1987 (which entered into force on January 1st, 1989) provides that claims arising out of the hindrance of competition are subject to the law of the market place in which such hindrance took effect. The FLC could there-

---

[1] The so-called principle of abuse prevention.
[2] Elimination of competition is occurring when existing competitors are forced out of the market or when potential competitors are prevented from participating in this market.
[3] *See* Schuermann/Schluep, Kartellgesetz, Preisüberwachungsgesetz, Zürich 1988, p. 697.
[4] Legal commentators point out that the provision as enacted is not very meaningful: if the newly created entity qualifies as a cartel-like organisation (which produces the detrimental consequences mentioned in Article 30 FLC), the Commission may start an investigation anyway (Article 29, 32 FLC).
[5] An investigation was opened in the merger between Schindler Holding AG and Flug- und Fahrzeugwerke Altenrhein AG in 1987. No results have been published yet. Preliminary inquiries were started in several mergers in 1988 but the Commission concluded in all these cases that there were no economically or socially detrimental consequences.
[6] Such orders may be appealed to the Federal Supreme Court in Lausanne.
[7] There are criminal penalties if recommendations accepted by the parties or orders issued by the FED are not observed.

fore theoretically apply to a foreign jvc.[8] The powers of the Commission are, however, limited to the territory of Switzerland.

Statutory defences vary slightly between the civil and administrative law parts of the FLC. A jvc that hinders third parties from competing may claim that legitimate interests justify its acts (Article 7 FLC). Defences to an investigation by the Commission may consist of claiming that the positive effects of the jvc for example, on costs, prices, quality, supply of goods or services, competitiveness of Swiss enterprises abroad or the interests of consumers or workers outweigh its harmful effects. The Commission must by law weigh these positive factors against the negative effects on competition of the arrangements. The law deems the exclusion (as opposed to mere hindrance) of third parties from competition as detrimental, unless there is an overriding benefit to the public interest.

3.10   Conclusions

The jvc has clear advantages over the contractual joint venture provided that the business project to be achieved justifies the higher formation and running costs. Foreign joint venturers will generally incorporate a jvc if they intend to do business in Switzerland.

---

[8] This provision presupposes that a Swiss court has jurisdiction. A Swiss company that is excluded from competition on the Swiss market by acts of foreign-based companies may, e.g., obtain jurisdiction if these companies have branch offices in Switzerland or if the claimant obtains an attachment (freezing order) on the assets of the foreign companies.

CHAPTER 8

UK joint ventures

1. GENERAL INTRODUCTION

With the exception of the European Economic Interest Grouping which pursuant to Commission Regulation 2137/85 became a part of the law of the United Kingdom ('UK') on July 1st 1989,[1] there exists neither a single body of UK law nor a distinct legal entity, dedicated to the formation and operation of joint ventures. Instead, a combination of legal disciplines, most conspicuously those comprising contract, taxation, company law, partnership law and competition law have served to govern the great variety of commercial relationships that fall under the term 'joint venture'.

Lacking a dedicated body of law and against a background of great variety in terms of implementation, it is perhaps not surprising that the term 'joint venture' confers no precise judicial meaning. For the purposes of the text that follows, we propose to by-pass much of the complex economic and legal debate and define a joint venture broadly as any arrangement between two or more unrelated parties to co-operate in the establishment and management of a commercial (including research and development) project or enterprise. Within that rather broad parameter, four basic joint venture structures can be identified in current UK law and practice:

(i)   contractual joint ventures (other than partnerships);
(ii)   partnership joint ventures;
(iii) limited partnership joint ventures; and
(iv)   joint venture companies or 'jvc's.

2. CONTRACTUAL JOINT VENTURES

2.1 Introduction

A contractual joint venture[2] is, as its title implies, entirely governed by contract but falls short of the carrying on of a business in common as required for a partnership. Unlike the partnership and jvc joint venture structures, the arrangement does *not* involve the establishment of an independent legal entity or 'vehicle' (for example the partnership 'firm' or the joint 'company') capable,

---

[1] *See* further, Chapter 1.
[2] They are also frequently referred to as co-operation agreements.

inter alia, of owning property, contracting in its own right with third parties, undertaking an independent business activity and acting as a profit centre. Instead, the parties define by means of one or more contracts between them the manner in which their joint objectives will be achieved. Given the absence of a joint venture vehicle in which the parties have respective equity interests, it is particularly important that the contractual arrangements between them address such matters as the ownership and rights to property generated or acquired by the contractual joint venture, the calculation and distribution of profits, which party (if any) will contract with third parties and the respective liability of the parties to such third parties. Often the line between a contractual joint venture and a partnership is a thin one as a partnership is also governed largely by the law of contract (*see* 2.3 (ii) below); however partnership normally requires both mutuality of interest and a desire to create profits whereas in the case of a contractual joint venture the parties may approach the project with quite distinct objectives or with a simple agreement to share the costs of an exercise which is beneficial to both. It must be appreciated however that in this chapter the term contractual joint venture is restricted to those contractual joint ventures which do not constitute partnerships.

2.2 Advantages

(i) *Ease of formation*. The lack of an independent vehicle and a body of law prescribing formalities that need to be observed in the formation of a contractual joint venture, ensure that such arrangements can be set in place simply and economically. The position can most clearly be contrasted with the formation of a jvc where the dictates of the Companies Act 1985 mean that the process of formation is more complex, time consuming and costly (*see* further paragraph 5.3(i) below).

(ii) *Ease of operation*. The absence of a dedicated body of law, coupled with the absence of an independent entity in which the parties have an equity interest, all mean that contractual joint ventures can be operated in a relatively informal and flexible manner. There is no entity to manage in the sense of a jvc or partnership, merely a commercial contract to adhere to. The position can, in particular, be contrasted with the jvc joint venture structure, where the dictates of the Companies Act 1985, for example, in respect of board meetings, general meetings and directors' duties, requires a much more formal administrative framework.

(iii) *Liability*. In a typical contractual joint venture, each member will be liable for his own acts and omissions. In contrast, under a partnership structure, each partner is liable to a third party not only for his own acts and omissions but also for the acts and omissions of all other partners (*see* further 3.3(i) below).

(iv) *Ease of termination*. Given that they are prescribed solely by contract and typically address a specific business project, contractual joint ventures are far easier to terminate than partnerships or jvcs. Lacking an independent vehicle, the problems of returning capital and other assets contributed by the parties are largely absent. Equally, there are no statutory rules to be observed, in contrast, for example, to the Insolvency Act 1986 rules on liquidation and Partnership Act 1890 rules on dissolution. Complexities may arise where the contractual joint venture has given rise to the acquisition or generation of jointly owner property, for example, intellectual property in the context of joint research and development. Here, if the parties have failed to address at the outset (i.e. in the contract(s) between them establishing the joint venture) their respective title and rights to exploit the relevant intellectual property, the difficulties are likely to be considerable (*see* further 2.8 below).

(v) *Tax transparency.* The contractual joint venture structure offers total tax transparency. The tax position is discussed at 2.6 below below but it will be noted that the absence of a joint entity leaves the joint venturers to deal with the tax on their own profits in accordance with their own circumstances. Each of them can therefore plan its own tax affairs without interference from the other joint venturer.

(vi) *Secrecy.* In contrast to a jvc, there is no obligation to register details of the constitution of the joint venture, its officers or accounts with a indepen-dent body such as the Registrar of Companies. The structure thus offers a greater level of secrecy than a jvc and an equivalent or greater level than a partnership.[3]

2.3 Disadvantages

(i) *Limited field of use.* The lack of an independent vehicle capable of, *inter alia*, representing the interests of its members and contracting with third parties means that this structure is suitable only for specific types of collaboration; in essence those designed to achieve collaboration short of the establishment of an independent jointly owned and managed trading enterprise. The structure does not conveniently lend itself to the establishment of a common profit centre and is therefore typically limited to activities below the level of sales to third parties (*see* further 2.4 below).[4]

(ii) *The unintentional creation of a partnership.* No formal documentation is required to bring a partnership into being. The definition of a partnership is very broad; namely, '... the relation which subsists between persons carrying on a business in common with a view to profit ...'.[5] It is in each case a question of fact as to whether parties are carrying on business in partnership. The result is that a partnership can be established unintentionally by the parties.

---

[3] Note that registration of the agreement(s) under the Restrictive Trade Practices Act 1976 poten-tially jeopardises the advantage that the structure offers in terms of secrecy (*see* further 2.9 below).

[4] Note that the use of a contractual joint venture as a common profit centre may imply the existence of a partnership (*see* further 2.3(ii) below).

[5] Partnership Act 1890, s.1.

The resulting application of the Partnership Act 1890 (considered in greater detail in 3 below) will, *inter alia*, alter the relationship not only between the parties *inter se* but also in their dealings with third parties. Thus each venturer will, *prima facie*, be able to bind his co-venturers and each venturer will be liable to any third party not only for his own acts and omissions in respect of the joint venture business but also for those of his co-venturers. In summary, several of the 'advantages' attaching to the contractual joint venture structure, most notably those relating to ease of formation, ease of operation, liability and ease of termination (*see* 2.2(i), (ii), (iii), and (iv) above) will be lost if a contractual joint venture is held to constitute a partnership.

2.4   When to select

The contractual joint venture is well suited to specific commercial collaborations where the aim is not to create a jointly owned and operated trading enterprise. Typical examples comprise activities below the level of sales to third parties where the joint venture activity is strictly ancillary to the activities of its members, for example, collaboration in specific stages of manufacture and production; the joint production or processing of essential components or raw materials; or collaboration in packaging or distribution. The use of the contractual joint venture structure for collaboration in joint research and development should be approached with caution in view of the relatively complex process involved in addressing at the outset the ownership and rights of the parties to any intellectual property developed (*see* further 2.8 below). The structure is also frequently used for property developments where the parties have different objectives. Although one normally identifies the structure with 'horizontal' arrangements, that is arrangements between parties at the same level of trade, a variety of other commercial relationships can also come under the category of contractual joint ventures, for example, distribution, licensing and sub-contracting arrangements.

2.5   Formation documentation, key aspects

As stated, there are no formalities prescribed by statute. The parties will set out their respective rights and obligations contractually. Against a background of great commercial variation, the contract can be expected to address, *inter alia*, the following factors:

2.5.1 Funding

There is little of general applicability that can be stated. The contractual arrangements will specify the extent and manner in which each party will contribute to the attainment of the objective. Funding is likely to involve not just the contribution of money but also the provision of plant and machinery, the secondment of personnel and the licensing of intellectual property rights.[6] As there is no independent vehicle, contributions will not result in any form of equity share. The basis of contribution and return will, as stated, be governed solely by the terms agreed in contract between the parties.

2.5.2 Liability to third parties

As stated above, the typical position is one of 'several' liability, that is to say, each will assume liability for its own acts and omissions. The contractual document recording the terms of the collaboration between the parties typically will buttress this position by providing that each party will be indemnified contractually in respect of any liability to a third party incurred as a result of his co-venturer's default. Thus, in the case of joint production of components, party A would ordinarily be indemnified from a third party claim to the extent that it resulted from the act or omission of party B and vice versa.

2.5.3 Liability between members

The complexities, as prescribed by statute, in the case of partnership joint ventures and jvcs are absent. There is no concept, for example, of one venturer being liable for the acts and omissions of all other venturers as in a partnership joint venture (*see* further 3.3(ii) below), or of the obligation incumbent upon a joint venturer to act in the best interests of the company and its shareholders in a jvc joint venture. The relationship between the members is governed solely by the terms of the contract between them. As a minimum, a contractual joint venture can be expected to prescribe that the arrangement is terminable upon the default of party B if party A (in its discretion) elects to serve notice requiring the default to be remedied and party B fails to do so within a specified period. Beyond this minimum, there are a great variety of economic and commercial inducements that are used to ensure compliance by the parties, for example, the loss of exclusivity in a distribution arrangement, if the distributor fails to achieve specified economic targets.

2.5.4 Management

In contrast to the jvc structure, there are no statutory rules governing the management of a contractual joint venture. The manner and extent of super-vision and monitoring of the performance of the collaboration will typically be agreed between the parties and specified contractually.

---

[6] Given the absence of an independent vehicle that will employ personnel, it should be noted that, in the absence of agreement to the contrary, intellectual property rights generated by seconded personnel will belong to their employers (i.e. the joint venturer procuring their availability).

2.5.5 Allocation of profits and losses

Given the lack of a 'vehicle' and of any equity interest reflecting the ratio of the parties' contributions (financial or otherwise) to the collaboration, a contractual joint venture will specify the level and manner of 'return' to the co-venturers.

As a contractual joint venture typically operates at a level below that of sales to third parties and is not generally an independent profit centre, the reference to 'profits and losses' in the heading will in most cases be inappropriate. The contractual joint venture agreement will specify the manner and proportion in which the benefits accruing to the collaboration (for example, the price and other terms governing the supply of jointly produced components) are to be allocated to the parties. That process can be expected to take due account of the respective expenses and contributions incurred by the parties (*see* funding at 2.5.1 above).

2.5.6 Resolution of disputes

Complex structures, such as the put and call options that typically occur in the context of a jvc and which are notable for their somewhat exotic titles (for example, 'Texas shoot-out', and 'Savoy clauses') have no place in respect of a structure lacking an independent vehicle in which the parties have no equity interest. Reliance is generally placed upon one of three alternatives, sometimes applied in combination:

(i)   reference of a dispute for resolution to senior management;
(ii) reference of a dispute to an independent expert or arbitrator;
(iii) reliance upon contractual remedies in the High Court of Justice.

2.5.7 Leaving the joint venture

A contractual joint venture will typically be established for a relatively short timescale, rarely in excess of five years. The parties would not ordinarily be entitled to terminate their arrangement 'at will' during the initial fixed term. In contrast a party would expect to be able to terminate the collaboration at any time for 'cause', i.e. upon the material breach, insolvency (or possibly) upon a change of control of a co-venturer. Given that a contractual joint venture does not comprise a separate entity or vehicle into which the parties vest assets in return for a share of the equity and given that it is not governed by a dedicated body of law,[7] there are none of the complexities that arise upon a dissolution of a partnership or the liquidation of a company. Upon a termination of the joint venture, each party would expect to retake possession and/or

---

[7] In the sense that the Companies Act 1985 or the Partnership Act 1890 govern the formation and operation of companies and partnerships.

control of any assets made available or employees seconded. Similarly, licensing arrangements in respect of intellectual property would ordinarily terminate.

2.5.8 Termination of the joint venture

Termination will be legislated for in the contractual agreement between the parties. In contrast to partnership and jvc structures, no rules of law apply, for example, that under section 32 of the Partnership Act 1890 in respect of the dissolution of a partnership or those under the Companies Act 1985 and Insolvency Act 1986 in respect of winding-up and insolvency. Typical grounds for termination comprise:

  (i)   a failure to agree upon a strategic matter requiring a common position;
 (ii)   a material (and unremedied) breach of the joint venture contract;
(iii)   insolvency; and
 (iv)   a change of control of one of the parties.

2.6   Tax

Since the participation of each joint venturer in a contractual joint venture is simply the performance by that venturer of a contract in the course of its own business, that venturer will be taxed on the profits or losses it makes in accordance with its own circumstances. Where it participates in the joint venture as part of its overall trade the results of that participation will be taken into account as part of the profits or losses of that trade. Amongst the consequences of this transparency:

(a)   The deductibility of its proportion of any joint expenses and the avail-ability of any capital allowances will be ascertained by applying the statutory tests to its own trade.

(b)   Maximum flexibility is available in the use of losses. Where participation in a contractual joint venture is treated as part of an overall trade any losses will be included in the overall losses of that trade and relieved accordingly. Inter alia such losses will be available for carrying forward against future profits of the whole trade.

(c)   A contractual joint venture is not in general treated as a person for VAT. Each participant in the joint venture will normally be carrying on a business and will be registered or not according to its own turnover and other circumstances. They may well make taxable supplies to each other pursuant to the joint venture agreement and these must be taken into account in determining whether turnover limits are met. It should be borne in mind that Customs and Exercise have power in certain circumstances to direct that a number of persons be regarded for VAT as a single person carrying on a single business and thus registrable, even though the persons in question are not actually partners. Such directions can only be made where those concerned have structured their activities to avoid registration.

2.7   Foreign involvement

Non-residents who participate in a UK joint venture will need to consider their liability to UK tax. Under UK law a non-resident will be within the charge to UK tax on trading profits if its trade is carried on wholly or partly in the UK. Frequently, this charge will be restricted by the terms of a double tax treaty and consideration will need to be given as to whether any establishment used by the joint venture could be a UK permanent establishment for treaty purposes.

2.8   Acquisition/use of business assets and intellectual property rights

The absence of an independent vehicle and the relatively short duration of contractual joint ventures will tend to rule out the sale or the outright assignment of assets and/or intellectual property rights to the joint venture by the parties. As stated under funding (2.5.1 above) the parties will typically make available certain assets (for example, plant and machinery and personnel) under the terms of the contract between them. Such process will frequently include the licensing of identified intellectual property rights, for example, patents, copyright, registered designs, trade and service marks and know-how.

As stated above, the use of the contractual joint venture structure for any type of collaborative project or enterprise that will or can reasonably be expected to generate intellectual property rights gives rise to a number of matters requiring careful consideration.

(i) *Title to the intellectual property rights.* Given the absence of a joint venture vehicle capable of employing persons in its own capacity, the persons responsible for the generation of the intellectual property rights (be they, for example, copyright, design right or patents) will typically[8] be in the employment of one or more of the joint venturers. Under the Copyright, Designs and Patents Act 1988, the Registered Designs Act 1949 (as amended) and the Patents Act

---

[8] Where outside contractors are used for a part of the collaboration, an additional factor presents itself, since the basic position (unless rebutted by contractual agreement between the parties) will be that the intellectual property rights belong to the outside contractor. Note that there is an exception in the case of unregistered and registered design rights (*see* Copyright, Designs and Patents Act 1988 ss.215(2)).

1977 the basic position will be that intellectual property rights generated by such employees will belong to their employers.[9] Thus where the employees of the joint venturers have both performed discrete functions within the general ambit of the collaboration, their respective employers (the joint venturers) will each own discrete elements of the overall product of the joint research and development. Not only may this not match the commercial objective (and spirit) behind the collaboration, it may also leave the parties in the position where neither has title to commercially useful or viable intellectual property rights without reliance upon a licence of the other's rights. Alternatively, it is quite possible that the intellectual property rights will be jointly owned by the parties, either as a result of express assignments between them or because the rights were jointly invented/generated by their respective employees.[10]

While joint ownership of trade and service marks is permissible under the Trade Marks Act 1938 (as amended),[11] that Act makes clear that the joint registration would become invalid where the mark is used independently by either venturer (for example, upon termination of a joint venture).

(ii) *Exploitation of the intellectual property rights.* Where each joint venturer owns intellectual property rights outright, there will, *prima facie*, be no limitation upon his ability to exploit such rights. However, as noted, practical and technical considerations may in fact mean that a party cannot apply his rights usefully without access to the 'balance' of rights held by his co-venturer. In the case of jointly owned patents, each joint venturer will in essence be free to exploit the jointly owned rights for his business purposes without accounting (in the form of royalties or otherwise) to the other but (in the absence of agreement to the contrary) neither will be able to license or assign his rights to a third party without the consent of the other party. Thus in the absence of agreement to the contrary, either joint venturer potentially has the power to block the commercial exploitation of the patent *per se* (as opposed to its incorporation in marketed products).[12]

(iii) *Other intellectual property rights.* Whereas statute offers some guidance on the subject of the joint ownership of patents, design rights, copyright and trade and service marks, common law principles will govern other forms of intellectual property, most obviously confidential information and know-how.

---

[9] Copyright Designs and Patents Act 1988, ss.11(2), 215(3) and 267(2) and Patents Act 1977, s.39(1). Note that the position in respect of copyright is subject to the existence of a contrary agreement and that the position in respect of patents is materially qualified by the provision of sub-clauses (a) and (b) of s.39(1). The Patents Act 1977 also makes provision for the payment of compensation to an employee/inventor where a patent of commercial benefit and value passes to his employer, when (i) the patent for the invention is of outstanding benefit to the employer, and (ii) it is just that compensation should be awarded. It is the patents, not the invention, which must be of outstanding benefit (*see* Patents Act 1977 s.40).

[10] *See, inter alia*, Patents Act 1977, ss.7 and 36. Section 10 of the Copyright Designs and Patents Act 1988 allows for works of joint authorship. However, joint authorship will only exist when the contributions of the two authors cannot easily be separated.

[11] Trade Marks Act 1938, s.63.

[12] Note the provisions of the Patents Act 1977, s.37(1)(b) enabling a party to apply to the Comptroller of Patents where exploitation of a patent is being frustrated.

In such cases, it is submitted that the question of title and the ability of the parties *inter se* to exploit the rights will turn primarily upon the nature of the agreement between them. If there is no agreement between the parties, then the rights in question will belong to the party who generated them. There could clearly be difficulties in establishing the true facts of any given situation.

Although by appropriate cross-licences and express agreements between the parties, for example in respect of third party commercial exploitation, a number (if not all) of the difficulties outlined above can be overcome, it remains the case that these relatively complex issues (not easily accessible to non-specialists) must be addressed in some detail at the outset. The nub of the problem can be ascribed to the contractual joint venture's lack of legal personality and its ensuing inability to hold property. It is as a result that the jvc joint venture structure would ordinarily be the preferred structure where the joint generation of intellectual property rights is contemplated. The jvc, as a legal entity, is capable of owning intellectual property rights outright in its own name, and either of employing persons direct or securing the services of employees made available by the joint venturers upon the basis that any intellectual property rights generated will belong to the jvc. As legal and beneficial owner, there is no fetter upon the jvc's ability to exploit the intellectual property rights that are or become its property (*see* further 5.8).

2.9   Competition law considerations

The contractual joint venture agreement will, *prima facie*, be subject to the Restrictive Trade Practices Act 1976 ('RTPA'). The RTPA is the principle mechanism by which UK law seeks to control the anti-competitive effects of commercial arrangements. In contrast to Article 85 EEC Treaty, which might be said to be 'effects' based, the RTPA is formalistic, concentrating in the first instance not upon the actual or likely anti-competitive consequences of given arrangements, but upon whether their 'form' (i.e. the contract between the parties) is of a type that is covered by the Act. In summary, an agreement (which need not necessarily be in writing) between two or more persons carrying on business in the UK pursuant to which two or more persons accept restrictions of a type covered by the Act will require to be notified to the Office of Fair Trading ('OFT'), who in turn will be charged with the responsibility of procuring an assessment of its anti-competitive effects. In essence, restrictions of a type covered by the Act are those which in respect of goods or services influence the terms or conditions under which goods or services are supplied or acquired. The following are typical examples of restrictions caught by the Act: covenants by the co-venturers not to compete with the joint venture activity; agreements controlling the prices at which goods are to be made available by a reseller; agreements as to the classes of person to or from whom goods or services are to be supplied or acquired. The RTPA 76 is a notoriously difficult piece of legislation to apply and recourse will always be necessary to the specialist texts[13] and the legislation itself. Notwithstanding such observation, the following general points should be noted:

(i) the consequences of failing to notify an agreement falling subject to the Act carries with it serious consequences. The relevant restrictions (which tend to be commercially significant, for example, non-compete covenants), will be void and unenforceable; and a party giving effect to them will be liable, *inter alia*, to an action for damages by a third party;

(ii) it is possible to notify agreements to the OFT upon a 'failsafe' basis to counter the difficulty of assessing whether they are notifiable or not;

(iii) the RTPA may be replaced by a body of law strikingly similar in form and content to Article 85 EEC Treaty.[14] It is proposed that the new law will apply retrospectively. Accordingly, agreements that satisfy the 'formalistic' assessment of the RTPA may yet fall subject to an 'effects' based analysis.

In addition to the RTPA, the joint venture agreement will be subject to the Resale Prices Act 1976. In essence, this legislation is designed to prevent the control by a supplier of a reseller's prices. The legislation is most obviously of relevance in joint ventures where the parties are in a relationship of supplier and reseller.

If the joint venture is conducted in an anti-competitive manner, one or all of the parties may become subject to a complaint to the OFT by an aggrieved third party under the Competition Act 1980.[15] This body of legislation bears a loose resemblance to Article 85 EEC Treaty insofar as it is 'effects' based. However, it lacks the significant 'teeth' afforded by Article 85(2) EEC Treaty which provides that agreements (or where severable the offending provisions) falling within Article 85(1) which have not been negatively cleared and/or exempted are automatically null and void.

Under UK law, conduct the subject of a Competition Act complaint will continue unhindered and without invalidity until such time as the OFT intervene. In practice, the Competition Act 1980 has not proved an effective remedy in respect of anti-competitive practices, largely as a result of the difficulty of persuading the OFT to intervene.

Finally, a contractual joint venture will, in theory, be open to investigation under the terms of the Fair Trading Act 1973 upon the grounds that it gave rise to a monopoly in the relevant market that might be expected to operate

---

[13] For example, Commercial Agreements and Competition Law by Nicholas Green, Graham & Trotman 1986.

[14] *See* the White Paper of July 1989, Command Paper 727.

[15] Note that the Competition Act 1980 and the RTPA 76 are mutually exclusive. Thus, conduct arising under or as a result of an agreement registered (and approved) under the RTPA 76 is incapable of being the subject of a Competition Act complaint (Competition Act 1980, s.2(2)).

against the public interest (*see* sections 6, 7 and 8 Fair Trading Act 1973). The application of this 'monopoly' legislation to a discrete commercial venture is, in practice, unlikely.

For a consideration of EEC competition law issues, see Chapter 1.

2.10   Conclusion

The contractual joint venture, lacking the establishment of a jointly owned and managed independent legal entity, in some senses offends the common understanding of a joint venture. Although it enjoys notable advantages in terms of ease of formation, ease of operation, ease of termination, tax transparency and several liability, it remains strictly limited in its breadth of application. Lacking an independent legal personality, it is not well suited to any collaboration that requires or contemplates direct contractual relations with third parties, the establishment of a common profit centre or the generation or acquisition of property. It follows that the structure is typically (although not invariably) limited to collaborations in the processes of manufacture and production below the level of sales to third parties, for example, in the joint production or processing of raw materials or components.

3.   PARTNERSHIP JOINT VENTURES (OTHER THAN LIMITED PARTNERSHIPS)

3.1   Introduction

In contrast to the contractual joint venture structure, the establishment of a partnership gives rise to a vehicle that can be used for the creation and operation of a jointly owned business. The formation and conduct of a partnership is governed primarily by the Partnership Act 1890 and a substantial body of associated case law. Some partnerships, known as 'limited partnerships', are also subject to the Limited Partnerships Act 1907. These are dealt with separately, at 4 below. Accordingly in this part references to partnerships are references to general partnerships only.

A partnership or 'firm' offers a joint venture a seemingly independent persona or identity. However, the 'independence' of the partnership from its members is not strictly speaking recognised in English law (the position is different in Scotland where a partnership is treated as a person). Although the firm may operate under a name that differs from its partners, may open a separate bank account, may sue or be sued in its own name, may be assessed in the first instance to tax and may not 'appear' to be affected by the comings and goings of partners, it is not, as a matter of law, regarded as being an entity independent of, or having separate interests from, its members or partners. This gives rise to fundamental and critical differences between this joint venture structure and that employing a company (the jvc joint venture considered in 5 below).

In the case of a partnership, the law looks not to the identity of the firm but to the identity of the individual partners. What may be regarded as the property of the firm is in law regarded as the property of the partners. The firm cannot contract in its own name (it cannot for example be a tenant of leasehold property). Instead each partner is entitled to contract on behalf of the firm and his act, providing he is acting within his authority, will bind (as that of an 'agent') all other partners as if they had entered into the contract themselves. In essence, each partner performs a dual role: binding other partners in the capacity of agent and in turn being bound by the acts of other partners in the capacity of principal. Perhaps most critically of all, the partnership structure, in contrast to a jvc, renders each and every partner personally liable for all partnership debts (and other liabilities) irrespective of the quantum of their respective capital contributions or whether the partnership has sufficient assets to discharge such obligations. The position can be contrasted with the concept of limited liability pertaining to a UK registered company. In such cases the joint venturers (or shareholders) will not ordinarily be personally liable for the debts (and other liabilities) of the joint venture vehicle (the jvc) save to the extent that there are amounts outstanding and owing in respect of their shares.

The liability of partners for each other's acts and their unlimited liability to third parties for, *inter alia*, partnership debts, has in general limited the use of the partnership structure as a commercial joint venture between corporate undertakings. Perhaps its most frequent use is to be found in the context of cross-border corporate joint ventures, where the availability of tax transparency (*see* further 3.2 below) offers a particular advantage over the jvc structure. The structure is also on occasion used for property joint ventures.

3.2 Advantages

(i) *Ease of formation.* As stated in 2.3(ii) above, the lack of formality prescribed under the Partnership Act in respect of the formation of a partnership, coupled with the broad definition of what constitutes persons carrying on business in partnership (see section 1 Partnership Act 1890) is such that parties frequently create a partnership unintentionally. Although the Partnership Act (as supported by a substantial body of case law) will infer a partnership from a course of conduct, it is in practice rare that parties will intentionally enter into such an arrangement without a carefully prepared partnership agreement. This primarily reflects the fact that the Partnership Act will imply a substantial number of terms governing the relationship between the parties which may not match their commercial objectives and which may only be rebutted by contrary agreement. Thus, and by way of example only, in the absence of an express or implied agreement to the contrary:

(a) all partners are entitled to share equally in the capital and profits of the partnership and must contribute equally to losses;[16]
(b) no partner is entitled to interest on capital subscribed before the ascertainment of partnership profits;[17]
(c) every partner is entitled to participate in the management of the partnership business;[18] and
(d) no partner is entitled to remuneration for his services to the partnership.[19]

Although the preparation of a partnership agreement may in some measure dilute the 'ease' with which a partnership may be formed, the process is generally less complex and bound by formality than the formation of a jvc (*see* further 5.3(i) below).

(ii) *Flexibility*. The Partnership Act 1890 does not, *inter alia*, prescribe the mechanisms by which a partnership must be managed or control the manner or extent to which profits are distributed or capital contributed or withdrawn. By comparison with the relatively lengthy provisions of the Companies Act 1985, in respect of, for example, board meetings, shareholders' meetings, the issue and allotment of share capital and the reduction or repayment of share capital, the partnership structure offers a vehicle of notable simplicity and flexibility. Subject to the preparation of an agreement establishing the rights of the partners *inter se*, there are few statutory restrictions in terms of management, operation, the distribution of profits and the injection and withdrawal of capital.

(iii) *Termination*. The rules governing the termination or 'dissolution' of a partnership[20] are considerably simpler and less formalistic than those governing the winding-up of a company. Upon a termination of a partnership, the value of the partnership assets will be realised, a general statement of account drawn up and a distribution made. Section 44 of the Partnership Act 1890 lays down rules for the payment of losses and the distribution of assets in the absence of agreement between the partners. The process is markedly more simple and flexible than the series of shareholder and creditor meetings that are required in the case of companies (*see* the Insolvency Act 1986, Part IV).

(iv) *Secrecy*. The constitution of a company (comprising its Memorandum and Articles of Association), the issue and allotment of its share capital, the appointment of its officers and its audited accounts must all be filed with the Registrar of Companies and will be open to public inspection.[1] In contrast,

---

[16] Partnership Act 1890, s.24(5).
[17] Partnership Act 1890, s.24(6).
[18] Partnership Act 1890, s.24(1).
[19] Partnership Act 1890, s.24(4).
[20] *See* Partnership Act 1890, ss.32–5 and paragraphs 3.2(v) and 3.5(c) below.
[1] In the context of the jvc joint venture structure, subject to the possibility of registration under the RTPA 76 (*see* 2.9 above), the contents of the Shareholders Agreement, which will contain the true commercial terms of the collaboration between the parties, will not be open to public inspection.

there are no filing requirements in respect of the constitution, management, capitalisation or audited results of a partnership. Clearly, though, where a partnership consists solely of corporate partners, the contribution of the partnership to each corporate partner's results may be ascertainable from their individual returns to the Registrar of Companies.

(v) *Tax*. The partnership structure offers a number of tax advantages:

(a) *Tax transparency*. As explained in 3.6 below partnership profits generally only bear tax by reference to the position of the partner and not by reference to that of any joint venture vehicle.

(b) *Greater flexibility to off-set losses than with a company*. For corporate partners the relatively complex and restrictive rules for consortium relief do not apply, but direct offset is available. Individual partners will also normally be able to offset their share of losses against other income.

(c) *Roll-over on capital gains*. A partner's liability to pay tax on its share of partnership gains can often be deferred (*see* further 3.6 below).

(d) *Taxation rules on 'distributions' not applicable*. The distribution by a partnership of monies to its partners is not subject to the rules on distributions by corporate entities set out in the Income and Corporation Taxes Act 1988. There is, for example, no requirement to account in advance for tax on partnership distributions (*see* further 3.6 below).

(vi) *Ease of variation*. It is a corollary of the general lack of procedural regulations governing the formation and conduct of partnerships (see (i) and (ii) above) that their form and constitution are notably more easy to change than with a company. In practice the parties would simply vary the terms of the partnership agreement.[2]

(vii) *Foreign participation*. Prior to deciding whether a joint venture involving a non-resident should take the form of a partnership or a jvc, a comparison should be made between the effective tax rates which in turn will depend on the provisions of any double tax treaty.

3.3 Disadvantages

(i) *Liability to third parties*. A partner's liability in respect of the debts and other liabilities of the partnership is not limited. All partners are personally liable for the full amount of all partnership liabilities. The position can be contrasted with the jvc structure (*see* 5.2(i) below).

(ii) *Liability inter se*. Each partner is constituted the agent of all other partners. Providing he is acting within his authority, he will bind and render liable all

---

[2] Note that as a matter of law, 'variation' can be inferred from a course of conduct, Partnership Act 1890, s.19.

other partners for his acts and omissions. In the absence of a carefully defined management and decision-making structure, the capacity of a partner to bind all other partners without their consent is considerable. The position can be contrasted with the position of a limited liability company, where a shareholder would not be liable for the acts and omissions of the company, its directors or other shareholders.

(iii) *Limited ability to carry forward losses*. The availability of relief for losses carried forward may be slightly more restricted in the case of a partnership than in the case of a jvc.

(iv) *External finance*. For a joint venture requiring significant external finance, the partnership structure carries with it distinct disadvantages. This results from the fact that UK securities and banking law and practice are in large measure dedicated to the making of loans to and the obtaining of security from limited liability companies. Most notably, a partnership is not able to grant a floating charge over its assets as security for a debt[3] or constitute and allot loan stock or other marketable debts on a security (*see* further 3.6 below).

(v) *Lack of permanence as a structure*. The Partnership Act 1890 contains a number of provisions[4] providing for both automatic dissolution and dissolution by a court (upon application) upon the occurrence of specified events. For example, death or bankruptcy (including, almost certainly, the dissolution of a corporate partner)[5] will bring about automatic dissolution whereas conduct injurious to the partnership business and a wilful and persistent breach of the partnership agreement are grounds for dissolution upon an application to court. The position can be contrasted with that of a jvc, where a change in the shareholding structure or a breach of the shareholders agreement will have no impact upon the continued existence of the company. It is important that parties entering into a partnership joint venture bear in mind the wide ambit of the statutory rules on dissolution.

(vi) *Limited ability to transfer partnership interest*. The inability to transfer an interest in a partnership (such that the transferee becomes a partner) without the consent of all other partners is sometimes cited as a 'disadvantage' of the partnership structure.[6] However, in the context of a joint venture, it is likely that such 'inability' will substantially meet the parties' commercial requirements. The selection of a joint venture partner is an essentially personal matter. Parties will not typically wish to have a change in the identity of the parties imposed upon them. Note the similarity between this position and restrictions on the transfer of shares in the context of a jvc (*see* further 5.5(vi) below).

---

[3] This, in general, forces the partnership to rely upon 'fixed charges' (which typically restrict the ability of the chargor to deal with the assets) and/or personal guarantees from the partners. Both are less attractive propositions than a floating charge.
[4] Partnership Act 1890, ss.33–5.
[5] Section 33 of the Partnership Act 1890 is subject to 'any agreement between the partners' to the contrary. Partners frequently elect to continue the partnership in such circumstances.
[6] This implied provision of the Partnership Act 1890, s.24(7) may be disapplied by express or implied agreement between the partners.

3.4 When to select

As a matter of UK commercial practice, the partnership structure is employed relatively infrequently in the context of joint ventures. Although, as with the jvc, it provides a mechanism for the establishment of a vehicle pursuant to which two or more parties can jointly own and operate a business, clients (by which are meant corporations rather than individuals) are, as a rule, disinclined to form a partnership, not only as a result of the specific disadvantages highlighted in 3.3 above, but also as a result of their general lack of familiarity with partnership law and practice. It is the availability of tax transparency that, in general, dictates the choice of a partnership, either because of the presence of a non-resident undertaking or because of the specific requirements of the transaction.

3.5 Formation documentation, key aspects

In practice, a partnership is usually formed by an agreement in writing notwithstanding the implied terms of the Partnership Act 1890. Save in the case of limited partnerships and in contrast to jvcs (*see* respectively 4 and 5 below) there are no statutory requirements to file, inter alia, the terms of the constitution of the partnership or particulars in respect of its officers or annual accounts. Although partnership agreements inevitably show enormous variation in terms of their commercial content, they will generally provide as a minimum for the following.

(a) *Name*. Partnerships are entitled to trade under a distinct name, i.e. one separate from those of the individual partners. The choice of name (where it does not consist of the surnames or corporate names of all the partners) must comply with the requirements of the Business Names Act 1985,[7] which, *inter alia*, restricts the use of certain types of name (for example, those incorporating the words 'British' or 'international') and lays down requirements for the display of the name (for example, upon partnership stationery).

(b) *Purpose and scope*. The nature of the joint business to be undertaken will be described. This will provide:

(i) a commercial and practical focus to the aims of the parties;
(ii) a basis and reference point for the definition of each partner's 'actual' authority to bind his fellow partners in the conduct of partnership business; and
(iii) a foundation for the obligations of the partners, *inter alia*, set out in sections 28 and 30 Partnership Act 1890, to account for any benefit

---

[7] The choice of name will also be subject to registered trade and service marks and the common law rules on 'passing-off'.

derived from any transaction concerning the partnership's business and for any profits derived from a competing business.

(c) *Duration/termination.* The duration and termination of a partnership can be provided for in a number of ways. A partnership can be expressed to expire upon the occurrence of a specified event (for example, the completion of a project) or after the lapse of a given period of time. In the absence of an express provision as to duration, the partnership will be deemed to be a partnership at 'will' and will be terminable at any time at the option of any one of the partners.[8] Note that the death or bankruptcy of an individual partner will bring about an earlier termination irrespective of the stated fixed term.[9] In the case of corporate partners, the dissolution of a company equates to an individual's death. Insolvency does not, however, bring about an automatic termination but will almost certainly be grounds to apply to court to have the partnership wound up.[10] A partnership may also be dissolved, irrespective of the stated fixed term, upon an application by a party upon the occurrence of any one of the circumstances set out in section 35 Partnership Act 1890, for example, where a partner becomes incapable of performing his partnership obligations, where a partner is guilty of conduct prejudicial to the interests of the partnership or where a partner is in wilful or persistent breach of the partnership agreement.

(d) *Management.* The agreement will address the scope of each partner's responsibility in terms of the conduct of the partnership business, i.e. the extent to which he can contract in the name of the partnership and bind his fellow partners. While this defines the partner's 'actual authority', note that a third party will not be bound by its provisions where he does not have notice. In practice, each partner's acts and omissions will bind all others if, to a reasonable outsider, they appear to fall within his usual or expected sphere of authority. Voting, the establishment of management committees, holidays and the remuneration of partners for their services are all likely to be addressed under this heading.

(e) *Provision of capital.* The proportions in which capital is to be contributed will be provided for. In the event of an unequal provision of capital, it is necessary to provide expressly for the payment of interest on capital prior to the distribution of any profits, for otherwise such payment is prevented by the Partnership Act.[11] The point on interest is rendered more critical in view of the fact that under the Partnership Act, the distribution of assets will not automatically follow the proportions in which capital is contributed. Indeed, in the absence of contrary agreement, all partners are entitled to share equally in all profits.[12]

---

[8] Partnership Act 1890, s.26(1).
[9] Partnership Act 1890, s.33(1) and *see also* Partnership Act 1890, ss.33(2) and 34.
[10] Partnership Act 1890, s.35(f) and *see* Lindley on Partnership, Sweet & Maxwell 1984, at p. 694.
[11] Partnership Act 1890, s.24(1).
[12] Partnership Act 1890, s.24(1).

(f) *Allocation of profits and losses.* As stated, in default of express or implied agreement to the contrary, profits and losses will be borne equally by the partners. The partnership structure affords considerable flexibility in the nature and extent of distribution. In view of the fact that the extent of profits or losses will not be known until the end of the year, it is customary to allow drawings in anticipation of future profits. 'Profit' is generally defined. For example, book debts are frequently taken into profit subject to a provision for bad or doubtful debts.

(g) *Accounts.* The agreement will typically provide, *inter alia*, for the keeping of proper books of account, for the preparation of half-yearly and/or yearly general accounts and for a declaration that the accounts once signed shall (in the absence of manifest error) be treated as conclusive.

(h) *Dissolution/Termination.* In the absence of agreement to the contrary, the death or bankruptcy of a partner will bring about the automatic dissolution of the partnership.[13] It is generally thought that an analogous provision will be implied in the event of a corporate partner being dissolved[14] but not in the case of its insolvency.[15] In the case of a partnership between individuals it is customary to disapply the rules on the automatic dissolution and winding-up of the partnership by providing that the remaining partners will carry on the partnership business (this is usual in the case of professional partnerships). Note that different considerations will almost certainly apply in the context of a partnership structure used for the purposes of a joint venture between corporate undertakings. In such circumstances, the cessation of one of the corporate undertakings is almost bound to bring the joint venture to an end. A partnership agreement will generally provide for the dissolution or termination of the partnership upon the occurrence of a number of specified events, for example, incapacity of a partner, breach of the partnership agreement, neglect of the partnership business or insolvency. As an alternative, partners can reserve to themselves rights of expulsion of a partner who commits, for example, any one of the acts specified above.

(i) *Entitlement of outgoing partner.* Where a partner ceases to be a partner as a result of death, bankruptcy, expulsion or otherwise, the agreement will provide for the mechanism by which his interest in the capital and profits of the partnership is to be valued and accounted for. A number of differing mechanisms are adopted for the purposes of valuation.

(j) *Non-compete covenants.* such covenants typically require a partner not to compete with the business of the partnership or to solicit or endeavour to entice away its employees upon his cessation as a partner. In the context of a joint venture, such covenants would also typically be extended to cover non-competition and soliciting of employees during the currency of the joint venture.

---

[13] Partnership Act 1890, s.33(1).
[14] For example, where it is struck off the register.
[15] *See* Lindley on Partnership, Sweet & Maxwell 1984, at p. 694.

3.6   Tax

(a) *Liability to tax generally.* An English partnership is not an independent legal entity (although this is not the case in Scotland, Scottish and English partnerships are in fact taxed by reference to the same rules). A partnership offers tax transparency, that is to say that tax is only borne once by reference to the tax position of the partners although, as will be seen, in some circumstances this tax may actually be a liability of the partnership. In the case of income, the regime under which tax is levied depends upon whether one of the partners is a company. In the case of capital gains, the UK revenue regard a partnership as 'look-through' with each partner owning its part of each asset.[16]

(b) *Taxation of income – partnerships with no corporate partners.* For income tax purposes, tax on the trading profits of a partnership (which in practice may be extended to include certain investment income) is computed in one sum and assessed on the partnership. Although the tax so charged is a joint liability of all the partners, it will be computed by reference to their individual positions and their respective proportion will be treated as tax paid by them in settling their overall tax liabilities for the year. Normally the partnership accounts will be drawn up in a way which seeks to allocate the burden of the tax fairly between the partners and there will also be provision in the Partnership Deed providing how that tax is to be allocated on changes in partnership shares.

The taxation of a partnership consisting of individuals is a highly complex subject but the following points might be regarded as particularly noteworthy:

(i)   As is generally the case in the UK where individuals carry on a trade, tax is levied on a preceding year basis. This means that save in the early or closing years of a trade where special rules apply, the profits on which the charge for a particular year of assessment (i.e. year to 5th April) is based are those for the accounting period of the partnership ending in the preceding year of assessment. Those profits are, however, treated for tax purposes as split between the partners in their shares for the year of assessment itself. This inconsistency can cause complications when profit shares change.

(ii)   Where there is a change in the composition of the partnership, whether an old partner leaves or a new partner joins, the partnership is treated as ceasing and a new partnership as beginning unless the partners make an election for the partnership to continue.[17] Whether or not an election is advantageous will depend on a number of factors. In general

---

[16]   *See* generally Inland Revenue Statements of Practice, 17th January 1975 and 12th January 1979. The position on capital gains is different where the partnership amounts to a unit trust for the purposes of s.93 CGTA. This, however, would normally only be the case where it was used as a vehicle for the joint holding of passive investments and even here there are a number of statutory exceptions.

[17]   ICTA 1988 section 113.

it is probably right to say that the election is advantageous where profits are rising and disadvantageous when they are falling, although it should be noted that the rules governing the taxation of a partnership following a deemed cessation are different from those which would apply to a new business.

(iii) The share of any trading losses attributable to an individual partner is apportioned to him for use according to his circumstances. There is provision for an individual to off-set such losses against his general income provided certain conditions are met. Losses may be carried forward indefinitely for use against the individual's share of taxable profits of the partnership. It should be noted that the position here may be more restrictive than that of a joint venturer who might be able to use his losses against the future profits of a broader trade.

(iv) Capital allowances of a partnership are initially given to the partnership as a whole and deducted in its tax assessment. Each partner is entitled to his share of surplus allowances and may, subject to certain conditions, with the consent of his partners, claim to have those allowances added to trading losses available for off-set against his own general income. Balancing charges will be brought into account in taxing the partnership trade. Charges on income have to be allocated among the partners and can be used to reduce their tax liabilities.

(v) Investment income of a partnership is not included in the partnership assessment but is directly attributed to partners for tax purposes. In practice, however, this is often dealt with by simply including it in the partnership profits.

(c) *Taxation of income – partnerships with corporate members.* A partnership of companies is dealt with rather differently. Here the profits and losses are computed as though the partnership were itself a company without in the first instance taking account of capital allowances, charges on income or losses carried forward. Each partner is then allocated its share of the profit or loss, capital allowances and charges on income and is taxed separately by reference to these. The partner is treated for corporation tax purposes as though those shares derived from a separate trade carried on by it. In computing the profits of the notional company no account is taken of changes in the partners where one company is a partner both before and after the change. As each partner is essentially taxed separately it has freedom as to how it wishes to use losses or surplus allowances. Losses carried forward can, however, only be used by a partner against its share of the partnership profits.

Where partners include both individuals and companies the initial computation is carried out as for companies but those profits attributable to individual partners are then dealt with in accordance with the income tax regime. Various rules are laid down for making the attribution.

(d) *Tax on capital gains.* Since each partner is treated as being entitled to its share of partnership assets, when the partnership disposes of property each partner is treated as making a gain (or loss) on its interest in the asset disposed of. This is not simply a question of apportioning a partnership gain since different partners may have acquired their shares in the asset for different costs (e.g. where a partner bought into the partnership after the date on which the asset was acquired his cost would reflect the price at which he purchased his interest). When changes in partnership shares occur there is a part disposal of assets by those partners whose shares reduce and an acquisition by any partners increasing its share. Where no consideration is given and the assets have not been revalued the transfer will normally be treated for tax purposes as taking place at a price which gives rise to no gain or loss.

In applying roll-over relief[18] under which gains on certain assets which are used in a trade (such as land or goodwill) can be rolled over into the cost of replacement assets, the partners are looked at separately, each of them being entitled (subject to the terms of the relief being satisfied) to roll the gain on its interest in the asset in question either into its interest in a new eligible partnership asset or into new eligible assets which it or its group companies may acquire for other trades. This gives a flexibility for roll-over not available when a trading asset is disposed of by a jvc.

(e) *Distributing profits.* In the case of a partnership, profits bear tax as they arise and no further tax is levied on the repayment of the partnership accounts which reflect those profits.

(f) *VAT.* Persons carrying on business in partnership are normally registered in the name of the firm. Accordingly the partnership will make VAT returns in respect of partnership transactions and the partners will not be treated as making VATable supplies to each other simply because they perform normal partnership duties.

3.7   Foreign involvement

Where a foreign corporate partner participates in a UK partnership it will normally pay UK corporation tax on its trading profit. It will need to consider whether the terms of the relevant double tax treaty make it advantageous to participate through a UK resident subsidiary.

3.8   Acquisition/use of business assets and intellectual property rights.

Considerable care must be taken in the context of a partnership to distinguish between 'partnership property' in the strict sense of the term and property belonging to an individual partner and made available for use in the partnership business. The point can quickly be illustrated to have a number of material repercussions:

(a)   increases in the value of partnership property will belong to the partner-

[18] Section 115 Capital Gains Taxes Act 1979.

ship; increases in a partner's personal property will belong to the partner concerned;

(b) creditors (judgment or otherwise) of the partnership will be entitled to recover against the partnership assets; but not against property belonging to an individual partner unless the partnership assets have been exhausted;

(c) land belonging to a partnership is regarded as 'personalty' nor 'realty', this reflects, *inter alia*, the fact that upon a dissolution of the partnership the land (as with all other partnership assets) will require to be sold. Thus a party who has been left a deceased partner's 'realty' will have a material interest in whether the land has become partnership property (i.e. 'personalty'). In practice, the above points turn upon the express or implied agreement between the parties. Accordingly, at the time of the formation of the partnership and under the terms of the partnership agreement, it is important that the issue is fully documented.

A partnership, as stated at the outset, is a vehicle which can be employed for the joint ownership and conduct of a business. The process by which the partnership is vested with the means to carry on business inevitably shows great variation in practice. The question of whether assets (including intellectual property rights) should be assigned outright to the partnership (thus becoming partnership property) or merely made available under licence, will in each case turn upon largely commercial considerations, for example, the intended duration of the joint venture. In the case of the assignment of assets to a partnership, it should be noted that, in the absence of agreement to the contrary, such assets will be allocated upon a dissolution (net of returns of capital and the discharge of other partnership debts) to partners in the same proportions in which the partners shared profits and losses. This may not necessarily reflect the parties' respective levels of contribution.

Where employees of a partnership in the course of their employment generate or create intellectual property rights, such rights will generally belong to their employer, i.e. the partnership.[19] The intellectual property rights will constitute part of the general body of partnership assets. In the absence of express agreement, any intellectual property rights would fall subject to the statutory rules as to the distribution of partnership assets generally (*see* the Partnership Act 1890, section 44 *et seq.*) upon a dissolution of the partnership. In essence the value of the intellectual property rights would be realised through a sale and the proceeds applied in the final settlement of the partners' respective accounts. Although this may not meet the joint venturers' commercial requirements at the time, it is submitted that it is impractical to try and legislate in advance for the devolution of partnership property upon a dissolution – if the parties wish to depart from the statutory rules (for example,

[19] *See* Copyright, Designs and Patents Act 1988, ss.11(2), 215(3) and 267(2) and Patents Act 1977, s.39(1).

by cross-licences, joint ownership or otherwise) then the only practical solution is for them to agree to do so at the time.

3.9   Competition

The partnership agreement, as with any contract in support of a contractual joint venture, will, *prima facie*, be subject to the provisions of the Restrictive Trade Practices Act 1976 ('RTPA 76') (*see* 2.9 above). Likely provisions in the partnership agreement to be caught under the RTPA 76 are covenants given by the parties not to compete with the partnership business both during and upon their cessation as partners.[20]

The conduct of the partnership will, as with the conduct of a contractual joint venture and a jvc, be subject to on-going regulatory control under the Competition Act 1980 and the Fair Trading Act 1973 (*see* further 2.9 above).

In certain circumstances the establishment of a partnership joint venture structure may give rise to a qualifying merger under section 64 of the Fair Trading Act 1973 (*see* further paragraph 5.9). For a discussion of the application of Articles 85 and 86 EEC Treaty to joint ventures, see Chapter 1 below.

3.10   Conclusion

The partnership joint venture structure is by comparison with contractual joint ventures and jvcs, relatively infrequently employed. Although, in comparison to jvcs, easy and unformalistic to establish and offering considerable flexibility in terms, *inter alia*, of the distribution of profits and management, the perceived 'negatives' of this structure, most obviously the lack of limited liability and the difficulties associated with external funding, in general lead corporate undertakings to adopt a jvc structure where their collaboration contemplates the establishment and operation of a jointly owned business. The one notable exception are collaborations involving a foreign undertaking, where the partnership structure, in view of the availability of 'tax transparency', offers peculiar advantages.

4.   LIMITED PARTNERSHIPS

4.1   Introduction

A special type of partnership was introduced by the Limited Partnership Act 1907, which comprises two distinct types of partner; 'general partners' who are responsible for the management of the partnership and who have unlimited

---

[20] It should be noted that the exemption from the provisions of the RTPA 76 now applying to certain of such provisions in shareholders' agreements does not extend to partnership agreements (*see* SI 1989/1081 and SI 1989/1082).

liability (in the same way as a partner under a classic partnership, *see* 3 above); and 'limited partners' who are not able to participate in the management of the partnership but whose liability is *limited* to the amount of their respective capital contributions to the partnership.[1] The structure has rarely been used in the context of UK joint ventures, primarily because the statute reduces the role of the limited partner to that of a 'sleeping partner'. Limited partnerships have now, however, become the accepted structure for UK venture capital investment funds.[2]

4.2 Advantages

Notwithstanding the requirements as to registration in respect of a limited partnership,[3] which to a degree lessen the ease of formation and secrecy of a limited partnership (*see* 3.2(i) and (iv) above), it is submitted that limited partnerships enjoy a majority of the 'advantages' outlined in respect of general partnerships (*see* generally 3.2 above).

4.3 Disadvantages

The principle disadvantage of the limited partnership comprises the inability of the limited partners to participate in the management of the partnership. While the liability of limited partners is limited to their capital contribution and such persons are unable to bind the firm (not being entitled to participate at all in its management), the liability of the general (managing) partners both to third parties and *inter se* is essentially as set out for ordinary partners (*see* 3.3(i) and (ii) above). Subject to the above, the disadvantages set out in 3.3 above will apply generally. A peculiar difficulty with limited partnerships is the inadequacy of the governing statute itself, which leaves a number of important questions as to the rights and obligations of the parties unconsidered.[4] These 'statutory' uncertainties are compounded by a lack of judicial precedent, in itself a reflection of the infrequent use of the structure.

4.4 When to select

As stated, the structure, with the exception of very specific applications (as a fund for certain investments being an example) is generally unsuited to a genuine collaboration between undertakings in view of the restrictions as to the rights of the limited partners to participate in the management. Note in

[1] Limited Partnership Act 1907, s.4(2), but note that the limited liability can be lost: (i) where the partnership is not registered; and (ii) where the limited partner takes part in the management.
[2] *See* British Venture Capital Association Memorandum published 26th May 1987.
[3] Limited Partnership Act 1907, s.5 *et seq.*
[4] *See* Lindley on Partnership, Sweet & Maxwell 1984 at 930.

this regard that a limited partnership must consist of a combination of general and limited (i.e. sleeping) partners.

Following clarification by the Inland Revenue and the Department of Trade and Industry of a number of technical problems, the limited partnership structure has become increasingly popular as a tax effective onshore vehicle for raising venture capital investment funds, the use of which is likely to be extended to other types of investment fund. As the limited partners will be the investors in the fund, the restrictions on management by limited partners will not normally be a problem as, in the nature of such a fund, investors will be looking to the investment manager (who will be the general partner) to manage and administer the fund on their behalf.

4.5   Formation documentation

In addition to the statutory requirements as to registration, a partnership agreement will be required. This will address a majority of the issues outlined in 3.5 above, although making due allowance for the differing rights and obligations of general and limited partners.

4.6   Tax and accounting

Limited partnerships are merely a form of partnership. Accordingly, the statements set out in 3.6 above will apply. Legislation was, however, introduced in 1985 to ensure that limited partners' tax losses were restricted by reference to the commercial losses that they had actually suffered. This stopped various tax schemes under which limited partners had a large share of partnership losses but in the end did not bear them because of limited liability.

4.7   Foreign involvement

See the statements set out in 3.7 above.

4.8   Acquisition/use of business assets and intellectual property rights

See the statements set out in 3.8 above.

4.9   Competition

See the statements set out in 3.9 above.

4.10   Conclusion

The limited partnership has been considered only briefly. This reflects the incidence of its use in the UK as a joint venture structure. While it offers limited liability to a section of the partners (the 'limited partners'), it is generally the case that the inability of this last group to participate in the management of the partnership will frustrate the use of this structure in commercial joint ventures.

5.   JOINT VENTURE COMPANIES

5.1   Introduction

The joint venture company ('jvc') is by some margin the most common form of joint venture structure for collaborations between UK corporate undertakings where the parties' objectives contemplate the creation and operation of a jointly-owned business. The collaboration in such circumstances takes the form of the establishment of an independent legal entity (the jvc) which unlike a partnership, will have distinct and separate interests from its members (the joint venturers). The resulting relationship that subsists between the parties is that of shareholders in a commonly owned and controlled company. Although the constitution and operation of companies and the rights and obligations of shareholders therein are to a large extent prescribed by statute and case law, it is customary to legislate expressly (a) for the manner in which the jvc will be funded, operated and controlled; and (b) in respect of the nature of the joint venturers' rights as shareholders in two principal documents: respectively the Shareholders Agreement and the Articles of Association.

5.2   Advantages

(i) *Limited liability*. In the case of a jvc, the maximum liability of the shareholders in respect of the liabilities of the company is the amount paid-up on their shares, or in the case of nil or partly paid-up shares, the amount owing in respect of their shares. This 'limited liability' can be contrasted with the position under a partnership (*see* 3.3(i) above) where each partner is personally liable for the debts and liabilities of the partnership irrespective of the quantum of his capital contribution. Although the availability of limited liability is, *prima facie*, a clear advantage of the jvc structure, there are a number of legal and commercial constraints upon its availability, for example:

   (a)   in the case of joint venturers whose shares are listed,[5] the market

---

[5] i.e. corporate shareholders whose shares are listed on the UK Stock Exchange or Unlisted Securities Market.

for and value of their shares are likely to be seriously and negatively impacted by the financial 'failure' of a subsidiary jvc;

(b)   where the jvc is a 'subsidiary' of a joint venturer, it is likely that the joint venturer would in practice be unable to allow the jvc to become insolvent without triggering default provisions in its external loans documentation;

(c)   in certain circumstances the law will disapply the protection of limited liability or 'lift the corporate veil', for example, where the number of members of a company falls below two;[6] in the event of fraudulent trading;[7] and in the instance of fraud or improper conduct;[8] and

(d)   if the jvc is of limited financial substance, banks and contractors, *inter alia*, are likely to require shareholder guarantees and bonds.

(ii) *Separate entity*. Unlike a partnership, a jvc is a distinct legal entity whose interests are separate from those of its members. A jvc is thus able under its own name to sue (or be sued) and to enter into contracts with third parties. In addition, the ownership by the jvc of property in its own right (whether acquired or generated by its own employees) is essentially clear-cut. The potentially difficult overlap between property belonging to partners and property belonging to the partnership is absent in the case of a jvc where there is a clear separation of the interests of the members (as shareholders) from that of the company. The structure is accordingly well suited to collaborations involving or contemplating the joint ownership and operation of a trading enterprise necessitating, amongst other things, contractual relations with third parties, the ownership or creation of property and the establishment of a common profit centre. The separateness of the corporate identity from that of its shareholders avoids many of the potential difficulties implicit in carrying on business in partnership, for example:

(a)   the ability of all partners to bind the partnership when acting within their usual authority;

(b)   the potential for confusion between individual and partnership property; and

(c)   the implied right of all partners to participate in the day to day management of the partnership.[9]

(iii) *Commercial understanding/familiarity*. Although not at first sight a very concrete advantage, there is no doubt that corporate undertakings favour the jvc structure because it operates within a body of law and practice with which they are familiar. Conversely, undertakings avoid the partnership structure in part as a result of a general unfamiliarity with the workings of partnership

---

[6] Companies Act 1985, s.24.
[7] Companies Act 1985, s.630.
[8] *See Gilford Motor Co. v Horne* 1933 Ch. 935.
[9] *See* generally 3.5 above.

law and practice. In selecting the 'vehicle' for a joint venture, it cannot be doubted that to select one with which the parties are familiar is an advantage.[10]

(iv) *Basis for further expansion.* In contrast to the partnership structure, the jvc through its ability to form subsidiaries and effect corporate reorganisations, offers a very effective base from which to expand the joint venture's operations. Different activities can be undertaken in separate companies within the jvc's corporate group and holding companies can be established. In short, there is an almost limitless number of possibilities in terms of structure. Finally, the corporate structure offers the possibility of an application for listing of the jvc's shares on the London Stock Exchange.[11]

(v) *Transferability of interests.* In contrast to the difficulties of assigning an interest in a partnership (*see* 3.3(vi) above) an interest in a company's equity can be transferred in a relatively simple manner by the execution of a stock transfer form. In practice, private companies, and in particular a private jvc, will control and limit the extent to which shareholders can transfer their shares. Nevertheless the underlying simplicity with which interests in a company can be transferred arguably confers an advantage over the partnership structure.

(vi) *Permanence as a structure.* As stated in 3.3(v) above, a partnership (subject to contrary agreement) dissolves automatically and upon application to the court in a wide variety of circumstances. Although, in practice, the effect of this rule is often mitigated by express provisions in the partnership agreement and by elections as to the basis of tax assessment.[12] The structure can be contrasted in this regard to the jvc, which remains unaffected by, *inter alia*, changes in the identity of shareholders.

(vii) *External finance.* As a general point, it is the case that banks and other third party lenders[13] are primarily used to dealing with companies and that, in consequence, a jvc will be considerably better placed to obtain external finance than a partnership. However, more substantive reasons exist for this advantage, for example: (a) the ability of a company to grant a floating charge over its assets; and (b) the ability of a company to constitute and allot loan stock or loan notes. The floating charge is a form of security that, in contrast to a fixed charge, is not attached to specific items of a company's assets but which, as its name implies, floats over the totality of the company's assets. Until such time as the charge is called-in by the lender (at which time it is said to 'crystallise') the floating charge permits the company to buy, sell and otherwise deal in its assets without requiring the chargee's consent. The floating charge is of considerable commercial importance as a flexible form of security and is not available in the case of partnerships. Loan stock or loan notes

---

[10] It will be interesting to observe to what extent the lack of previous experience of an EEIG will inhibit its employment by businessmen. Certainly the example of the French Groupement d'interet economique (upon which the EEIG is based and which was little used in practice) offers little encouragement.

[11] This might comprise a (full) listing on the London Stock Exchange or listing on the Unlisted Securities Market.

[12] *See* 3.3(v) above.

[13] e.g. venture capital funds.

are both written instruments constituted or created by a company with a view to evidencing debt. In structuring such finance, thought will need to be given to whether any loss sustained will be allowable for the purposes of tax on capital gains. Since the widening of the definition of qualifying corporate bonds in the 1989 Finance Act this has become more difficult. However, specific reliefs are available under ss136 and 136A Capital Gains Tax Act 1979.

5.3 Disadvantages

(i) *Formation.* The formation of a company (or the acquisition of a ready-made company),[14] the preparation (or in the case of an acquired company) the alteration of its Memorandum and Articles of Association, the issue and allotment of its share capital and the filing of all associated 'returns' to the Registrar of Companies are but illustrations of the greater administrative complexity attached to the use of the jvc structure. To the statute-based formalities must be added the essentially commercially driven requirement to prepare, *inter alia*, a shareholders agreement setting out the rights of the parties to manage and control the jvc.

(ii) *Lack of flexibility.* In comparison to a partnership, the operation of a company, whether in terms of decision making (i.e. through the Board of Directors and in General Meeting), alterations to its 'constitution' (the Memorandum and Articles of Association), alterations to the nature and form of its share capital (the issue and allotment of different types or 'classes' of share) or the return of capital (for example upon a winding-up of the company) is governed by a relatively complex body of law[15] and associated judicial precedent. Although the basic structure permits great variation in terms, for example, of different shareholding structures (which in themselves are capable of giving expression to differing combinations of rights to voting, dividends or capital), nevertheless in comparison to the operation of a partnership, the process is more rigid and statute bound.

(iii) *Termination.* Whereas a partnership is relatively easy to terminate or dissolve (*see* 3.2(iii) above), the winding-up of a company will involve the parties in a lengthy series of procedures.[16] Although the relative 'permanence' of the jvc is seen as an advantage over the partnership (which is capable of dissolution in a wide variety of circumstances), the eventual winding-up of the structure is a time consuming and expensive task. In practice, the parties are likely to avoid this difficulty by stripping out the assets of the jvc and leaving it as a dormant or non-trading 'shell' company (as to the tax consequences of this, *see* 5.6(iii) below). It should be noted that the jvc, in contrast to a partnership,

---

[14] Ready made companies can be acquired at a price of approximately £150 although modifications will inevitably be required to be made to the name, registered office, Articles and other constitutional matters.

[15] To a large extent contained in the Companies Act 1985 and the Insolvency Act 1986.

[16] The nature of the procedures will vary according to the nature of the winding-up, *see* the Insolvency Act 1986, Part IV.

exposes shareholders to a double tax charge upon a winding-up: the jvc will be liable to tax upon a disposal of its assets; while the shareholders will be liable to tax upon receipt of their share of the surplus assets in the liquidation (if any) – *see* 5.6(v) below.

(iv) *Lack of secrecy.* A registered UK company is required to file with the Registrar of Companies, *inter alia*, its annual audited accounts, copies of certain resolutions adopted by the shareholders, particulars of all changes in the identity of its directors and secretary, details of the structure and ownership of its share capital and copies of its Memorandum and Articles of Association. In comparison with a partnership, there is substantially less scope for keeping the identity and nature of the joint venture confidential. In the case of a jvc, it is customary to keep as much as possible of the essentially commercial (and confidential) content of the collaboration out of the documents open to public inspection (e.g. the Articles of Association) and to place them instead in the Shareholders Agreement.[17]

(v) *Tax.* The jvc, as a separate legal entity, will be liable to tax in its own right. In comparison with a partnership, the structure is in at least three respects, arguably less favourable:

(a)   the absence of tax transparency;
(b)   less flexibility in the use of loss relief; and
(c)   the requirement to account for advance corporation tax in respect of dividends and other distributions of profit.

All of the above issues are described more fully in 5.6 below.

(vi) *Foreign participation.* The lack of tax transparency coupled with, *inter alia*, the non-availability of consortium relief to non-residents may make the jvc structure less attractive from the perspective of a foreign participant.

5.4   When to select

In view of the substantive advantages listed in 5.2 above and the general commercial prejudice against the employment of partnership structures (except in very specific applications) the jvc is almost always the preferred choice for a joint venture contemplating the establishment and operation of an independent business involving contractual relations with third parties, the acquisition or creation of property rights and the operation of a common profit centre. Against this, it would generally be unnecessary and uneconomic to use a jvc structure where the type of commercial activity contemplated could be operated by means of a contractual joint venture. In general this will be the case where the collaboration falls short of the establishment of a jointly owned and operated business, *see* further 2.4 above.

---

[17] Note that the Shareholders Agreement, and similarly the Partnership Agreement, may nevertheless become open to public inspection as a result of the application of the Restrictive Trade Practices Act 1976, *see* 2.9 above.

5.5   Formation documentation, key aspects

JVCs can be divided into two broad categories:

    (i)   those specifically formed by would-be joint venturers to undertake a given venture; and

    (ii) those already trading and in which one or more joint venturers participate by means of a subscription for shares.

The documentation governing the on-going control and management of both types of jvc will be in practice substantially the same and will comprise two key elements: a Shareholders Agreement and specifically modified Articles of Association. However in the case of an investment or subscription for shares in an existing trading company ((ii) above), it is customary for the investing joint venturers to require and obtain contractual warranties and indemnities as to the assets, liabilities and trading status of the company. The form and nature of such warranties and indemnities and the identity of the persons giving them will vary in practice, but in general, they will be given by the existing shareholders and will broadly resemble those to be found in a sale and purchase agreement for a private company.

The Shareholders' Agreement in respect of a jvc, like the Partnership Agreement in the case of a partnership, will inevitably show considerable variation in practice. Nevertheless, the following major headings are likely to be addressed.

(i) *Issue and allotment of share capital.* The agreement will typically record the manner in which the share capital is to be subscribed for and allotted among the joint venturers. It is customary to allocate a different class of share to each party, for example, 'A', 'B', 'C' Ordinary Shares, depending upon the relevant number of participants. The jvc as a structure permits considerable ingenuity in terms of framing and adjusting the respective rights of shareholders to, *inter alia*, voting, dividends and return of capital through the creation of classes of share conferring different rights and obligations.[18]

Subject to the obvious dangers of generalisation, it is usually the case that complex share structures in the context of joint ventures are limited to outside investments by venture capital funds (or other third party investors) where the proportion of the investor's equity in the company will be adjusted by reference to its solvency and performance. In the case of a straightforward joint venture between two or more corporate undertakings, the structure, as often as not, comprises solely an appropriate number of separate classes of ordinary share (viz: 'A', 'B', 'C', etc), ranking equally as to rights (e.g. in respect of voting, dividends and distributions upon a winding-up) with each class having the right to nominate a particular number of directors.

(ii) *Funding.* This will take one of two basic forms (frequently applied in combination): (a) by the joint venturers themselves; and (b) via recourse to

---

[18] The subject generally lies outside the scope of this work, but note, for example, the use of preference shares (cumulative, participating, redeemable), convertible shares and deferred shares.

third party external funders. The abolition of capital duty on the issue of shares has removed one major difference between subscriptions for equity and loans to the jvc. However, there are important differences between the tax treatment of interest and dividends (*see* 5.6 below). In addition, whereas in general capital losses on share capital are deductible for UK tax on capital gains, more care has to be taken to ensure that losses on loans will be so available (*see* 5.2(vii)).

However, in a more practical sense, it can be argued that the provision of funding by means of loans affords the joint venturers considerably more flexibility in the event that the collaboration is not a success and the parties wish to withdraw. If the parties have funded the jvc by means of equity, they will only be able to obtain the return of their investment by following the relatively time-consuming and costly procedures of a corporate winding-up.[19]

The procurement of external funding ((b) above), for example, from a bank to cover normal overdraft facilities, will almost certainly rely upon the creation by the jvc of a floating charge over its assets.[20] In practice, the attempt to procure external finance for a start-up jvc, may have an almost immediate effect of removing the availability of 'limited liability' for the joint venturers, for unless the jvc has, from the outset, material assets, it is unlikely to be able to provide adequate security for a loan and the joint venturers themselves may find themselves under an obligation to guarantee repayment of the loans in the event of the jvc's default.

(iii) *Constitution of the Board of Directors.* The right of the joint venturers to appoint directors to the Board of the jvc will typically be expressed as a class right, that is to say, the A Shareholder, B Shareholder, etc. will each be entitled to appoint (and remove) a specified number of directors to the board of the jvc. The provisions relating to the constitution of the Board will typically be addressed both in the Shareholders Agreement and the Articles of Association and will address, *inter alia*: the minimum number of directors necessary to form a quorum; the ability of a specific shareholder's nominated director to cast the votes of other of his nominated directors not present at a meeting of the Board; the manner in which appointments and removals are to be effected;[1] the mechanism for the appointment of a Chairman of the Board.[2] The Chairman's casting vote is generally disapplied.

(iv) *Minority protection.* This, in a real sense, constitutes the heart of a Shareholders Agreement in that it lays down a requirement for common accord amongst the shareholders on a variety of material issues affecting the jvc's

---

[19] There is an argument that a reasonable level of equity subscription gives the jvc a semblance of solidity and permanence. This is true, although, in practice, very substantial levels of capitalisation will be required before recourse to the joint venturers themselves is likely to be avoided in the context of, *inter alia*, performance bonds on contracts and guarantees in support of third party loans.

[20] Note that a partnership is not able to grant a floating charge and must rely instead upon fixed charges over identified assets or personal guarantees from the partners.

[1] Typically simply by serving a notice on the Secretary of the jvc, although it is sometimes specified that the other joint venturers must approve the selection of a new director.

[2] The 'Chairmanship' typically will rotate annually between the joint venturers' nominated directors.

business, constitution and operations. The term 'minority protection' reflects the fact that in a typical joint venture, none of the parties will have a controlling interest in the jvc's voting share capital, i.e. each will be in the position of a 'minority' shareholder and will be capable of being outvoted by a combination of the other parties. Issues typically requiring 'common accord' comprise, *inter alia*, changes to the Memorandum and Articles of Association of the jvc; the issue and/or allotment of share and loan capital; the granting of charges, mortgages and other forms of security over the jvc's assets; the entry into of material contracts or contracts outside the usual course of business; the incurring of capital expenditure above a specified minimum; the incurring of debt generally above a specified minimum; the employment of key personnel; or variation to the terms of employment of key personnel. The process of ensuring that the jvc does not undertake any of the foregoing without the consent of all the joint venturers needs to be considered both at the level of the Board and at the level of the Company in General Meeting. At the level of the Board the minority protection is typically achieved by specifying in the Shareholders Agreement that none of such actions shall be taken without the unanimous approval of the Board or without a board Resolution in respect of which the 'nominated' directors of each of the A, B, etc. shareholders shall have voted in favour. Although it is possible to entrench such rights in the Articles of Association, it is generally preferred to keep the commercial detail in terms of control at the level of the Board in the Shareholders Agreement since this document, unlike the Articles of Association, is not subject to filing with the Registrar of Companies and public inspection.[3]

In the case of minority protection, at the level of the Company in General Meeting, a distinction can be made between a 50:50 deadlock jvc and a jvc containing two or more shareholders. In the former case, since neither party is capable of forcing through either an ordinary or special resolution, neither requires protection from the other and the shareholding arrangements typically would only address minority protection at the level of the Board.[4] In the second case, however, each shareholder will require protection in General Meetings of the Company, either because his co-venturer alone has greater than 50% of the voting shares or because two or more co-venturers might combine to achieve more than 50% of the voting shares. In relation to those items where protection is required at General Meeting level, such as changes to the jvc Memorandum and Articles of Association, alterations to the share capital and the removal of directors, minority protection is generally achieved by stipulating either:

(a)   that changes to any such matters are deemed to constitute variations

---

[3] Note that the Shareholders Agreement may become liable to public inspection as a result of the application of the Restrictive Trade Practices Act 1976, *see* 2.9 above.

[4] Even this protection is technically not necessary if both parties have the right to appoint an equal number of directors. In such circumstances it is common to specify that all 'material' decisions will require unanimous approval.

to each class of shares and therefore require the consent of the majority holders of each class; or

(b)   that in respect of such matters each class of shares has only one vote which can be exercised by the decision of the majority of holders of each class.

(v) *Disharmony and termination.* The agreement only to undertake certain key actions by common accord raises the question of the parties' failure to agree. Notwithstanding the existence of certain statutory rights,[5] it is customary to legislate for the resolution of disputes in the Shareholders Agreement. The following are examples of typical solutions to the problem of deadlock or a failure to agree:

(a)   the referral of a dispute to the Chairman (or other senior management) of the respective joint venturers;

(b)   the entitlement of any joint venturer to require the matter to be considered in a General Meeting of the jvc;[6]

(c)   referral of the dispute to arbitration or a nominated expert;

(d)   the granting of a casting vote to a director of the Board who is independent of the joint venturers;[7]

(e)   termination of the joint ownership of the jvc structure, typically by one of the two mechanisms described below. Note the distinction between the termination of joint ownership (which impliedly contemplates the withdrawal of one or more joint venturers) and the disbandment or dissolution of the joint venture structure itself, i.e. the jvc;

(f)   upon a failure to resolve the dispute and as a last resort termination of the joint venture and the winding-up of the jvc.

(vi) *Termination of the joint ownership of the joint company.* Two methods are commonly used.

(a)   The first consists of buy and sell options (often referred to by the slightly over-romantic names of 'Russian roulette', 'Savoy' or 'Texas shoot out' clauses). They all involve a procedure whereby one party may serve a notice on the other (1) offering to buy the shares of the other party at the price specified in the notice or (2) offering to sell his shares to the other party at the same price (i.e. that specified in the notice under (1) above). The party receiving the notice is entitled within a set period to elect either to sell his shares to the first party or to buy the shares

---

[5]   A shareholder could apply to Court under Companies Act 1985, s.517(1)(g) to have the jvc wound-up on the 'just and equitable' ground; or apply to Court under Companies Act 1985, s.459–61 upon the basis that the company's affairs were being conducted in a manner unfairly prejudicial to his interests.

[6]   (a) and (b) above keep the dispute within the control of the joint venturers but remove it from the context of the Board.

[7]   (c) and (d) above take the dispute out of the control of the joint venturers. For such reason they are, on the whole, unpopular solutions. It is, in addition, questionable whether it is practical to ask independent parties (most conspicuously in the case of (c)) to judge essentially commercial issues.

of the first party at that price. The procedure is designed to ensure that the party delivering the notice states a 'fair' price, since it must be one at which he is prepared to both sell and buy the shares. If the other party makes no election, the first party may elect whether to buy or sell at the stated price. The mechanism as described here assumes that the parties have equal shareholdings. The mechanism works in respect of unequal holdings (say 60:40) and can be adapted to apply in circumstances where there are more than two parties providing the prices underlying the put and call options are calculated on a per share basis. This neat mechanism is sometimes said to be so fair that it is never put into use! It certainly has a clear disadvantage where the two shareholders are of uneven financial standing – one party may be bought out simply because he cannot meet the price offered by the other party for his shares. It may not therefore be suitable for joint ventures where there is a financial imbalance between the joint venturers. It should also be noted that there is a risk that the Revenue will deny consortium relief and the reliefs outlined at 5.6 below where such arrangements exist. In practice, however, it is doubtful whether this point is taken.

(b)   An alternative solution is to utilise the 'pre-emption rights' that would typically be contained in the Articles of Association of the joint company. Pre-emption rights are a mechanism that prevents the diversification of the ownership of a company by providing that a shareholder who wishes to sell his shares must first offer them to the other existing shareholders in proportion to their holdings, i.e. the shares must first be offered to the 'club' of existing shareholders. The selling shareholder can sell his shares to an outside party only where the existing shareholders elect not to buy. The process which in practice is more complex and refined than that described above is typically started by the serving of a notice (a transfer notice) indicating a wish to sell. The party wishing to terminate can procure the serving of a transfer notice on the other parties. If the other parties do not purchase the first party's shares and no third party purchaser can be found, the first party typically is entitled to serve a further notice threatening to wind up the joint company. There then typically follows a 'cooling off' period during which the parties have an opportunity to resolve their differences. If they fail to do so, the first party can serve a further notice and the parties will then be contractually bound to wind up the joint company as soon as practicable. The principal problem with this route is that the procedures for winding up are slow and complex, particularly where the jvc is a trading company.

Perhaps not surprisingly, there is no truly satisfactory solution to the problem of deadlock. If the parties are having fundamental disagreements then the joint venture will simply cease to function properly and undoubtedly it will be in both parties' interests to negotiate a mutually acceptable settlement. However, it is generally held that the various mechanisms outlined above are of use. Even if they are not put into practice,[8] their mere existence can serve to concentrate the minds of the parties and encourage them to reach a settlement. Parties frequently rely upon a combination of the above, for example, (v)(a) failing which (v)(b), failing which (v)(e).

(vii) *Transferability of shares*. With the exception of the pre-emption rights (*see* (v)(e) above) restrictions on the transferability of shares are typically set out in the Shareholders Agreement. Restrictions on transfer in a practical sense restrict the parties' ability to leave the joint venture. The nature of the restrictions vary, the following are examples showing a sliding scale of lock-in to the jvc:

(a) at the top of the scale is an absolute restriction on transfers without the consent of the other party;
(b) less severe is a restriction on transfer without consent for a stated period and thereafter transfers are permissible but subject to compliance with pre-emption rights (*see* (v)(e) above);
(c) less severe still is a simple requirement to comply with pre-emption rights; and
(d) primarily as a qualification of (c) above, there may also be a category of permitted transfers such as those between members of the same group of companies.

(viii) *Termination*. The Shareholders Agreement will typically legislate for a number of circumstances that will bring about the termination of the jvc. The following are typical examples:

(a) A failure to agree, *see* (v) above.
(b) Insolvency of the jvc. Note that the parties may for a number of reasons be compelled to keep the jvc solvent, for example, cross default provisions on loan agreements whereby the insolvency of a subsidiary will trigger a 'default' or more general commercial reputation considerations.
(c) Breach of the joint venture agreement. As an alternative to contractual remedies for damages, the parties may provide that a material breach of the Shareholders Agreement will give rise to rights under the put/call

---

[8] Note that in the case of a jvc that is a subsidiary of a listed company, it may be necessary to consider carefully the timing requirements in respect of these types of provision under the Yellow Book rules, since the disposal by a listed company of its shares to its co-venturer may, *inter alia*, amount to a class 4 transaction requiring shareholders' prior approval. It is also possible in the case of a listed company that the acquisition of shares may require shareholders' approval and the issue of a circular as a transaction falling within classes 1 to 3 of the Yellow Book rules.

option mechanism described at paragraph (v)(i) above or that, for example, the defaulting party shall transfer its shares to the other party either at a fair price to be decided upon by the auditors or, sometimes, at a price which, as a disincentive to the breaching party, is less than the fair value.

(d)   Insolvency or change in control of one of the parties. In these circumstances it is common to provide for the non-affected party to have the right to require the transfer to it of the other's shares. In the case of insolvency, provision should be made to ensure that the non-affected party has all necessary rights, including in particular all requisite intellectual property rights, to carry on the jvc's business on its own.

(e)   Completion of the joint venture's objectives. If the jvc has been set up for the fulfilment of a limited purpose and that has been achieved, then it is usual to provide for the mechanics of dissolution in advance.

(ix) *Future funding.* Unless it is clear how much money the jvc is going to need, legislating for the requirements of future funding is not easy. Where the two shareholders both have equal financial strength, a provision to the effect that future finance should be provided equally by them is frequently included, breach of which will amount to a material default under the Shareholders Agreement. An alternative is to provide that a shareholder is entitled to an increased share in the equity if the other refuses to provide further finance upon the basis agreed. The problem is made more difficult where the two shareholders are of disparate financial size. The smaller may not wish to see its share in the joint company reduced merely because it cannot put up the further finance required.

(x) *The purpose of the joint venture company.* The purpose and scope of work of the jvc should be described in the Shareholders Agreement. This is particularly important where the area of the jvc's activities will overlap with the activities of the shareholding companies or their corporate groups. In these circumstances there will almost certainly be various non-competition covenants between the shareholding companies (and their respective groups) and the jvc. In order to define the scope and nature of such covenants it will be necessary to define what the jvc is going to do. Clearly, the nature and scope of the jvc's work can always be changed at some later date by mutual agreement if the definition proves too restrictive.

(xi) *Mutual confidentiality.* Each joint venturer will typically be required to keep confidential all information relating not only to the business and affairs of the jvc but also that relating to the business and affairs of all other joint venturers.

(xii) *Non-competition.* Each joint venturer typically will be required to covenant not to compete with the business of the jvc[9] during the currency of

---

[9] Note that such covenants, *inter alia*, may bring the agreement within the terms of the Restrictive Trade Practices Act 1976 and make it notifiable to the Office of Fair Trading, *see* 2.9 above.

the agreement. Note that the covenant may benefit from the exemption set out in the Restrictive Trade Practices (Sale and Purchase and Share Subscription Agreements) (Goods) Order 1989 (SI 1989 No. 1081).

(xiii) *The rights to and use of intellectual property rights created by the joint company. See* generally 5.8 below.

(xiv) *Dividend policy.* Parties will frequently try and agree this in advance. Where not possible it will typically be a matter requiring the agreement of the joint venturers' nominated directors (*see* (iv) above and 5.6(iii) below).

(xv) *Costs.* It is usual for the parties to bear their own costs. If the parties wish the jvc to bear the start-up costs then the financial assistance implications under section 151 Companies Act 1985 will need to be considered.

In the case of a jvc, there are likely to be a number of important ancillary documents. In addition to the Shareholders Agreement and Memorandum and Articles of Association some or all of the following will be required: collateral contracts, for example, in respect of the licensing-in of intellectual property rights or the supply of goods or services by the joint venturers to the jvc; service agreements in respect of the employment of key personnel; and property documentation in respect of the jvc's occupancy of land.

5.6 Tax

A jvc, as a separate legal entity, is subject to the normal rules for the taxation of UK companies. In particular:

(i) Corporation tax is paid on profits, normally nine months after the end of the accounting period in which they arise. If the Finance Bill 1991 is enacted as first published the rate will be 34% for the year ended March 1991 and 33% for the year ending March 1992 although lower rates are available in the case of certain small companies. Under the 1991 Finance Bill as first drafted this relief would only apply where profits are less than £1.25 million, although this threshold has to be shared with certain 'associated' companies.

(ii) In general a UK-resident jvc which is either a trading company or an investment company (as defined in the Taxes Acts) should be able to obtain a deduction for interest on its long-term borrowings or on interest paid to a bank. However a number of areas need to be watched:

(a) A UK company paying such interest is normally obliged to deduct tax at basic rate unless either the interest is being paid to a bank carrying on a *bona fide* banking business in the UK or to a lender protected from tax on interest by a double tax treaty.

(b) Certain interest (for example most interest which depends on the profit of the jvc or interest on certain convertible instruments) is treated for UK tax purposes as a distribution. In these circumstances no deduction is available from profit but ACT is payable as mentioned in (iii) below. The provisions of s209 ICTA 1988 need to be considered carefully in choosing a structure.

(c)   Short interest (very broadly that on borrowings for less than a year) is, unless paid to a bank carrying on a *bona fide* banking business in the UK or certain other privileged lenders, only allowable as a deduction in computing trading profits (i.e. only available if the jvc is carrying on a trade).

(d)   In arriving at a loan structure, thought should be given to the taxation of any gain or loss made on any loan instrument. These could be capital or income, or outside the scope of tax altogether, depending on the nature of the instrument used.

(iii) Following payment of a dividend or other distribution (and this may in some circumstances include the payment of interest on certain loan stocks) normally (but subject to the exception mentioned in 5.7 below) the company will have to pay to the Inland Revenue an amount of advance corporation tax ('ACT') currently equal to one third of the amount of the distribution. This can, within certain limits, be offset against the jvc's liability to corporation tax and so is often merely a cash flow disadvantage. UK shareholders who are entitled to such a dividend will receive a tax credit equal to the ACT paid. In the case of a UK individual, this will be offset against his tax liability (it also forms part of his taxable income) or, where he has insufficient liability, can be reclaimed in cash. In the case of a UK resident corporate shareholder, the credit, together with the dividend itself, constitutes franked investment income which (subject to (iv) below) should not bear tax in the shareholder's hands. Such franked investment income may be used by the recipient to justify the payment of its own dividends without ACT. Foreign shareholders are not generally entitled to a tax credit as such although they are often able to claim a part of it under the relevant double tax treaties.

(iv) Since UK-resident corporate shareholders will generally be liable to tax on any gain realised on the sale or liquidation of a jvc but do not pay tax on receipt of a dividend, it is usual to pay out available reserves by way of dividend prior to a sale or liquidation taking place with a view to reducing the taxable gain and putting a corresponding sum into shareholders' hands. It is important to note here that the Inland Revenue have power under Section 26 Capital Gains Tax Act 1979 to add back material dividends received in computing any gain ultimately realised on the disposal of the shareholders' shares. Although the power is wide in theory, it has not generally been applied where the dividends represent the extraction of profits of the company as they arise. For this reason the dividend policies of joint ventures are often framed as being to distribute the profits as they arise subject to such retentions as are required to cover present and future liabilities. It should also be noted that any loss created by dividend stripping is likely to be disallowed under Sections 280 and 281 Taxes Act 1970.

5.7 Group relief

Group relief provisions under which losses and other reliefs may be surrendered between members of certain 75% groups are extended to cover what are known as consortium companies. These would include a UK-resident jvc which carried on a trade where firstly 75% or more of its ordinary share capital is owned by other UK-resident companies, none of which holds less than 5% or as much as 75% ('the members of the consortium') and, secondly, various tests going to the commercial substance of this relationship are satisfied. Broadly, this relief permits the consortium members to take surrenders of their proportion of trading losses and certain other reliefs. It is also possible for them to surrender their own losses and reliefs against their proportion of the profits of the jvc company. In order to ensure that a commercial balance is maintained it is usual for those receiving losses or reliefs under these provisions to pay for them, the price being the amount of the tax saved. Such payments do not themselves attract tax.

Relief under these provisions can also be available where the jvc is a holding company which has a 90% trading subsidiary and in such circumstances reliefs can be surrendered to and from the trading subsidiary. Under s406 ICTA 1988 there are also provisions for surrender of reliefs between a jvc which is a consortium company and companies in the same groups as the consortium members.

It is important to note that one of the restrictions to relief under these provisions is that there must be no arrangements under which the consortium company could become a member of the same 75% group as a consortium member (or indeed any other company). The Inland Revenue have stated that the existence of untriggered provisions under which members must offer round their shares on their leaving the consortium will not impair their ability to claim relief. It should be noted that arrangements such as Texas shootout and Savoy clauses (*see* further 5.5(iv)) fall outside the scope of the Revenue's statement, probably because the Revenue are not aware of them. In practice it does not appear that the Revenue object to such arrangements although there must remain a risk that they will disqualify relief.

(i) *Payments of dividends and interest gross.* Section 247 ICTA 1988 provides that a consortium company may pay dividends to its members without ACT and interest to its members without deducting basic rate tax. Provisions in the 1989 Finance Act restrict this relief in a manner analogous to the restrictions on consortium relief.

(ii) *Foreign involvement.* In summary, the availability of consortium relief largely mitigates the danger of losses being locked into a jvc and the absence of tax transparency in the jvc structure. One significant disadvantage to be borne in mind, however, is the non-availability of the reliefs to a non-resident company. Since the introduction of a non-resident company as a joint venturer can also deprive other joint venturers of the relief, non resident companies are frequently introduced through a UK subsidiary. They will then depend on the terms of any applicable double tax agreement for any reliefs they are able to obtain.

5.8   Acquisition and use of business assets and intellectual property rights

There is relatively little of general application that can be said here. Clearly, as with a partnership, there is a fundamental choice as between outright acquisition and the provision under collateral contracts of goods and services by the jvc shareholders. As a rule long-term jvcs will seek to acquire outright the assets necessary to conduct their business, whereas short-term ventures will rely on collateral contracts. As a practical matter, the reliance of a jvc upon material collateral contracts, for example, the licensing-in of key intellectual property, presents a number of difficulties:

(i)   *de facto* control: where there is an imbalance as between co-venturers in the provision of goods and services, one party (the key provider) may acquire a greater degree of *de facto* control;

(ii)   in practice it is difficult to avoid the termination of a collateral contract, and consequent loss of the goods or services, upon the cessation of the relevant party as a shareholder;

(iii)   it is important to try and establish 'common control' of the terms of and conditions governing collateral contracts (particularly those in respect of price). As a result it is quite frequently provided in the Shareholders Agreement that their terms cannot be altered without the consent of the parties' nominated directors. Disputes on future price increases are sometimes legislated for by reliance on index linking, for example, by reference to movements in the Retail Prices Index.

As stated above, the jvc is well suited to the ownership of property, whether realty, chattels or intellectual property rights and whether acquired by assignment or as a result of the endeavours of its own employees, those seconded to it[10] or the activities of third parties commissioned to perform the work.[11] As with the partnership structure, it is considered impractical to attempt to legislate at the outset in respect of the eventual ownership and rights of the parties to use intellectual property and assets vested in the company upon the termination of the joint venture. The circumstances of termination, the value of the assets and even the identity of the parties remaining are all likely to influence the matter in a manner that cannot be foreseen at the outset. The parties must be left to reach whatever appropriate commercial arrangement they can devise at the time.

---

[10] Note that unless expressly agreed to the contrary, intellectual property rights created by employees seconded to the jvc by the joint venturers will generally belong to the joint venturers and not the jvc.

[11] Commissioned works, with the exception of registered and unregistered design rights (Copyright, Designs and Patents Act 1988, ss.215(2) and 267(2)) will, in the absence of contrary agreement, belong to the party carrying out the commission and not the party placing the order.

5.9 Competition law considerations

The Shareholders Agreement and all other ancillary documents will be subject to the Restrictive Trade Practices Act 1976, *see* 2.9 above.

The on-going conduct of the jvc will be subject to regulatory control under the provisions of the Resale Prices Act 1976, the Competition Act 1980 and the monopoly provisions of the Fair Trading Act 1973, again *see* 2.9 above.

In certain circumstances the establishment of a jvc may constitute a qualifying merger under the provisions of sections 64 *et seq.* of the Fair Trading Act 1973. For example, if a company was already trading in a particular market and a joint venture was formed by the subscription by another company for shares in that company, (now the jvc), and if the new shareholder transferred a portion of its business to the jvc, it is possible that the two business enterprises may have ceased to be distinct and that a qualifying merger will have taken place within the terms of section 64 FTA 73. Although a full discussion of the issue lies outside this Chapter, a qualifying merger will in practice require 'prior clearance' by the Secretary of State for Trade and Industry if parties are not to risk the possibility of forced divestiture upon the grounds, *inter alia*, that a concentration of market share in the supply of goods or services can be expected to operate against the public interest. It should be noted that the above description of a qualifying merger would apply no less in the case of a partnership.

For a consideration of EC competition law issues, *see* Chapter 1.

5.10 Conclusion

The jvc structure, notwithstanding the greater formality and cost attaching to its formation and operation, will in the vast majority of cases be the preferred structure for a joint venture between UK individuals or corporations whose commercial objectives contemplate the formation and operation of a jointly owned business. In general, only specific tax considerations or the presence of a foreign participant will favour the selection of a partnership structure in such circumstances.